Citizen Lobbyists

Citizen Lobbyists

Local Efforts to Influence Public Policy

Brian E. Adams

Temple University Press
PHILADELPHIA

Temple University Press
1601 North Broad Street
Philadelphia PA 19122
www.temple.edu/tempress

∞ The paper used in this publication meets the requirements of the American
National Standard for Information Sciences—Permanence of Paper for Printed
Library Materials, ANSI Z39.48-1992

Library of Congress Cataloging-in-Publication Data

Adams, Brian E., 1973–
    Citizen lobbyists : local efforts to influence public policy / Brian E. Adams.
      p.   cm.
    Includes bibliographical references and index.
    ISBN 13: 978-1-59213-569-1   ISBN 10: 1-59213-569-2 (cloth: alk. paper)
    ISBN 13: 978-1-59213-570-7   ISBN 10: 1-59213-570-6 (pbk.: alk. paper)
    1. Lobbying—United States—States—Citizen participation.   2. Local
government—United States.   3. Lobbying—California—Santa Ana—
Citizen participation—Case studies.   4. Santa Ana (Calif.)—Politics and
government—Case studies.   I. Title.

JK2498.A33 2007
324'.40973—dc22   2006015935

2   4   6   8   9   7   5   3   1

Contents

Acknowledgments

I would like to thank several people who have read and commented on parts or the entirety of early drafts. My dissertation committee—Mark Petracca, Katherine Tate, and Helen Ingram—provided constructive criticism and valuable insights. Lina Newton, Kim Haselhoff, and Molly Patterson also provided helpful comments (and much needed encouragement) in the early phases of this project. Part of this book was written during a fellowship at the Kettering Foundation in Dayton, Ohio, which greatly enhanced my perspective on the issues discussed in these pages. At Kettering, I benefited greatly from conversations with Randy Nielsen, Christopher Kelley, John Cavanaugh, Julie Fisher, and John Dedrick. Finally, I would most especially like to thank all of my colleagues in the Political Science Department at San Diego State University. I am truly fortunate to be in a department that has both a vibrant intellectual life and a friendly and supportive atmosphere. My colleagues have provided an endless amount of support and encouragement, without which I doubt I would have been able to complete this project.

Citizen Lobbyists

PART I

Introduction

1 Citizen Lobbyists

Citizens' political activity in local government can take three basic forms. First, they can partake in elections, voting for local officials, volunteering for political campaigns, giving campaign contributions, or running for office themselves. Second, citizens can engage the policy-making process directly, prodding officials to take desired policy actions. Toward this end, citizens can attend city council meetings, organize protests, circulate petitions, or engage in a host of other activities. Third, citizens can bypass local governments altogether and address community issues through civic organizations, working with their fellow citizens to make positive improvements to their communities outside of the formal channels of government.

This book examines the second type of activity: engaging the local policy-making process. When thinking about this form of political participation, there are four central research questions:

1. Who participates?
2. What issues do they try to influence?
3. What activities do they engage in?
4. Are they effective?

All four questions are interrelated. Who participates will influence what issues generate the most participation. Also, citizens may engage in different activities depending on the issue, and their effectiveness may be a partial function of who is participating and how they participate. Although the four research questions are interrelated, separating them is valuable because they constitute four distinct aspects of citizen participation. Despite their connections, each question focuses on a different piece of the participation puzzle, and each needs to be answered to develop a complete picture of how citizens engage policy making.

Political scientists have generally focused on the first and the last question: who participates and are they effective. I focus on the second and third questions. Citizens—with limited time to devote to politics and an endless array of issues—need to decide which issues they will try to influence. Why do they choose to participate on issue A and not issue B? To pose the question from a different angle, what types of public policies will generate high levels of participation? This line of questioning examines the patterns of participation across local policies, observing what types of issues generate the most interest and participation from citizens.

Once citizens decide to participate, what activities do they engage in to accomplish their political goals? On a local level, citizens have many options for participation: attending public meetings, contacting officials, petitions, protests, and other activities. Which of these activities do they utilize in their participatory efforts? I also study the strategies that citizens employ. Do they engage in pressure tactics in an effort to force officials to accede to their demands or do they try to persuade officials on the merits of their position? Do they rely primarily on formal channels of participation (such as public meetings) or do they utilize informal channels to accomplish their goals?

A case study approach was chosen for this research because it allows for a thorough and deep examination of the nature of citizen engagement with the policy-making process. It allows us to develop a comprehensive picture of citizen participation, which is more than just an aggregation of individual participatory acts. The details of citizens' participatory activity and how specific activities fit together into overall strategies are important elements in understanding the dynamics of citizen engagement with policy making. Further, a case study approach creates opportunities to examine in detail the patterns of participation across policies, not just documenting which policies generate the most participation but also exploring how the characteristics of those policies influence participation patterns. The richness and depth afforded by a case study approach is particularly important given the lack of scholarly attention to the research questions addressed in this study and the absence of prior conceptualization of how citizens engage the policy-making process.

The downside to a case study approach is one cannot make reliable generalizations. The city chosen for this study—Santa Ana, California—is not a "typical" city, and it is doubtful that there is any such creature. I do not present the findings from Santa Ana as applicable to all cities in all circumstances. I suspect that many of the findings capture the essence of participation in other cities, but verification of that argument will have to wait for further research. The goal of this research is not to make sweeping generalizations about all cities, but rather to conceptualize the nature of citizen engagement with the policy-making process. Even if the findings from Santa Ana do not apply to all cities, the evidence presented in this book will advance the research on citizen participation by developing a framework for understanding how citizens participate in policy making. It can also help us explore the implications that it has for local democratic practices more generally; we can use the findings from Santa Ana as a platform from which to examine the actual and potential impact of this form of citizen participation on the quality and extent of democratic decision making in local government.

With a population of 320,000, Santa Ana is an older suburb of Los Angeles located about thirty miles south of downtown. Santa Ana's size makes it a good venue to study citizen participation: it is small enough to allow citizens to get directly involved in policy making, but it is still large enough to have significant urban problems and thus a broad range of policies on which to participate. Santa Ana was once a largely Anglo middle-class suburb, but it is now a diverse city with a majority Latino population and economic challenges. It shares some common characteristics with other older suburbs in terms of its demographic transformation, infrastructure problems, and loss of tax revenue. However, it also has some unique features, such as an extremely high Latino population (over 75 percent) and a major problem with overcrowding.

Santa Ana is also a good setting for exploring citizens' engagement with the policy-making process because of its political diversity. The politics of Santa Ana reflect both the city's status as a "suburb" and its large minority population, with a variety of different types of issues on the public agenda. Many different groups of citizens participate in Santa Ana politics on issues ranging from traffic mitigation to school overcrowding to public safety. Its politics are multi-dimensional without one overriding issue. The diversity of Santa Ana politics allows for an examination of participation in different contexts and by different groups. Its political diversity is not only a unique feature that sets it apart from many other cities, it also contributes to the value of Santa Ana as a case study by presenting a setting where different types of issues are on the public agenda and various groups of participants are active in political life.

Citizen Engagement in Local Policy Making

Citizen engagement with the policy-making process encompasses both citizens' selection of issues on which they participate and the specific activities they perform to influence those issues. Of the many issues local governments tackle every year, only a handful will generate any participation from citizens. When citizens choose to participate on issue A rather than issue B, they determine the context in which they enter the policy-making process. Once citizens decide what issues they will try to influence, they can perform a variety of political acts to accomplish their goals, including everything from talking to officials, to speaking at public meetings, to street protests. Further, citizens can insert themselves into the policy-making process at different points in time, ranging from when an issue is first being discussed by officials to the implementation stage. They can engage policy making in a confrontational mode, attempting to influence policy through pressure, or they can try to work with officials to persuade them of the merits of their policy views. Citizens have many choices regarding how to approach political activity, and the choices they make will influence the manner in which they engage the policy-making process.

We can sort through this variation by identifying a few ideal-types of how citizens engage the policy-making process. Below are five descriptions of roles that citizens perform in relation to local policy making. These categories highlight different approaches to participation rather than discriminating between participatory activities and/or participant motives, although each approach varies along these criteria. This scheme is a conceptualization of the relationship between participants and governmental decision makers, not a classification of the participation itself. The roles are not mutually exclusive, and citizens can engage in different roles at various times. Though they do not present a stark either-or choice for citizens, this classification scheme is valuable because it highlights the different ways that citizens can engage the local policy-making process and can provide a structure to analyses of citizens' political activity by identifying general approaches to influencing government.

1. *Citizens as Watchdogs.* Most citizens are not politically active, have little interest in public affairs, and consequently do not participate extensively (Putnam 2000; Dahl 1961). However, many citizens participate occasionally, particularly when government is proposing to do something undesirable. Here, citizens enter the policy process as watchdogs. They generally do not participate but will do so to prevent unwanted actions by local governments. Their participation is reactive; rather than setting the agenda themselves, they respond to the agenda set by government officials. Their participation is also obstructionist in that their goal is to prevent government from doing something unwanted rather than proposing a solution to a specific problem. Their obstruction may be beneficial to the community (e.g., by preventing a land use decision that will reduce the community's quality of life), but its fundamental goal is to prevent government from doing something rather than solving community problems. In most cases, government officials will disagree with the participants' views (given that they were the ones who placed the issue on the agenda to begin with), and thus citizens' strategies will focus on pressuring officials rather than persuading them.

2. *Citizens as Collaborative Problem Solvers.* Some scholars promote participation as a way to address difficult political and social issues that communities face (Boyte 2004; Mathews 1999). Rather than reacting to the government's agenda, collaborate problem solvers proactively address issues that they feel are important to the community, or ones on which they can have a positive impact. To accomplish these goals, citizens work with policy makers to develop solutions to the problems identified. Although most participation focuses on solving perceived problems, what separates this approach is that participants collaborate with policy makers rather than confront or pressure them. Much of their work may occur outside of the formal policy-making process, where they address community problems without government involvement. When they do engage the

policy-making process, their work mode is one of deliberation and collaboration with officials to develop mutually satisfactory policy. Their political activities will mostly be informal and private, working one-on-one with officials. When they do engage in public activities, they will avoid confrontation with officials to maintain good working relationships.

3. *Citizens as Lobbyists.* The third role citizens can assume is that of lobbyist. Here, citizens identify issues of importance to them, develop a set of political goals, and lobby government to accomplish them. They differ from community problem solvers in that their work mode is not necessarily collaborative or deliberative, resorting to pressure tactics as needed. Further, their focus is likely to be on more specific issues: collaborative problem solvers may tackle "big" issues, such as affordable housing or poverty, whereas citizen lobbyists will turn their attention to neighborhood issues, such as the construction of a particular low-income housing project. Unlike watchdogs, they are sometimes proactive in setting the agenda and defining issues. Citizen lobbyists engage in the same activities as conventional lobbyists, such as attempting to persuade officials, pressuring them, mobilizing other citizens, and conveying information to both the public and officials. Although they differ from conventional lobbyists in that they are not paid by a third party for their services, their engagement in the policy-making process is the same: they identify issues of importance to them, develop political goals, and engage in a variety of political activities to accomplish those goals.

4. *Citizens as Pawns.* The previous three roles have citizens taking some initiative in deciding on which issues they will participate and the types of activities in which they engage. However, we can imagine scenarios where they do the bidding of elites either within or outside of government. Rather than determining which issues to participate on, citizens would follow the lead of elected officials or interest groups who coordinate and mobilize citizens to participate. In this role, citizens' political activity is coordinated by elites who organize rallies, start petition drives, or mobilize citizens to attend public meetings. Citizens willingly partake in this activity because they believe in the goals they are trying to achieve (i.e., they are not being misled or

manipulated), but they are not deciding the manner in which they participate. In other words, their engagement with the policy-making process is directed and coordinated by elites.

5. *Citizens as Ideological Activists*. Finally, citizens may participate to push ideological agendas. Here, citizens choose which issues to participate on according to their relevance for a larger ideological agenda. The issues may not directly influence them or have significant impact on the community, but they are important within the context of ideological battles. This approach differs from the first three in that decisions concerning what issues to participate on and how to participate are informed by a larger partisan context, rather than the specifics of the issues themselves. Of course, all participants are likely to have an ideology that informs their participation, but what distinguishes this approach is that participation is derivative of participants' ideological goals, rather than just being influenced by them. Given the nature of the issues they attempt to influence, their activity is likely to be confrontational and public. They may collaborate with sympathetic officials, but they are more prone to pressure tactics.

I assess which of these models represents citizens' engagement with the local policy-making process and argue, as the title suggests, that in Santa Ana most participants engaged the policy-making process as lobbyists. Citizens approached policy making in the same way as conventional lobbyists, engaging in a variety of political activities to accomplish specific goals. At times, participants exhibited some of the characteristics of the other roles, with occasional ideological battles and a few efforts to solve broad social or political problems. There were also one or two instances where citizen participation was directed and managed by elites. However, the dominant mode of participation was as citizen lobbyists. Participants' focus was typically on narrow neighborhood issues rather than overarching social problems, and at times, they were proactive in setting the agenda. As do lobbyists, they relied heavily on social networks and informal communication in their participatory efforts. Thus, the citizens-as-lobbyists model captures the nature of their engagement with local policy making in Santa Ana.

The Patterns and Forms of Citizens Participation

This book is divided into four parts: an introduction, one section
each on the two central research questions, and a concluding chapter. Both research questions (What issues do they try to influence?
and What activities do they engage in?) explore aspects of citizen
engagement with local policy making and examine why citizens
resemble lobbyists in their participatory activity. Below are brief
summaries of the findings.

1. Patterns of Participation

Part II asks why some local issues generate significant participation
whereas others do not. To address this question, I explore the
validity and implications of four possible answers. My methodology
in this section is primarily inductive; these four answers suggested
themselves in interviews conducted with participants (described
below). I assess the validity of each of these factors by drawing on
the qualitative data collected from participant interviews, analysis
of meeting minutes, and media information. The focus is largely
exploratory: my goal is to examine whether these four propositions
are feasible explanations for participation patterns in Santa Ana and
to draw out the implications of these findings.

Policy Characteristics. Policies differ in how they impact citizens.
Some policies have a direct impact on citizens' lives and have clear
implications for how they live on a day-to-day basis. Other policies
are more obscure, may have nebulous effects, and may only indirectly influence citizens' daily routines. I argue that these differences
influence the likelihood that citizens will participate on an issue. The
decision to participate on a given policy is not based on an abstract
notion of the importance or salience of an issue, but on a more specific type of salience derivative of the nature of the policy's impact
on citizens. Policies that have direct and clear effects on citizens are
more likely to generate participation than those policies that do not
have these characteristics. The policies that generated participation
in Santa Ana were not necessarily those that were perceived as the
most important in some general sense, but those that had the most
direct and clear impact on citizens. In other words, the nature of a

policy's impact, rather than its extent, is the critical influence on citizens' participatory choices.

Policy Entrepreneurs. One influence on patterns of participation are policy entrepreneurs, citizens who promote a policy agenda or solution to a social problem. A policy entrepreneur could come up with an idea and through their promotion of it, generate interest and participation, acting as a mobilizing force. If such an incident occurs, then we can explain some of the variation in participation by reference to policy entrepreneurs: policy A received more participation than policy B because it was pushed by an entrepreneur who was able to get it on the public's agenda and mobilize other participants. The conclusion I draw from my analysis of entrepreneurs in Santa Ana is that they influence participation patterns by creating opportunities to participate. By putting an issue on the agenda, developing a strategy for addressing it, and mobilizing interested citizens, policy entrepreneurs create an opportunity to influence local policy that was previously lacking. With the opportunity presented to them, citizens are more likely to participate. Although policy entrepreneurs in Santa Ana did not generate groundswells of participation, and the issues receiving the most participation were not necessarily the focus of policy entrepreneurs, they did have a limited impact on participation patterns by shifting some activity toward the issues and agendas they promoted.

Media. Do newspapers increase citizen activity on the issues they cover? Given the importance of newspapers for informing citizens about local government, we might expect to see some relationship: newspapers familiarize citizens with a pressing local issue, prompting a few of these newly informed citizens to get involved. Of the four factors analyzed, however, this factor is the only one that lacks empirical support. The manner in which newspapers cover local events minimizes their impact on participation: they generally do not cover events until after the fact and offer sparse information on how citizens can get involved. Further, participants rely on social networks and personal experience, rather than newspapers, for information on local politics. Even though the average citizen may get most of his or her information about local politics from newspapers, active citizens have other sources of information that reduces the importance of newspapers as an information source and as a prompt for participation.

Urban Visions. One possible explanation for participation patterns is that they reflect patterns of social conflict: the policy issues that represent major social cleavages, the fault lines in society, are the ones that generate the most participation. In other words, citizens will participate on those issues that serve as proxies for larger debates. If this argument is true, then we should see the greatest level of participation on the issues that are representative of, or have implications for, major social conflicts. The social cleavage that repeatedly emerged from participant interviews—and one that I argue is an important force in organizing participation—is the debate over "urban visions." An urban vision is a conception of the functions and organization of the city. What purpose do cities serve? Whose needs should they meet? What should be the primary goals of city policy? Participants in Santa Ana fundamentally disagreed over these questions, which oriented many of the debates over local policy issues. The issues in Santa Ana that generated significant participation often had implications for the urban visions debate, explaining the interest in the issue and the controversy surrounding it. Not every issue generating participation was relevant to the urban visions debate, but enough of them were to conclude that a connection to this debate was a factor in generating citizen participation: citizens were more likely to participate on an issue if it had implications for the urban visions debate.

2. How Citizens Participate

When citizens try to influence policy decisions, how do they go about doing it? The goal of Part III is to analyze how citizens attempt to influence local policy. According to my analysis of citizen participation in Santa Ana, citizens utilized both formal and informal channels of influence and applied both public and private pressure on officials. Citizens typically attempted to persuade officials of the merits of their argument, primarily through personal communication with officials and comments at public meetings. If persuasion did not produce the desired result, public pressure tactics were utilized, although these were less common. Citizen participation was multifaceted (in that citizens engaged in many activities to accomplish their political goals), but participants usually lacked well-structured strategies.

Two facets of citizen participation—the role of public meetings and the value of social networks—stood out as being particularly important for citizen efforts to influence local policy, and thus are discussed at length in Chapters 8 and 9, respectively. Public meetings are frequently attacked as useless democratic rituals that lack deliberative qualities and fail to give citizens a voice in the policy-making process. Though many of the criticisms leveled against public meetings have merit, I argue that they do have a role to play as a venue for citizen participation. They may not be very good at accomplishing their primary goal of giving citizens the opportunity to directly influence decisions made by governing bodies, but they can be used to achieve other ends, such as conveying information to officials and setting the agenda. Attending and speaking at public meetings was such a common activity among participants in Santa Ana because it helped them accomplish a variety of political goals connected to their efforts to influence local policy.

Social networks also played a key role in citizen participation. I argue in Chapter 9 that social networks are a political resource akin to time, money, and civic skills that facilitate participation by helping citizens achieve various political tasks. In the same way that campaign contributions enhance access to officials, free time increases the capacity to circulate petitions, and oratory skills help citizens make persuasive arguments at public meetings, social networks assist citizens in gathering information, mobilizing allies, pooling resources, and performing other political activities. In Santa Ana, participants relied heavily on social networks in their efforts to influence local policy, making these networks an important resource.

Methods

Both the City of Santa Ana and Santa Ana Unified School District (SAUSD) were included in this study. The Santa Ana city government is organized on a council manager basis. The city council has seven members, which includes a directly elected mayor. SAUSD, like all school districts in California, is a separate entity from the municipal government. Comprised of five members elected at large, the school board governs a district of over 60,000 students. The district is geographically smaller than the city, containing about 85 percent of the city within its borders, with the remaining 15 percent in neighboring school districts.

Politics in Santa Ana was quite contentious in the 1990s, the time period for this study. The city council consistently had one or two members vociferously opposed to the council majority led by Mayor Dan Young and, later, his protégé Miguel Pulido. The five-member school board had one or two conservative Christian members who also consistently opposed the majority of the board. These divisions led to a great amount of conflict and personal animosity. There was also conflict between the City and the school district, leading to an inability of the two governments to cooperate effectively.

Two primary data sources inform my analyses: interviews with citizens active in Santa Ana politics and minutes of city council and school board meetings.

Participant Interviews

The data I rely on most heavily are interviews with citizens active in Santa Ana politics. Respondents were selected through a variety of means: some names were gathered through newspaper reports of citizen activities, some were culled from the minutes of city council and school board meetings, some names were given to the researcher by respondents already interviewed, and others came from a list of neighborhood contacts provided by the City of Santa Ana's Neighborhood Development office. To be considered for inclusion in the study, a citizen needed to be active in attempting to influence Santa Ana city or school district policies.

Through these methods, a list was compiled of citizens who were active in Santa Ana politics. I found contact information (mailing address, phone number, and/or e-mail) for eighty-five potential respondents. Between March and July 2001, I interviewed fifty-five of the eighty-five citizens on the list.[1] Most of the remaining twenty-nine citizens did not respond to a request to be interviewed, by either not returning phone calls or responding to a letter. The contact information for a few citizens turned out to be incorrect, and a few others were contacted but refused an interview.

Table 1.1. Organizational affiliations

Organization	Number of affiliations*
Neighborhood associations	41
City committees	40
Nonprofits	22
Business organizations (chamber of commerce, etc.)	14
School district committees	10
PTA/PFO/school-site council	10
Political party organizations	9
Other	12
Total	158

*The number of times an organizational affiliation was mentioned, not the number of respondents who had affiliations with each organization. If a respondent mentioned two different organizations in the same category, both were included. For example, many respondents belonged to more than one city committee or were active in both their own neighborhood association and Commlink (an umbrella organization of neighborhood associations). In these cases, each mention of an organizational affiliation was included. Thus, even though there were forty-one affiliations with neighborhood associations and Commlink, the actual number of respondents who were affiliated with these organizations is lower.

To get a better idea of the study population, we can look at the types of civic organizations to which they belonged. During the interview, respondents were asked to list their affiliations to civic organizations and committees (only those organizations that have a connection to local politics were included). Results are in Table 1.1. On average, respondents identified just under three organizations or committees each. Affiliations with neighborhood associations and Commlink, an umbrella group for the neighborhood associations, topped the list. They were followed by city boards, such as city advisory commissions and ad hoc committees. Rounding out the list were nonprofits, business organizations, parent–teacher associations, school district committees, and political party organizations.

Table 1.1 identifies interview respondents as citizens highly active in local political life. Although respondents may be more active than the average citizen, the types of positions that respondents held were not positions that conferred extensive political power, and thus we would be remiss to conclude that respondents represent an "elite" class based on their extensive organizational affiliations. Take, for example, being an officer in a neighborhood association. Neighborhood associations in Santa Ana do not have any formal policy-making authority and do not have the power to force residents to pay dues (although some collect voluntary dues). The only authority that an association president has is to speak on behalf of the neighborhood, and even that is curtailed if few participate in association meetings. Similarly, serving on a city advisory commission is not a prestige position. Although being a city commissioner has its benefits, such as increased access to information and some ability to frame issues and alternatives, they do not have much formal authority outside of making recommendations. Therefore, while respondents were highly active in local political life, it does not necessarily follow that they were also highly influential.

Many of them held formal positions (e.g., president, treasurer) within civic organizations, but few could draw upon extensive institutional resources to achieve political ends, and thus were relatively less powerful than many other political actors, such as union leaders and developers (who have such resources). Generally, respondents were citizens who were highly involved in local politics but could not be considered "political elites." There were four exceptions: three former elected officials (one city councilman and two school board trustees) and the president of the Santa Ana Chamber of Commerce. The remaining fifty-one respondents were not elites, just people who were more active than the average citizen.

The respondents interviewed for this study are not meant as a representative sample of the citizenry at large. I take the population of activists as given: I am looking at the political behavior of citizens active in local politics, not all citizens. Thus, the fact that respondents may not be representative of all citizens is irrelevant: none of my arguments rest on the claim that those interviewed are a reflection of all citizens.[2] I do, however, claim that they are representative of active citizens. The basis for this claim is twofold. First, the multiple avenues through which I identified respondents resulted in a pool of citizens who were active in different contexts and on a variety of different issues. Second, during interviews respondents articulated a wide range of opinions, beliefs, and ideologies about politics. Included in the study were extreme conservatives, extreme liberals, and multiple shades of moderates. Further, respondents expressed a myriad of opinions on Santa Ana politics, from those who wholeheartedly supported the existing leadership to those who were harsh critics. The diversity of political views expressed, along with the variation in political activity itself, led me to conclude that the fifty-five respondents represent the diversity of participants in Santa Ana.

Interviews were semistructured and asked participants about their activities in trying to influence city and school district policy. The interviews were focused on activities, not opinions: I wanted to know in what issues citizens participated and how they went about doing it, not what they thought about the issues or about policy debates. Of course, respondents spent a great deal of time during the interviews offering opinions on everything from electoral politics to the ethics of certain elected officials to social issues; respondents found it difficult to separate descriptions of participation from their opinions on the policies targeted by their participation. Further, at times respondents were asked to offer opinions on specific subjects (e.g., whether they think speaking at public meetings is a valuable political activity). Despite these discussions, the primary goal of the interview was to get the respondent to describe their political activity, not for them to offer opinions on local policy.

Meeting Minutes

The city council and school board hold biweekly board meetings. The Ralph Brown Act, the California law regulating local meetings, requires that all legislative decisions be conducted in public meetings (with a few exceptions for personnel issues, lawsuits, and other sensitive topics). Further, it requires that the public be given an opportunity to comment on items before the council or school board, and have an opportunity to make general comments on nonagenda items. Though televising the meetings is optional, local governments in California are required by the Brown Act to keep minutes of the meetings, which describe the proceedings, including what decisions were made and comments made by the public.

I reviewed the minutes for the school board and city council from January 1, 1990, to December 31, 2000. Most governmental decisions are of a routine nature and are made without comment from officials or the public. These routine decisions are not relevant for this study because they rarely generate any citizen participation. To eliminate routine decisions from the study, only nonunanimous votes, or unanimous votes opposed by at least one public speaker, were included. For each one of these votes, basic information (e.g., date, a description of the issue, the ayes and nays) was collected, along with the number of public speakers. At a minimum, all the meeting minutes listed the number of speakers on each issue. In many cases, they also listed the speaker's address, their organizational affiliation (if applicable), and whether they were speaking for or against the item. Minutes also report petitions or letters received, although this information is not consistently reported.[3]

The city council and school board cast a total of 730 controversial votes between 1990 and 2000: 332 and 398, respectively. These figures include nonunanimous votes, unanimous votes with public speakers in opposition, and votes to table items, but does not include procedural motions (such as continuations) and closed-session votes because the public is not given an opportunity to speak on those items. Of these 730 decisions, 210 had at least one member of the public who spoke, with 2,377 speakers total. The city council also received 2,118 written communications, which are letters sent to the city clerk by those who either cannot or do not want to come to the council meeting. This number, however, is rather deceptive: for only twenty-five policies did the city clerk receive any letters, and three issues account for 94 percent of the letters.

In addition to the information gathered from meeting minutes, I also analyzed media coverage of the 730 controversial issues. Santa Ana has two major English-language newspapers, the *Los Angeles Times–Orange County Edition* and the *Orange County Register.* Both of these papers cover local politics in all thirty or so cities in Orange County, of which Santa Ana is the largest. I conducted database searches of each of these papers to find articles pertaining to policies identified as controversial city council or school board votes. I tabulated the number of articles on each decision and combined the totals with the data collected from meeting minutes.

The Benefits and Drawbacks of Citizen Lobbying Activity

Understanding how citizens engage the local policy-making process through an analysis of the patterns and forms of their participation can illuminate the benefits and drawbacks of this activity. The role that citizens play in relation to policy making can vary, and this variation alters the impact of their participation. With an understanding of how citizens engage policy making, we can assess the implications of this participation for local democracy.

Citizen lobbyists in Santa Ana gained a variety of benefits from their political activity. First, they enhanced their political knowledge. Engagement with the policy process serves as a venue where citizens can learn the fine art of politics and gain a deeper understanding of policy making. As lobbyists, they did more than just partake in isolated activities: they also formulated strategies, mobilized other citizens, and developed a set of political goals. They were enmeshed in the policy-making process itself, which helped them gain insights into how politics works and how policy is formulated. In addition to gaining political knowledge, citizen lobbyists also had an opportunity to develop civic skills, such as public speaking, organizing public events, and networking.

Second, citizen lobbyists in Santa Ana built social capital through their activities. Lobbying government is fundamentally a group activity; citizens need to work with others to accomplish their goals, and consequently rely heavily on their social networks in their participatory efforts. Participation also serves as an incentive to form social networks beyond one's immediate circle of friends and neighbors. The development and use of social networks for political ends can have the effect of increasing the trust, respect, and norms of reciprocity that comprise social capital (Putnam 2000).

Finally, citizen engagement with the policy-making process provided a venue where they could have their voice heard. Their voice was not always heeded, and there were many cases where citizens were unsuccessful in their efforts. However, citizen lobbyists were able to express their views through their activity. Engaging the policy-making process may not always be the most effective way to express opinions, but it does provide an additional outlet to do so. There is a downside, however, to having citizens express views through participating in the policy-making process. Participants in Santa Ana were not representative of the public at large and their views did not always represent public sentiments, which distorted the messages that officials heard. Nevertheless, for citizen lobbyists, engaging the policy-making process provides a venue where they can pursue their political goals and voice their opinions.

Benefits accrued to citizens in terms of developing political skills, building social capital, and providing a venue where their voice can be heard, but there are limits to the value of this form of participation. In particular, citizen lobbying efforts in Santa Ana did not enhance government's capacity to address major social problems. Citizen lobbyists have a tendency to participate on neighborhood issues rather than issues with citywide implications. The examination of participation patterns in Part II reveals that most citizen participation was focused on narrowly defined issues, and citizen participants usually did not operate as community problem solvers. This limitation decreased their contribution to the government's problem-solving capacity. Many scholars argue that government alone cannot solve pressing social problems; they need the resources and knowledge that citizens can bring to the table (Weeks 2000; Fischer 1993; Durning 1993). These resources were not forthcoming from citizen lobbying efforts. In order for these benefits to materialize, citizens would need to engage policy making in a different way, focusing on a different set of issues and engaging in alternative activities.

This analysis of how citizens engage the local policy-making process helps us understand the functions that this type of participation can and cannot serve. The value of citizen lobbying efforts lies in the benefits that accrue to participants; as the following analysis will show, citizens gained a great deal from their participation. There were fewer benefits to the policy-making process itself. Not only were participants unrepresentative of the public at large, leading to distorted messages to officials, but they did not bring many resources to the process. The types of issues they tried to influence and the manner in which they went about influencing them did not increase governmental problem-solving capacity. With a realistic assessment of the benefits and limits of citizen attempts to influence local policy, we can better understand how this activity fits into the larger picture of local democracy and policy making.

2 Citizen Efforts to Influence Local Policy

A Review of the Literature

When thinking about citizen efforts to influence local policy, there are four general areas of inquiry:

1. Players: Who participates?
2. Objects: What policies do citizens try to influence with their participation?
3. Activities: What tactics and strategies do citizens employ when trying to influence local policy?
4. Effectiveness: Is citizen participation effective?

These questions could be asked of all forms of political participation, but in this chapter I focus specifically on nonelectoral participation on the local level. By not analyzing the literature on electoral activity and participation in national policy making, we can concentrate on the unique nature of local participation and on how citizens lobby their local governments.

Who Participates? Explanations for (Non)Participation

There are two central issues concerning who participates in local policy processes. First, what are the barriers and incentives that inhibit or promote participation? This line of research attempts to explain the overall level of participation in local politics. Second, why do some citizens participate and others do not? The finding that citizens with higher socioeconomic status (SES) participate more than those with lower SES applies to both electoral and non-electoral participation (Verba, Brady, and Schlozman 1995; Berry, Portney, and Thomson 1993; Verba and Nie 1972). The task undertaken here is to review the literature's explanations for why we see biases in nonelectoral participation.

Barriers to, and Incentives for, Participation

A central concept in the study of participation is the problem of collective action (Olson 1965). Simply put, individuals have a disincentive to participate because their own, personal participation is not likely to have an impact on political outcomes, although collectively citizen political activity may. Given limited time and resources, citizens will decide to be "free riders" and let others in the community participate to secure desired public goods. The question then becomes why do citizens participate at all, given the incentive not to. This issue has been most thoroughly researched in the context of voting: why would citizens spend the time and effort to vote, when the chance that their one vote will change the outcome of an election is slim? (See Leighley 1995 for an overview.)

The free rider problem, however, is not as powerful of a force in local politics, at least by the logic of its argument. There may still be incentives to be a free rider, but the ability of one citizen to make a difference at the local level is greater due to the relatively small number of total citizens participating. Thousands or even millions of citizens vote in an election, whereas only a handful typically participate in local policy making at any given time. Further, unlike voting in which participation is limited (citizens can only vote once in each election), there is no formal limitation for participating on a local policy issue. Thus, one additional participant may make a significant difference (as my analysis of policy entrepreneurs in Chapter 4 will demonstrate). Further, because the scale is smaller, a single citizen who mobilizes friends, family, and neighbors in a collective political action can potentially have a great impact on policy outcomes. The same cannot be said of a presidential election or attempts to influence congressional legislation. Thus, we might hypothesize that the free rider problem would be smaller when dealing with citizen lobbying efforts at the local level than it would in elections or attempts to influence national policy.

Though the free rider problem may be mitigated somewhat on the local level, another problem is exacerbated: citizens may choose to leave a jurisdiction rather than try to change policy. In his 1970 work, *Exit, Voice and Loyalty*, Albert Hirschman argues that there are two ways that citizens can respond to decline in political and economic organizations. They can express displeasure in the hope that their speaking out will lead to positive changes or they can leave and seek a better situation elsewhere. These options are identified by Hirschman as "voice" and "exit," respectively. On the scale of national politics, the exit option, for most people, is not feasible. Leaving the country because of disagreement with political decisions is not something that most people contemplate given the expense and effort involved with moving, as well as an emotional attachment to the country. On the local level, however, moving is much easier. Citizens unhappy with their city's policies can move to a neighboring city with relative ease; most of their life will remain intact. Tiebout (1956) hypothesizes that, in fact, citizens "vote with their feet" and will move to the jurisdiction that best suits their desired "bundle of goods and services." Citizens have a much greater exit option on the local level, and so if they are displeased with local policy, they can simply leave rather than participate to change local policy. Thus, citizens' ability to exercise their exit option is a potential disincentive for participation in local politics.

Even if citizens do not exercise their exit option, they may still opt out of participating in local politics because multiple and diverse localities may affect the public goods that they consume, making participation in their home locality less important. As Briffault (1990b) points out, a citizen may live in one city, work in another, and shop in a third. This fragmentation of political jurisdictions may dampen participation: why try to influence policies in the city you live in when the city next door (where you work) has a greater impact on your quality of life? Because most political rights, such as voting, are conferred based on place of residence, citizens may have limited opportunities to participate in shaping policies that influence them, yet another factor that could depress local participatory activity.

The amount of citizen participation can also be influenced by barriers and incentives derived from the local political system itself. Opportunities can be created or closed off through decision-making and participatory structures. The existence of institutions that facilitate participation, such as neighborhood organizations, citizens' forums, public meetings, and the like, can increase the overall participation of citizens in local policy. Similarly, a closed decision-making process or inhospitable avenues for participation can reduce participation. In sum, although the free rider problem may not be as pronounced in local politics, other disincentives for participation are exacerbated on the local level, thus explaining why the smaller scale of local politics does not automatically translate into greater citizen participation.

Participation Bias

Above, I explored factors influencing the overall level of participation that we see in local policy making. Now, I will review the explanations concerning why some people participate and others do not. Needless to say, participation is not spread evenly across the population, and explaining this participation bias has been the primary preoccupation of the literature in this field. A consistent finding of the literature is that citizens in a higher socioeconomic class are more likely to participate in politics than those in a lower socioeconomic class (Verba and Nie 1972). All types of political participation are subject to socioeconomic status (SES) bias; for our purposes, studies have demonstrated that SES bias exists for non-electoral activities, such as attending public meetings (McComas 2001a) and joining neighborhood associations (Berry, Portney, and Thomson 1993).

One explanation for SES bias is that higher SES citizens participate more because they have greater political resources and skills (Verba, Schlozman, and Brady 1995). To participate in politics, citizens need to have information about issues being addressed, know how the political system works, have the time and money to participate, and have confidence in their ability to be effective. All of these attributes are more common among high-SES individuals. Another explanation for SES bias revolves around mobilization. Many citizens participate because they are asked to, but mobilization efforts are not spread equally across the population. Those who are already active in their communities are more likely to be asked to participate, and because high-SES individuals are more likely to be active, mobilization efforts are disproportionately targeted toward them (Rosenstone and Hansen 1993).

SES bias is the most common (and compelling) finding concerning participation patterns, but there are other variables along which participation varies. One is religious activity. Although some research has not found a connection between religious activity and participation (e.g., McKenzie 2001; Martinson and Wilkening 1987), the weight of the evidence suggests that there is a link between participation and religious involvement (Niles and Clawson 2002; Alex-Assensoh and Assensoh 2001; Greenberg 2000; Calhoun-Brown 1996; Harris 1994; Peterson 1992).

Age is another factor that can impact participation. The age issue is particularly important for local politics because it is highly correlated with mobility. Older people are more likely to stay in a community for a long time, which leads to a greater incentive to participate, whereas younger people are more likely to move out of the city in the relative short term, leading them to opt out of local politics. Although anecdotal evidence of older people with disproportional influence in local politics supports this hypothesis, the few studies on the topic do not. Burr, Caro, and Morehead (2002), using a survey of Boston residents, conclude that there is a curvilinear relationship between age and attending community meetings, with attendance decreasing after the age of sixty-five. The most thorough study of aging and participation, by Jennings and Markus (1988), found that though there is little drop off in voting, as people age their nonelectoral political activities decline.

One hypothesis presented in the literature is that living in a neighborhood with high poverty levels and social problems will decrease political activity, the logic being that they do not have access to the resources and skills needed to participate. There is, however, minimal evidence to support this contention (Lawless and Fox 2001; Alex-Assensoh 1998; Cohen and Dawson 1993). Race and ethnicity is another variable than can influence participation rates. Even though most racial differences in participation disappear when controlling for SES, the literature has explored other factors that account for racial differences in participation (Marschall 2001; Leighley and Vedlitz 1999; Bobo and Gilliam 1990).

In sum, the literature explores variables that influence who participates, with the goal of understanding sources of participation bias. Many of the variables that influence local participation have been analyzed, but researchers have overlooked a few seemingly important ones. First, we could hypothesize that metropolitan fragmentation will dampen participation, with citizens living in areas with multiple local jurisdictions participating less. Also, given the importance of local policy for property values and property taxes, home ownership may have a significant impact on local participation (Rohe and Stegman 1994; Cox 1982). Finally, length of residence may also impact participation rates because the longer one lives in a community, the more knowledge and interest one is likely to acquire about local politics. Given the absence of research into these variables, we have an incomplete picture of the factors that influence nonelectoral participation on the local level.

What Issues Generate Participation?

Few works in participation studies, urban politics, or public policy deal directly with variation in participation across public policies; most research focuses on who participates and the effectiveness of citizen participation, which are related but distinct research questions. Perhaps the only direct attempt to understand what issues generate participation is an analysis conducted by Verba, Schlozman, and Brady (1995, 84–91), based on their Citizen Participation Study. When respondents stated they engaged in a participatory activity, they were asked to identify the issue that motivated the participation.[1] The primary finding was that different political acts are motivated by different types of issues. For voting, taxes and the economy are dominant issues, but these issues do not motivate other forms of participation. Contacting officials is typically motivated by "human needs" and education, protests are frequently about abortion, and "community activity" is often related to education and crime. Verba, Schlozman, and Brady conclude that there is a division of labor among participatory acts because some are better suited to sending certain types of political messages to officials; voting, for example, is a better conduit for expressing concern about taxes than a personalized contact, whereas contacting is better suited to addressing issues of human needs than voting. Thus, we see a pattern where the issues motivating participation vary across the different types of participatory acts.

Although there are few studies similar to that of Verba, Schlozman, and Brady that analyze participation across policy areas, some research is available that can contribute to our understanding of why citizens choose to participate in the political process affecting some policies and not others. The research discussed below does not directly address this question; however, we can draw on ideas and insights it presents to explore what types of patterns we might see in our study of Santa Ana.

In a classic article on the dynamics of local politics, Charles Tiebout (1956) argues that citizens choose their home locality based on the relationship between the bundle of goods and services that the locality provides and the bundle of goods and services they personally desire. In this model, citizens are consumers, shopping around to find the locality that best matches their personal preferences. Tiebout's model does not deal with participation, as citizens unhappy with their locality will move rather than participate to change local policy. We can, however, use Tiebout's premises and logic to hypothesize about what participatory patterns we would see if citizens were unable to leave and had to participate to make the locality's bundle of goods and services more closely resemble their preferred bundle. Barring exit as a possibility, Tiebout's theory infers that citizens will participate in those policies that have the greatest impact on their preferred package of goods and services, with the goal of making the locality's goods and services package more similar to theirs. Thus, participation patterns will be a reflection of the patterns of policy preferences in the community. This is a basic "interests" model of participation: citizens have a set of preferences and participate in order to realize them. Tiebout's theory, however, cannot tell us anything about why citizens have those preferences, nor can it tell us why citizens consider some goods and services to be more important (and thus more likely to generate participation) than others. In a Tieboutian world, the nature of public policies does not influence interests; citizens have set preferences, and will use those preferences to determine which policies are most important and worthy of their time and effort.

James Q. Wilson's (1974) typology of cost–benefit distribution effects introduces policy characteristics into the equation. For Wilson, whether the costs and benefits of a policy are distributed widely or narrowly concentrated determines the extent and nature of organizational activity. Policies with widely distributed costs and benefits will not generate much organizational activity (and are very likely to be passed by legislatures) because groups will not have a great personal stake in the outcome. Policies with concentrated benefits and distributed costs are also very likely to be enacted, because there will be organized activity by those benefiting but few groups will have an incentive to oppose them. Distributing benefits widely but concentrating costs will lead to strong opposition, and thus are not very likely, whereas concentrating both benefits and costs leads to continuous organized conflict, as those affected by the policy will try to avoid costs and maximize benefits.

Wilson's argument offers an additional variable to the hypothesis that participatory patterns are a reflection of policy preferences within a community: participation not only reflects the interests of the citizenry, but also how policies distribute costs and benefits. Policies that have concentrated costs or benefits will generate more participation because the recipients of the benefits or those paying the bill have greater incentives to participate. With widely distributed benefits and costs, the incentives to put time and money into influencing a policy are less. Thus, the policies that receive the most participation may not be the ones that have the greatest impact on citizens' collective interests, but those that have the most concentrated costs or benefits.

We can also frame cost–benefit distribution in terms of citizen preferences themselves. I mentioned above that Tiebout takes preferences as given, and thus cannot speak to how citizens come to think of some policies as being more important than others. Wilson's typology offers one possible influence on this process: citizens will view those policies that concentrate benefits or costs on them as being most important. This hypothesis moves outside of Wilson's theory itself because he is concerned about the behavior of groups, not preference formation among individual citizens. Yet, his cost–benefit typology could be applied to citizens if the incentive structure behind the typology works for both groups and individuals. The implication here is that policies that concentrate costs or benefits might generate more participation even if those policies have a smaller impact on citizen preferences than other policies that distribute costs and benefits more broadly.

Peterson's (1981) typology of policy arenas offers additional insights into how the nature of public policies influences participation patterns. Peterson classifies local polices into three categories—developmental, allocational, and redistributive—and analyzes how the politics surrounding each policy arena varies. Developmental politics is relatively closed, centralized, and consensus driven, with limited participation by citizens and interest groups. Allocational policies are more conflictual, with organized groups (particularly labor unions) actively participating. Redistributive issues are highly controversial, and city leaders will try to avoid them and deflect minority group demands for redistributive policies. Peterson argues that the amount of participation will vary across these arenas due to the nature of the politics surrounding each. His argument assumes that the amount of participation on a policy is derivative of the nature of its politics, not of individual preferences concerning its importance. There is minimal participation in developmental policy, for example, because it is closed, noncontroversial, and centralized, not because citizens find it unimportant. The hypothesis we can derive from Peterson's theory is that participation patterns are a function of the nature of the politics surrounding each policy area, not of the preferences of individuals. Even though Peterson's and Tiebout's theories converge on many issues, the implications of each theory for patterns of participation are different. Extending Tiebout's logic, participatory patterns are derivative of citizen preferences, whereas Peterson's theory treats participation as a function of the politics surrounding a policy arena.

Logan and Molotch (1987) offer another insight into determinants of participation patterns. They argue that conflicts over growth are central to the organization of cities. The essential dynamic of these conflicts is a tension between exchange values, which are the worth of land or buildings on the open market, and use values, which are the capacities of the city to fulfill daily needs. Land can serve two purposes: it can turn a profit for its owner(s) by appreciating in value or it can be used to fulfill needs, such as providing a place of residence or an entertainment destination. On the one hand, businesses, property owners, and (in many cases) city officials concentrate on the exchange value of property; on the other hand, city residents focus on its use values, leading to frequent clashes between residents who want to maintain their neighborhood use values and developers and business owners who want to intensify land uses to enhance exchange values.

If this argument is correct, we should expect participation to be greatest on those policies that have significant impact on either use values or exchange values. Citizens care most about use values, therefore, they will consider those policies that influence use values as being most important, and thus will be more likely to participate in them. The same holds true for business owners and exchange values. Like the hypotheses we derived from Wilson and Peterson, this one concerns how policy characteristics can influence participation; it describes how variation in a policy's impact on use and exchange values can influence citizen participation. Further, like Wilson's cost–benefit typology, Logan and Molotch's work offers insight into why citizens consider some policies more important than others. However, because use values encompass everything from shopping to commuting to recreation, it does not offer a very precise concept for understanding participation patterns.

Cost–benefit distribution, policy arenas, and use–exchange values offer a compelling case against the pure-interests model of participation that we inferred from Tiebout's theory. Participation patterns reflect more than just the preferences of individual citizens; they also reflect the attributes of public policies. Citizens do not just participate in whatever policies most impact their preferred bundle of goods and services; they also participate based on the distribution of costs–benefits, the politics surrounding the policy, and whether the policy affects use or exchange values.

How Do Citizens Participate?

When citizens try to influence local policy, how do they go about doing it? I break down citizen participatory activities into three broad categories: working through formal participatory structures, informal attempts to influence policy, and working through community organizations. These three categories are not mutually exclusive and citizens may engage in any combination of them on a given issue. That said, they do offer a convenient way to organize the disjointed and diverse literature on this subject.

Formal Participatory Structures

On the local level, one of the most common methods of citizen participation is the public hearing: a survey of city managers and chief administrative officers found that over 97 percent of cities use it as a strategy for dealing with citizens (Berman 1997, 107). Public hearings, which are usually required by law, allow citizens to comment on a specific issue or proposal before a legislative or administrative body. The literature discussing the merits of public hearings as a participatory tool will be discussed in detail in Chapter 8. Given the widespread use of public hearings as a means of receiving citizen input, it is reasonable to expect these hearing to be a central component of the strategy of many citizen attempts to influence policy.

In part due to the dissatisfaction with public hearings as a participatory tool, scholars and practitioners promoting enhanced citizen participation have developed other mechanisms for receiving citizen input. These include citizen panels or citizen juries (Haight and Ginger 2000; Kathlene and Martin 1991; Crosby, Kelly, and Schaefer 1986), town hall meetings (Moynihan 2003; America Speaks 2002; Spano 2001, 102–17), deliberative opinion polls (Fishkin 1995; 1991), citizen surveys (Weeks 2000), and deliberative forums (Mathews 1999). None of these processes have gained widespread use, although collectively they present an impressive array of opportunities for citizens to influence policy decisions.

Another avenue for citizens to influence local policy directly is through initiatives and referenda. Although common (particularly in western states), local initiatives and referenda have not been a primary subject of scholarly attention save for a few case studies on transportation and growth referenda (e.g., Steelman and Ascher 1997; DeLeon 1992, Chapter 4; Whitt 1982, Chapters 2 and 3). Scholars have also written a handful of articles on local school bond referenda (Shock 2001; Sonstelic and Portney 1980; Giles, Gatlin, Cataldo 1976). These articles, however, are concerned with predicting voter behavior based on a host of demographic variables, and do not examine school bond elections as a means for citizens to influence education finance policy.

Finally, many federal programs require local participation and the creation of local participatory structures. The best known of these is the "maximum feasible participation" mandate in the Economic Opportunity Act of 1964, which promoted participation in community action programs (CAPs). The literature on CAPs centers on whether citizens are effective in influencing local poverty policy. For our purposes, the important point is that this legislation prompted the creation of new ways to participate, primarily through appointment to, and lobbying of, a local Community Action Agency (CAA) board. This particular participatory form was incorporated into future federal programs, most notably the Empowerment Zone program, where a local board is authorized to distribute a federal grant to community organizations. Sitting on this board, or lobbying the board for funds, constitutes a unique way that citizens can participate in local policy decisions.

Informal Participation

All of the ways to participate described above are formal mechanisms created by government to allow for citizen input into the policy process. Participation, however, is not limited to these formal means, as citizens have other opportunities to influence policy. One such way is by directly contacting government officials. Since Verba and Nie's (1972) initial conclusion that contacting is not explained well by the standard SES model, the literature has centered on identifying the variables that predict contacting activity. Variables tested in the literature include social well-being, need, efficacy, and awareness, with little agreement on which factors are most important (Thomas and Melkers 1999; Sharp 1986, 1984; Hero 1986; Thomas 1982; Brown 1982; Vedlitz, Dyer, and Durand 1980; Jones et al. 1977). Hirlinger (1992) argues that the contradictory findings in the literature are a result of variation in operationalizing "contacting," particularly the common practice of lumping together particularized contacting (i.e., contacts on matters of narrow concern to the contactor) and general referent contacting (on matters of concern to the community as a whole). Hirlinger's distinction identifies a significant shortcoming in the contacting literature. By focusing almost exclusively on the correlates of contacting behavior, the literature has neglected to analyze the nature of contacting itself, even though the literature has recognized that there are different reasons for contacting officials (e.g., Coulter 1992). Verba, Schlozman, and Brady (1995, 84–93) make some progress toward this end by breaking down contacting by policy area, but the literature has largely ignored research questions concerning what constitutes a "contact," the nature of the request, and the context in which the request is made.

In addition to contacting, citizens can influence local policy decisions by signing and circulating petitions, protesting, joining a board or commission, or working through community organizations. Most of the literature analyzes these activities in the context of community organizations (the topic discussed in the next section). One line of thought in the literature, however, deserves mention here—namely, "public acting." Public acting, as defined by Mathews (1999) and Boyte and Kari (1996), occurs when citizens address public problems themselves, rather than appealing to government for help. In public acting, citizens tackle tough policy issues by deliberating and acting themselves, not by lobbying government.[2] Public acting is still an attempt to influence local policy, if one defines "local policy" as the community's (not just government's) approach to solving a particular problem. However, it is a unique participatory activity in that unlike most of the others discussed, it does not involve directly lobbying local officials to take a desired action.

Community Organizations

Much of the literature on how citizens try to influence local policy is preoccupied with the activities of community organizations. One type of community organization is the neighborhood association (for an analysis of the origins of neighborhood associations, see Logan and Rabrenovic 1990). Berry, Portney, and Thomson's (1993) seminal study on neighborhood associations concludes that they act as a link between citizens and city officials and can be an effective tool for citizens to influence local policy (see also Thomson 2001, and Portney and Berry 1997, for further analyses of these data). Other research also documents how citizens can use neighborhood associations to influence policy, including studies of Cincinnati (Thomas 1986), Birmingham (Haeberle 1989), and Baltimore (Crenson 1983). The literature documents the political efficacy of neighborhood associations, but it is more pessimistic about whether they represent the public at large: Berry, Portney, and Thomson (1993) find the same SES biases in neighborhood organizations as in other forms of participation, and other scholars also question how well they actually represent citizens (Swindell 2000; Cnaan 1991).

In addition to neighborhood associations, other community organizations are also conduits for citizen participation. Most notable are those organizations following an Alinsky-style approach that combines relational organizing, pressure tactics and connections to religious organizations to accomplish their political objectives. Best known among these groups is the Industrial Areas Foundation (IAF) and its local affiliates, such as San Antonio's Communities Organized for Public Service (COPS), Los Angeles' United Neighborhoods Organization (UNO), and Baltimoreans United in Leadership Development (BUILD). The Pacific Institute for Community Organization (PICO) is another faith-based community organization that operates in California and the western United States. The Association of Community Organizations for Reform Now (ACORN), though not explicitly an Alinsky-style group, is also a community organization that engages in many of the same organizing and lobbying techniques as the IAF and PICO.

The main subject of research in this area is on organizing strategies and effectiveness; it asks whether community organizations are able to mobilize poor neighborhoods and whether their organizing efforts have enhanced the political power of their constituent neighborhoods. The research on ACORN is generally written by scholars affiliated with the organization, and thus it has a positive assessment of both its organizing practices and effectiveness (Russell 1990; Delgado 1985). Some of the literature on the IAF is a bit more critical. For example, Skerry (1993) critiques UNO as being unable to develop an effective strategy given Los Angeles' political characteristics, and concludes that their successes have been isolated and superficial. And though COPS has been more successful, over time the organization has lost its confrontational edge and, Skerry concludes, it is now the functional equivalent of a political machine, not a grassroots community organization.

Despite such criticisms, most research on the IAF (particularly COPS) is positive. Berry, Portney, and Thomson (1993) use COPS as an example of neighborhood associations that are successful, and Boyte (1990, 89) states that COPS is responsible for "delivering a series of stunning political and programmatic victories." Mark R. Warren (2001), in the most comprehensive research on the IAF to date, also gives a positive assessment. He argues that the IAF empowers poor and minority neighborhoods, and that "the key to reinvigorating democracy in the United States can be found in efforts to engage people in politics through their participation in the stable institutions of community life" such as COPS (M. R. Warren 2001, 15). He also contends that the relational organizing employed by COPS creates leadership capacity within constituent neighborhoods and, despite some setbacks, has led to improvements in neighborhood quality of life. Wood's (2002) analysis of PICO is also positive, leading the author to be "cautiously optimistic" about prospects for these organizations to revitalize democracy.

In summary, the research on how citizens participate is a disjointed collection of analyses and stories about how citizens use participatory mechanisms or community groups to achieve their goals. Because the literature is so disjointed, drawing conclusions about the nature of citizen participatory activity is difficult. We do not know why citizens choose to engage in one activity rather than another, and only have sporadic descriptions of how citizens use the participatory options available to them to accomplish their political goals. Both of these issues are addressed in Part III.

Is Citizen Participation Effective?

When citizens try to influence local policy, are they successful? The most extensive and coherent line of inquiry into this question has been the effort to identify the relative power of elites and citizens in the "urban power" literature. The other literature addressing citizen effectiveness is a potpourri of studies on a variety of different factors that may have an impact on whether citizen participation leads to desired outcomes.

Urban Power and Citizen Effectiveness

The central theme in the urban-power debate is whether the average citizen can influence governmental decisions, or whether major decisions are made by elites irrespective of citizen preferences. Robert Dahl's (1961) study of New Haven, Connecticut, presents the most compelling case for the former contention. Dahl concludes that power in New Haven is fragmented, with political resources widely distributed among various groups. Further, a different set of political actors are powerful in each policy arena, and no one individual or group dominates all political decisions (even though for any one decision, you may have such domination). Some citizens are more powerful than others, but all citizens have some political resources, and no group of elites make all the political decisions. Thus, citizens can be effective at influencing local decisions, as shown by Dahl's now-famous story of Mary Grava, a New Haven resident who led a successful fight against low-income housing in her neighborhood.

Other studies contradict Dahl's findings. Early studies (Mills 1956; Hunter 1952) identify a dominant elite and marshal evidence that they, in fact, make all the major decisions. Later studies attack Dahl's conclusions by arguing that his conception of political power (defined as the ability of A to get B to do something that he or she would not otherwise do) is thin and underappreciates the power of elites. One line of thought contends that political power is not just the ability to make a decision but also to set the agenda and prevent decisions from even being made (Gaventa 1980; Crenson 1971; Bachrach and Baratz 1962). Others argue that the capacity to create consciousness—the ability to influence attitudes and beliefs—is also a component of political power (Gaventa 1980; Lukes 1974).

With this broader conception of power, the methodology that Dahl employs—identifying decisions and then finding out who influenced them—does not necessarily lead to an understanding of political power in a community. Gaventa (1980), for example, contends that the power of the elite in an Appalachian community lies not just in their ability to make important decisions (which they had), but also in their ability to keep certain issues off the agenda and in influencing how citizens think about politics and the economy. When elites have these powers, they can limit citizens' political effectiveness. The issues that citizens may want to influence may not even be taken up by local governments, preventing citizens from effecting the change that they desire. Further, the capacity to define and frame local issues can alter citizens' perceptions, perhaps stifling action that citizens might have taken otherwise.

Starting in the 1980s, the urban-power debate took a turn away from the question of how much power elites have vis-à-vis citizens and focused instead on how people (elites or otherwise) are able to exercise power in an urban context. The theory that emerged to answer this question was regime theory. A regime is a set of informal arrangements that complement the formal mechanisms of government, and constitutes the way most communities are governed (Stone 1989, 3). These informal arrangements allow a group of individuals to have the capacity to make decisions for the community: by informally gathering resources from various political actors, a regime is capable of reacting to situations as they arise and developing a policy program to govern the community. Regime theory works from the premise that both formal and informal relationships are necessary to govern effectively; governing requires being able to react to situations as they arise, and these reactions require more than formal authority. Addressing local problems requires different segments of the community to pool their resources and work together to develop strategies and take actions that can be effective.

The most common regime is a growth machine dominated by the downtown business elite (Logan and Molotch 1987; Elkin 1987; Swanstrom 1985; Molotch 1976). In a growth machine, business leaders and elected officials form partnerships to promote growth and economic development in the community (usually in downtown business cores). The logic behind growth machines is that the intensification of land use will result in profits for private business and additional tax revenues for cities; thus, city officials and local businesspeople have incentives to promote growth. Business leaders are in a good position to form the basis of an urban regime because they control valuable political resources: business contributes heavily to a city's tax base and business leaders frequently are large contributors to candidates for political office. City officials need the cooperation of businesspeople to make investments in the city, and businesspeople rely on elected officials for tax incentives and building permits, creating a mutual dependence that provides incentives for both sides to work together.

Regimes empower those who belong; the raison d'être of a regime is to develop the power to govern effectively. This does not necessarily mean that citizens outside of a regime will be ineffective at influencing local policy, because regimes create the capacity to act, not merely shift power from one group to another (i.e., power is not zero sum). Nonetheless, people outside of a governing regime will likely have less influence over the direction of local policy than those inside: the incentive structures of regimes are such that they will pay most attention to those groups and individuals that contribute resources to the regime.[3] If a group of citizens does not contribute, then they are not likely to be effective. Thus, regime theory concludes that citizens who are able to join and contribute to a regime will be more effective at influencing local policy than those who do not. Given the prevalence of growth machines, whose major players are politicians and downtown business leaders, citizens in many cities may not play a major role in regimes, and thus may not be effective at achieving their political goals.

Other Research on Citizen Participation and Effectiveness

Outside of the urban power debate, scholars have explored what factors enhance or diminish the impact of citizen participation. One research question here is whether decentralizing power will enhance the control that citizens have over local policy. Supporters of decentralization (e.g., Altshuler 1970) argue that moving policy-making authority from the city government to neighborhood-based councils will lead to greater opportunities for citizens to influence policy. In the late 1960s and early 1970s decentralization experiments in school districts were conducted, and the research studying these efforts reveals mixed results (cf. Rogers and Chung 1983; Gittell 1980, 1972; LaNoue and Smith 1973; Fantini, Gittell, and Magat 1970). On a different note, Berry, Portney, and Thomson (1993) analyze the effectiveness of decentralizing municipal government through the establishment of neighborhood associations and find that neighborhood associations can set the agenda, compete with business interests, and can increase government responsiveness.

Scholars have also explored the capacity of participatory structures to enhance effectiveness. The research on whether public hearings provide an opportunity for citizens to influence governmental decisions generally concludes that, at least in some circumstances, citizen comments at hearings do have an impact (McComas 2001b; Chess and Purcell 1999; Gormley 1986; Gundry and Heberlein 1984; Rosener 1982; Mazmanian and Sabatier 1980). Mansbridge (1980), in her study of New England town meetings, argues that this form of participation can lead to effective participation if there are common interests and giving every citizen an equal voice is not essential (see Bryan 2004 and Bryan and McClaughry 1989 for a more positive view of the benefits of New England town meetings). And, as already mentioned, the literature on neighborhood associations suggests that these organizations can enhance citizen effectiveness (Mesch and Schwirian 1996; Berry, Portney, and Thomson 1993; Haeberle 1989; Thomas 1986).

Political scientists have also studied federal mandates of participation to assess whether they promote citizen influence over federal policy. Studies of CAPs have mixed results. In the most thorough study, Greenstone and Peterson (1973) argue that there is wide variation in CAP implementation due to differences in how the boards are appointed, city administrative structures, and the role of political groups. They conclude that the outcomes of CAPs are ambiguous. Marston (1993) has a more positive assessment, arguing that the CAP in Tucson, Arizona, institutionalizes citizen participation and brings about significant changes to the political landscape. Along these same lines, Sirianni and Friedland (2001) argue that CAPs create new forms of social capital that promote participation. The Empowerment Zone legislation passed in 1993 also mandates citizen participation, but the research to date reflects mixed results concerning the level and effectiveness of citizen participation (Bockmeyer 2000; Gittell et al. 1998).

Some research has analyzed the variables that impact the effectiveness of participation. Kweit and Kweit (1981) argue that effectiveness is contingent upon the structures of participation, the characteristics of target organizations, and environmental characteristics. For example, they propose that cities with a reformed governing structure exhibit greater levels of citizen effectiveness than machine-style cities. They conclude that the effectiveness of participation depends on the context in which it occurs. Along these same lines, Bass (2000) suggests that community organizations can effectively influence public safety policy, but that many factors (such as powerful police unions and institutional structures) can impede their capacity to participate. Scavo (1995) comes to the conclusion that central cities are more receptive to neighborhood empowerment than newer "edge cities" (Garreau 1991), leading to more effective participation in the former (given the history of machine politics and regimes dominated by business elites in older central cities, one might expect the opposite to be true). This distinction between older central cities and newer edge cities is a significant one, given their different political cultures, and deserves more attention in the literature.

Another research question on citizen effectiveness concerns whether confrontation or cooperation is the most effective way to participate. Classic studies ask whether cooperation leads to co-optation and neutralization of participation and conclude that it does (Piven and Cloward 1977; Selznick 1966). The research on the IAF and Alinsky-style groups picks up on this theme, but focuses more on whether these groups are able to maintain a confrontational stance even after gaining a measure of political power (for contrasting answers to this questions, see Skerry 1993 and M. R. Warren 2001). There are two key issues here: whether citizens (or community groups) are more effective in a confrontational or cooperative mode, and whether it is possible for groups and citizens with a confrontational stance to maintain it over time. Based on the research of Piven and Cloward (1977), the answer to the second question would appear to be negative. The first question, however, has not been dealt with in any substantive way.

In sum, the literature on the effectiveness of citizen participation has left us with a very unsatisfying "it all depends" conclusion. Regime theory tells us that the conditions that affect the impact of participation are the relationship of the participants to the governing regime and the resources they can bring to the table. Other research on effectiveness identifies a host of variables that can influence the impact of citizen participation. Yet the literature has not sorted through these variables to identify the ones that are most important in predicting when participation will be effective, nor has it offered convincing evidence for the variables it identifies as being important. Thus, we are left with the conclusion that citizen participation can be effective under some circumstances, but without much guidance as to what those circumstances would be.

Conclusion

In this chapter, I examined the literature on nonelectoral participation in local politics, breaking down this subject into four areas of inquiry: who participates, what issues they try to influence, how they participate, and whether their participation is effective. Although the literature is not unified, there has been substantial work on this topic, at least on who participates and whether citizen participants are effective. Of the four areas examined, the research on what issues citizens try to influence has been the least studied. Further, many studies explore how citizens participate, but they tend to pay attention to a particular mode of participation or a specific social movement. Missing from that literature are analyses of the overarching strategies that citizens employ when they participate. Parts II and III begin filling these gaps in the literature with an analysis of the patterns and forms of citizen participation in local politics.

PART II

Participation Across Local Policies

3 Policy Characteristics and Patterns of Participation

Why do some local issues generate significant participation while other do not? Citizens—with limited time to devote to politics and an endless array of issues—need to decide on which issues they will participate. Why do they choose to participate on issue A and not issue B? My goal in part II is to understand the variation in participation across local public policies and to analyze the choices that citizens make when they decide to participate in local affairs.

Typically, questions concerning participation patterns are cast in terms of personal versus community interests: do citizens participate on policies that affect their own personal interests (such as the amount of taxes they pay or the level of services they receive) or is their participation prompted by broader community concerns, such as maintaining a healthy environment or assisting those in need? This conceptualization is not very productive because distinguishing between personal interests and community interests is problematic. Are citizens' concerns about air pollution personal interests (they want to breathe clean air) or are they community concerns (they want to maintain a healthy environment for everybody in the community)? Personal interests are interrelated with community interests: since citizens live within a community, their own well-being is tied—at least to some extent—to the community as a whole. Determining whether citizens base their participation on personal interest or community concern is impossible because their interrelationship prevents us from developing adequate measures of each. Furthermore, we cannot ask citizens whether they are driven by personal or community interests, since many citizens equate their own personal interests with the community's interests—a variation of the now cliché "What's good for GM is good for America."[1]

Understanding the participation choices that citizens make, therefore, cannot be done using a framework of personal versus community interests. Rather than trying to understand the nature of the interests (i.e. personal vs. community) that drive participation, we need to understand the factors that influence citizens' understanding of which policies are most salient. Citizens participate on those issues that they feel are important, either important to them personally or important for the community at large. How do they come to understand which issues are the important ones and which ones are not? Answering this question is the key to analyzing the patterns of participation that we see in local politics. In this chapter, I explore how the characteristics of local public policies influence which ones citizens find important enough to stimulate participation. Some policies have a direct and clear impact on citizens' lives whereas others are more obscure, may have uncertain effects, and may only indirectly influence citizens. These differences influence how citizens view a policy's importance and, consequently, their participation.

Before I discuss how policy characteristics influence participation, an overview of participation patterns in Santa Ana is in order.

Which Policies Generate the Most Participation?

Public Speaking across Issues

We can use the set of controversial city council and school board votes described in Chapter 1 to identify which decisions generated the most participation, as measured by the number of public speakers. Though speaking at a public meeting is only one of many possible acts of participation, it serves as a good measure of participation generally. Public speaking is one of the most common forms of participation: 98 percent of interviewees said that they had spoken at a public meeting at some point. Of course, not all decisions are made by city council or school board votes, and participation in these administrative decisions will not be reflected in this analysis. Despite this shortcoming, an analysis of public speaking provides a good measure of which city council and school board decisions generate the most participation.

Tables 3.1 and 3.2 summarize public speakers by policy type. Categorizing policies is subjective because they often fit into multiple categories, and the categories themselves do not have

Table 3.1. Public speakers on city policies

Category	Speakers	Number of decisions	Speakers per decision
By substantive area			
Redevelopment	373	34	11.0
Public works	298	44	6.8
Land use	287	78	3.7
City rules and regulations	135	28	4.8
Public safety	81	16	5.1
Budgeting	65	26	2.5
Personnel	65	43	1.5
Other	42	31	1.4
Housing	39	8	4.9
Parks, rec. and library	30	6	5.0
Internal city rules	14	18	0.8
Totals	1,429	332	4.3
By type of decision			
Fiscal policy*	479	97	4.9
Land use	387	99	3.9
Regulations on individuals	326	25	13.0
Business regulation	84	27	3.1
Personnel	65	43	1.5
Other	62	21	3.0
Internal city rules	26	20	1.3
Totals	1,429	332	4.3

*"Fiscal Policy" is more inclusive than the "budgeting" category above in that it includes contracting decisions, CDBG grant decisions, and others fiscal decisions that are not directly related to passing a city budget.

clear boundaries. To account partially for this limitation, two different classifications are presented for city council decisions in Table 3.1. The first is by substantive area, which groups policies according to the department or function that the decision affects. The second is by type of decision, which categorizes decisions based on the nature of the activity, not on substantive area. Despite significant overlap, they offer two different perspectives on the distribution of public speakers. The school district policies are easier to classify (largely due to an easy distinction between facilities and instruction), and thus only one classification is presented in Table 3.2.

It is difficult to draw firm conclusions from these tables for two reasons. First, a handful of controversial issues can significantly

Table 3.2. Public speakers on school district policies

Category	Speakers	Number of decisions	Speakers per decision
School district policy	406	73	5.6
Facilities	233	58	4.0
Classroom instruction	130	36	3.6
Fiscal policy	87	47	1.9
Other	56	14	4.0
Grant applications	30	87	0.3
Internal matters	3	51	0.1
Personnel	3	32	0.1
Totals	948	398	2.4

influence the speakers per issue ratio (e.g., the "redevelopment" ratio is so high because of Community Development Block Grant allocation hearings). Second, the number of controversial decisions in each category is partially a reflection of the peculiarities of elected officials. For example, the school district had eighty-seven nonunanimous decisions on typically routine grant applications because two conservatives on the school board opposed the social programs (such as head start and health care) that the grants funded. These limitations aside, the two tables are valuable in that they provide some general (if crude) trends in the distribution of public speakers across different types of policy decisions.

On the City side, issues dealing with the built environment (redevelopment, land use, public works) generated the most participation. City regulations and service delivery also generated some speakers. The issues receiving the least participation were personnel issues and "internal city rules" (such as ethics codes and decision-making procedures). Among school district decisions, the "school district policy" category, which is an assortment of policies on a host of noncurriculum issues, received the most speakers. This category includes decisions relating to school uniforms, boundary changes, and various school programs. The building of new schools (facilities) and instructional issues also generated a fair number of public speakers. The issues that garnered the least number of speakers, not surprisingly, are personnel issues or internal matters (most

Table 3.3. Distribution of public speakers

Number of speakers	City decisions	Speakers (% of total)	SAUSD decisions	Speakers (% of total)
0	192	0 (0)	27	0 (0)
1–5	70	168 (12)	29	67 (7)
6–10	21	163 (11)	12	93 (10)
11–20	27	395 (28)	18	259 (27)
21–30	13	332 (23)	6	155 (16)
31 and over	9	371 (26)	6	374 (39)
Total	332	1,429	398	948

of which were obscure disagreements among school board trustees). Although issues dealing directly with classroom instruction received some interest from citizens, they were not the focus of most participation. This lack of interest is perhaps a bit surprising, as we might hypothesize that instructional issues would generate more participation, particularly in a school district with such a poor academic record.

Table 3.3 provides another perspective on the distribution of public speakers by examining the extent to which speakers were spread out among the 730 decisions made by the city council and school board. The majority of issues did not have any speakers, and only seventy-nine issues had more than ten speakers. However, these seventy-nine policies had 1,866 speakers, or 79 percent of the total. In other words, 11 percent of the decisions accounted for 79 percent of the public speakers. Speakers were clustered around a few decisions for both city and school district decisions, although the trend is more pronounced on the school district side with only twelve policies accounting for 56 percent of the total. Thus, we see a pattern where a handful of policies generates most of the public speakers. The question then becomes, what is it about these policies that generate so much attention whereas most other policies generate little interest?

To answer this question, Table 3.4 lists the policies that had at least thirty speakers.[2] Here are brief sketches of the issues on the list, based on newspaper articles and interview respondent descriptions.

Table 3.4. City council/school board decisions with the most public speakers, 1990–2000

Issue	Entity	Date	Description	Speakers, single meeting	Speakers, overall*	Letters**
Space-saver school	School district	2/1/94	Approval of a new school located next to a mall	67	149	NA
Floral Park traffic plan	City	6/19/95	Motion to make traffic diverters on Santa Clara and 19th streets permanent	64	64	1,218
School health clinics	School district	5/14/91	Approval of a pilot program to establish mobile health clinics in elementary schools	54	76	NA
School uniforms	School district	9/24/96	Proposal to require all elementary and junior high school students to wear uniforms	44	64	NA
CDBG grant allotment, FY 98–99	City	4/6/98	Public hearing on the allotment of $8,154,000 in CDBG funds	42	42	0
Approval of contracts for a new City jail	City	2/22/94	Approval of various contracts and other matters to allow for the construction of a new jail and police headquarters	40	76	38
CDBG grant allotment, FY 97–98	City	4/21/97	Public hearing on the allotment of $8,401,000 in CDBG funds	38	38	2
School District Budget, SY 91–92	School district	3/12/91	Plan to balance school budget through layoffs and program cuts	37	45	NA

CDBG grant allotment, FY 95–96	City	5/1/95	Public hearing on the allotment of approximately $7 million in CDBG funds	37	37	0
Floral Park traffic plan	City	4/5/93	Plan to place traffic diverters on Santa Clara and 19th streets	35	35	419
Floral Park traffic plan	City	12/2/91	Proposal to develop a traffic mitigation plan for the Floral Park neighborhood	33	48	0
Teacher dress code	School district	6/24/97	Approval of a teacher dress code	32	40	NA
Main Street pawn shop	City	4/20/92	Permit to allow the construction of a pawn shop	31	31	10
CDBG grant allotment, FY 94–95	City	6/20/94	Public hearing on the allotment of $6,675,000 in CDBG funds	30	30	7
17th Street medians	City	8/3/98	Construction of street medians on 17th street between Bristol and Broadway	30	30	0

*Includes speakers at meetings three months before or three months after the vote was taken.

**The school district does not report letters received.

Space-Saver School. Santa Ana is densely populated and has scarce open land, creating problems for a school district needing to build additional schools to accommodate a growing population. To address the issue, the school district decided to utilize a state program (called the "space-saver program") that provides funds to urban school districts to build schools in unusual places and proposed building a school adjacent to a strip mall. Under the proposal, the school district would buy a corner of the mall, relocate one of the buildings, and then build a three-story school on a relatively small piece of land. Opponents (mostly nearby homeowners) had three arguments against the plan: the school would cost too much, the school would generate significant noise and traffic, and the location was unfit for a school. Supporters (many of whom were active in school parent–teacher associations) countered these arguments, and claimed that the real reason for the opposition was racial: opponents were mostly wealthy white residents in the nearby Floral Park community, whereas the school would serve primarily Hispanic children.

School Health Clinics. This proposal was intended to fund a mobile health clinic that would travel among the district's intermediate schools. Opponents were primarily religious and fiscal conservatives who argued that schools should not be in the business of providing health care and feared that the program might be extended to include abortion counseling.

Floral Park Traffic Plans. Floral Park is one of the wealthiest neighborhoods in Santa Ana, very active politically, and primarily Anglo. All three votes listed in Table 3.4 involve a proposal to place traffic diverters (essentially barricades to reduce traffic) on two major streets running through the neighborhood. They were originally meant as temporary measures to mitigate increased traffic caused by freeway construction but were made permanent a few years later. Supporters claimed safety and aesthetic reasons for the diverters; opponents accused Floral Park of snobbery and elitism (most of the opponents lived in nearby communities who used the streets being blocked).

School Uniforms and Teacher Dress Code. After the school district voted to require all elementary students to wear uniforms, they followed up by passing a dress code for teachers (including a ban on T-shirts, jeans, and other casual apparel). Many of the speakers on the teacher dress code (and some on the school uniform issue) were teachers.

School District Budget, SY 1991–1992. In a time of dwindling state funding and an economic slowdown, the school district proposed laying off eighty-eight people and cutting athletic, music, and other programs.

Community Development Block Grant (CDBG) Allotments. When cities receive CDBG funds from the federal government, they are required to hold a public hearing on how they will disperse the funds. Almost all of the speakers at these meetings are representatives from social service agencies requesting funds.

City Jail. To deal with a serious crime problem and a lack of space at the Orange County jail, the City proposed increasing the utility tax from 5 percent to 6 percent in order to pay for a new jail and police headquarters. In a rather unusual scenario, the majority of residents in the surrounding neighborhood (Washington Square, a middle-class, majority white area) supported the jail, although there was some opposition from fiscal conservatives unhappy about the tax increase.

Main Street Pawn Shop. Approval of a new pawn shop was opposed by residents of a nearby neighborhood.

17th Street Medians. This proposal to create grassy medians on 17th Street, a major thoroughfare, generated significant controversy because it would alter traffic patterns. Not surprisingly, citizens who lived on streets that were likely to have more traffic opposed the plan (most speakers were in opposition). There was also opposition from business owners who feared that potential customers would have difficulty locating their businesses.

We will return to the question of why these issues generated so much participation, but first I present an overview of the evidence from participant interviews.

Participant Interviews

During the second part of the interview, respondents were asked to list two or three issues that they were personally involved with, and then open-ended follow-up questions were asked on each issue. Table 3.5 identifies the policies that respondents discussed (a complete list of the policies appears in the Appendix).

The list is dominated by transportation and land-use issues. The transportation category includes traffic mitigation measures, such as street barriers and stop signs, as well as an issue concerning a proposed light rail running through the city. Many of the responses in the land-use category were opposition to locally unwanted land uses (LULUs), such as a drug rehabilitation center, a blighted apartment complex, and a swap meet. The new schools category also includes opposition to what some consider LULUs, although about half of the responses here were from citizens in favor of building new schools. Proposed new schools generated opposition because of a perceived negative impact on quality of life, but some of the supporters of new schools stated their support was due to positive impact on the education of their children.

Measure C was a bond measure passed in 1999 that raised money for school construction and repair.[3] The rest of the list is fairly self-explanatory. The economic development category includes mentions of the empowerment zone and a major redevelopment project. Code enforcement constitutes efforts by citizens to eliminate visual blight, whereas the housing and overcrowding category includes issues such as creating affordable housing and limiting residential densities. School instruction includes references to bilingual education and to special education. The business regulation category includes two references to efforts to ban pushcart vendors downtown and two references to a liquor license application for a downtown restaurant.

We should note what is not on the list. First, issues dealing with controversial social issues are, for the most part, absent.[4] This exclusion is partly a function of the fact that cities and school districts do not routinely deal with issues such as welfare, abortion, and capital punishment. Even so, local governments occasionally address these issues, and citizens have opportunities to participate on these issues through decisions that local governments make. For example, both the City and the school district have affirmative

Table 3.5. Issues receiving participation by interview respondents

Categorized by policy area*

Policy area	Number of policies
Transportation	21
New schools	12
Land use (other than schools)	11
Measure C (school bond)	11
Parks, rec., and library	8
Economic development**	8
School instruction	7
Public safety	7
Code enforcement	6
Housing/overcrowding	5
Artists village/arts programs	5
Historic preservation	4
Business regulation	4
Personnel	2
Other–school district***	2
Other–city***	8
Total	121

*See Appendix A for a complete list of issues.
**Includes mentions of the Empowerment Zone.
***"Other" categories include policy areas that were mentioned only once.

action programs, yet this controversial issue did not generate any mentions among interview respondents. Participants did not pick ideological battles with the City or school district, and their participation was not geared to achieving policy change to make local policy more congruent with their ideological beliefs.

The specific policies that received attention are the result of the peculiarities of Santa Ana politics. Because Santa Ana is a dense city with a growing population, the siting of schools is a major issue, whereas in many communities it is not. Further, the focus on traffic is also a by-product of density and population growth, along with the fact that Santa Ana is a relatively old city that is not designed to handle the volume of traffic that currently exists. Thus, speculating about which specific issues receive the most attention from participants is not very useful: traffic may be a big issue in Santa Ana, but may be a nonissue in another city. We can, however, infer something about the general characteristics of policies that receive attention, a task undertaken in the next section.

Policy Impact and Participation Patterns

In this section, I explore how local government decisions vary in their impact on citizens, and demonstrate how this variation can explain participation patterns in Santa Ana. I identify two characteristics of policy impact, directness and clarity, that influence participation. Each will be discussed in turn.

Directness

Most functions that local governments perform impact citizens' lives. Local governments provide basic public services (e.g., public safety, education, sanitation) and maintain the physical infrastructure (e.g., repave streets and maintain parks). Localities also regulate economic, political, and social activity through such devices as zoning regulations, building codes, and public nuisance ordinances. To pay for these activities, they levy taxes and fees that are easily identifiable and ever present. All of these regulations, collectively, have a tremendous impact on citizens' daily routines and their quality of life. The activities of local governments matter for how people live their lives, the quality of services they receive, the education of their children, and the amount of taxes they pay.

Although local governments perform functions that affect citizens, not all local policies directly impact citizens' lives. By "directly" I mean the capacity of a public policy to have a noticeable impact that citizens can see, feel, and experience in their daily routines. Most decisions that governmental bodies make only tangentially affect the final outputs that government produces, and thus do not directly affect citizens. These policies may have some impact, maybe even a significant impact, but the influence is indirect: a governmental body takes an action, leading to other changes that, in turn, affect citizens. Sometimes, however, governmental bodies make decisions that have a direct impact on citizens' lives. Citizens, in going about their daily activities, will be able to see and feel the effects of the new policies and can attribute changes to them.

An example may clarify this point. Most citizens view public safety as an important governmental function and care deeply about safety in their community. Further, the safety of a community has significance for citizens' daily routines: Unsafe streets may require citizens to change their habits, such as not allowing their children to walk alone or avoiding night activities that require walking on the streets. Every now and then cities will make decisions that have a direct impact on public safety. For example, they may decide to hire a hundred more police officers to patrol the streets or they may decide to change to a community-oriented policing style. Decisions like these will result in more police officers on the street or altered police behavior (even though it may not have much of an impact on crime rates). Most public safety decisions, however, have an indirect impact. Take, for example, a city that decides to give police officers a 5 percent raise. This raise could have significant impact on the nature of policing: it may mean reductions in the number of officers, it may mean higher-quality recruits, it may mean higher taxes, and so forth. The impact is great, but it is indirect. None of these potential impacts directly affects the policing that citizens experience on a day-to-day basis. Citizens cannot see a 5 percent raise nor can they feel the impact of the raise in their daily lives. They may see changes (such as fewer officers on the street or more professional conduct), but the relationship of these changes to a pay increase is remote. The decision to give officers a raise will impact secondary activities of policing (such as hiring new recruits), which may, in turn, influence the quality of policing that citizens experience. In sum, within a given policy area citizens will be able to see the direct impact of some decisions, but the impact of others will be less direct.

Most decisions that local governments make have only indirect impacts on daily routines. If one browses through minutes of city council or school board meetings, one will see many personnel actions, contracting decisions, minor adjustments to city regulations, and other such decisions. Even when governmental entities make major changes, they are usually done in incremental steps, each of which only indirectly contributes to a significant impact. Local legislative bodies are generally concerned with day-to-day managing of the government and conducting routine business, the effects of which citizens rarely see or feel. There are, of course, times when decisions have direct impacts. Most land use decisions are good examples; a city's decision to approve a new housing development will have a direct impact on the daily routines of citizens near the proposed development. These decisions, however, comprise only a small portion of the decisions that local officials make.

There are three policy characteristics that significantly influence the directness of policy impact: target groups, policy chains, and policy tools. Schneider and Ingram (1997) define target groups as those groups of citizens whose behavior the policy is aimed to influence. Target groups will not necessarily experience policy impact directly, however, they are more likely to feel the consequences of a policy directly than will nontarget groups. For example, city employees will directly experience the effects of a change in personnel regulations, but most other citizens will not even notice the change. Similarly, a new housing development may directly impact nearby residents, but it may also have little direct influence on the rest of the city. Other policies, of course, may have a direct impact on both targets and nontargets or not have any direct impact on either. The point is that directness varies across groups as well as across policies and that the directness of policy impact is not uniformly distributed.

Another factor that can influence the directness of a policy's impact is the length of the policy chain. Schneider and Ingram (1997) illustrate that many policies have long chains comprising of multiple targets, where the ultimate target is not the direct focus of the policy. For example, Santa Ana's efforts to establish an artists' village (see Chapter 4) had as its ultimate target the citizenry at large (who were to benefit from having this cultural amenity), although the proximate targets consisted of developers and artists who received loans, grants, and assistance from the City. More proximate target groups will be more directly affected by policy impact, and those further down the policy chain will only indirectly experience the policy. Long policy chains reduce the directness of a policy's impact by having the effects of the policy work through the behavior of other target groups.

The use of various policy tools also impacts directness. Salamon (2002) argues that policy analysis should shift its focus away from programs and agencies and toward policy tools, which are the methods that are employed to achieve policy goals. Government employs many policy tools, Salamon continues, and its choice of tools has significant implications for policy effectiveness and impact. For our purposes, the point is that certain tools lend themselves to direct impact whereas others are more diffuse in their effects, and the same policy decision could have a more or less direct effect depending on the policy tools employed.

Table 3.6. Tools for policies generating participation

Tool	Number of policies
Social regulation	77
Land use/zoning regulation	58
Direct government	21
Grants	18
Contracting	9
Position taking	9
Taxes, fees, charges	8
Redevelopment	7
Direct loans/loan guarantees	4
Tax expenditures	0
Multiple tools	16
No tool involved	15
Other/unclear	16
Total	258

Directness and Participation in Santa Ana

In Santa Ana, policies with a direct impact generated the most participation. To demonstrate this fact, we can look at the target groups, policy chains, and tools employed by policies that generated participation. Starting with policy tools, Table 3.6 summarizes the tools used by the policies that generated participation.[5] The table includes all decisions from the policy table that had at least one public speaker and all policies mentioned by respondents (with duplicates deleted). Over half of the policies used social regulation or land use decisions (a specific type of social regulation) as the primary tool to accomplish policy objectives. These tools lead to direct policy impacts: the City or school district enacts an ordinance or makes a land use decision that regulates the behavior of citizens and leads to changes in either the built environment or the actions of citizens.

Moving further down the list, however, the policy impact is diluted by the nature of the tool used. For example, contracting decisions only have an impact on citizens through the performance of contractors. Redevelopment policy is usually indirect because the impact that citizens experience—redevelopment of the physical infrastructure in a neighborhood—is removed many steps from the decisions that the city council makes.[6] Tax policy has both direct and indirect elements. It is direct because decisions by the school board or city council lead straight to citizens paying higher taxes. However, on the opposite end, the impact of the additional tax revenue is usually indirect, as tax revenues cannot be traced to something that citizens experience unless they are earmarked for a specific purpose. Thus, most of the policies that generated participation employed policy tools that lead to direct impact on citizens.

If we examine the policies with the most public speakers (Table 3.4), we can see that most of them utilized tools that have a direct impact on citizens' routines. The Floral Park traffic mitigation efforts are the best examples of direct impact. We would be hard pressed to find a more direct way to alter the behavior of motorists than to block streets with concrete barriers, which is what these policies did. Building a school is also a direct way to impact citizens. The same goes for school uniforms, a bit of social regulation that has direct implications for both children and parents. There are a few exceptions to this pattern: The pawn shop only had indirect consequences for the neighborhood opposed to it because the shop itself was not going to radically change the area. Also, the health clinics issue had more to do with an ideological battle between conservatives and liberals than with its actual impact, which was minor. However, the fact that only one highly charged, ideological issue made the list indicates that the direct experience of policies matter more for generating participation at the local level than ideological debates.

A similar analysis can be done for the policies categorized in Table 3.5. The land use, transportation, and new schools categories are comprised entirely of policies that utilize policy tools that lead to a direct impact on citizens. The governmental decisions in these categories alter the physical plant of the City by building new structures or altering the uses of existing structures through regulation. Either way, the decisions have an impact on citizens' experience. Measure C is a case of a taxing decision that had direct implications for citizens on both ends. Not only was it a direct assessment on property, but it also specifically identified how the money generated was going to be used (this tactic was intentionally used by bond proponents to generate additional support). Some of the policies in the remaining categories do not utilize tools that lead to direct impact (such as the artists' village and school instruction), although the list is dominated by policies that do utilize these types of tools.

Moving on to target groups, the majority of participants were the proximate targets of the policies in Tables 3.4 and 3.5. The CDBG votes—where almost all of the participants were potential recipients—are illustrative. Few other citizens participated, despite the fact that large sums of money were at stake and the City had some flexibility as to how to distribute the funds. Also, traffic plan debates were dominated by those directly targeted, either as commuters using the affected streets or people who live on them. This finding is not surprising; of course street users will be most concerned about a proposed barricade, and potential recipients are going to be motivated to participate in a CDBG hearing. The interesting finding here is that policies, such as CDBG funding and traffic mitigation plans, that directly impact their proximate targets generated more participation than those that do not.

There are exceptions to this pattern, where the decisions did not have a very direct impact on proximate targets or where most participants were not proximate targets. The school health clinics issue generated participation from many citizens who were opposed to the program even though it would have minimal impact on them. Approval of the new city jail was another issue where many participants were not proximate targets. Participants were either opponents of the new tax used to finance the jail or supporters believing the new jail would reduce crime. The former group were proximate targets (because they were being taxed to raise the money to build the jail), and the latter group were targets many steps removed. Despite these exceptions, participants were generally citizens who were the proximate targets of the policies they tried to influence.

Along these same lines, policies generating participation usually had very short policy chains, meaning that there were few intermediate target groups between the initial action and the final desired outcome. For land use and transportation policy, the policy chains go from a decision to modify or regulate the built environment, to actually performing that task, to some desired outcome. Few intermediate target groups are needed. For example, the traffic mitigation plans involved a city decision to modify traffic patterns by erecting barriers or altering traffic rules, which would lead directly to changes in traffic patterns (the desired outcome). Another example of a short policy chain is the school uniform issue: The school district passes a regulation requiring students to wear uniforms, which directly influences the ultimate target (children). Most other policies had similarly short and direct policy chains, with few examples of chains that involved many target groups. Redevelopment policies, such as the efforts to establish the artists' village, are exceptions, as the link between the initial action by the City and ultimate outcomes are mediated by developers, business owners, and residents impacted by redevelopment. However, policies with such long policy chains usually do not generate much participation.

One more piece of evidence from the participant interviews can demonstrate the importance of directness for generating participation. After respondents listed two or three policies, they were asked why they decided to participate on each issue. Table 3.7 categorizes their open-ended responses. For over a quarter of the issues mentioned, direct, personal experience with an issue was given as the reason for their involvement. For example, those who participated on traffic mitigation issues stated that it was traffic on their street (or in their neighborhood) that provided the impetus to participate. A second response was to explain why the issue was important to the neighborhood or the city as a whole. For example, one respondent, when asked why he was involved in development of the artists' village, discussed the importance of the arts for society and community.

A third explanation given was that their participation was necessary to prevent a bad decision by the city council or school board. Citizens focused on preventing unwanted land uses in their neighborhood usually offered this explanation. For example, a respondent opposed to the building of a new school in his neighborhood offered this explanation for why he participated:

> I really didn't think this was the right place for a school and quite honestly haven't changed my mind. I saw a blatant, blatant disregard for the environmental impact that the school board presented. . . . Certainly, the traffic impact was just totally out of the question. It was so far wrong I thought a blind man could see it. I also felt we were paying too much money for that property.

Finally, many citizens got involved in specific issues because someone asked them to or because they belonged to organizations

Table 3.7. Reasons to participate

Reason given for participation	Mentions*
Personal experience	26.5
Important issue	25.5
Asked/encouraged by others	16
Affiliated groups were involved	12
Need to prevent bad decision	9
Total**	89

*If respondent gave two answers, each was counted as half (0.5) of a response. If there were more than two answers, only the first two mentioned were counted (this happened in only one instance).

**For thirty-two issues, no reason was given, either because the respondent did not respond or the question was not asked.

that were involved. Some involvement was generated through neighborhood groups: people would go to the monthly neighborhood association meeting, hear about an issue, and then get involved in it either as a representative of the neighborhood association or as just a concerned citizen.

The number of respondents who said that personal experience was their primary motivation is an indication of the importance of direct policy impact for generating participation. The personal experiences that respondents cited usually focused on various aspects of their daily routines or personal finances. For example, a citizen who led the fight for the Floral Park traffic diverters explained her participation this way:

> I think the reason I got involved was traffic mitigation. I bought my home eleven years ago and couldn't get in and out of my driveway because there was so much commuter traffic on my little residential street. ... [H]ere I'd made the biggest investment of my life in a home, and I had all the impact of local businesses and commuter traffic and no one willing to address it.

We see two interrelated reasons for participation here: traffic's impact on property values and its impact on the ability to leave and return home. The City's decisions to implement traffic mitigation measures will directly influence these aspects of daily life. An opponent of the traffic plan offered similar reasons:

Well, because it really affected me directly and it certainly affected most of the people in this neighborhood, in that anything that would have precluded our going down Santa Clara [one of the streets that was blocked] took us away from what was then one of the better, bigger business sites. Our bank was right there at the corner of . . . I guess it was Main and Santa Clara, and there were other businesses down in that general area that many of the people in this area patronize. So it was a matter of driving a couple of miles out of my way to get to the same place that I had gone to for years and years and years. That got me interested in it.

The prevalence of these explanations for getting involved is a result of the types of issues in which citizens were involved. Traffic and land use policies are the types of policies that have direct impact on how citizens go about their daily business. This situation illustrates my point precisely: citizens are more likely to participate on issues that have a direct impact than on issues that do not. Thus, Table 3.7 offers an explanation for the pattern that we see in Table 3.5: the reason why transportation and land use issues generate the most participation is because they have direct effects on citizens' lives, and these direct effects are what prompt citizens to participate.

Clarity

Clarity refers to the transparency of a policy's impact (as opposed to directness, which refers to the nature of the impact). The effects of some policies are clear and unambiguous, but for others the impact may be difficult to discern. For example, if a city passes a regulation reducing the speed limit, there are three possible results: people drive slower, they receive more speeding tickets, or the law has no effect. Drawing out the likely causal relationships here is not difficult. Other policies are less clear in their impact. Take a revision to the City's general plan concerning housing density. The impact of this change, in terms of impact of development patterns, city revenues, and quality of life, is not at all clear. Citizens (and government officials too) may have difficulty in determining what impact, if any, the revision will have. Arriving at conclusive determinations concerning the likely impact of a policy decision is always problematic, however, predicting policy impact is easier for some policies than others.

Policies often have multiple and varied impacts, some of which will be clear and others ambiguous. There is an intended effect on specific target populations, and also impact on groups not directly targeted (e.g., the space-saver school had an impact on the surrounding neighborhood, although it was not an intentional target for the policy). There may also be unintended consequences, which could lead to additional impacts on both target populations and others. Thus, the clarity of policy impact varies both across policies and within policies.

Like directness, clarity is influenced by the policy tools employed and the length of policy chains. Some policy tools, by the very nature of the activity, have clearer impact than others. For example, attempting to revitalize a blighted neighborhood through enhanced code enforcement will have a predictably clearer impact than doing so by creating a redevelopment area, as the latter could potentially have a variety of differing impacts. Even though we cannot claim that some policy tools always have clearer impacts than others, for any given issue the choice of policy tools will influence the clarity of the policy's impact. As for policy chains, the longer they are and the more targets they have, the less clear the policy's impact will be. Having multiple targets extends the possible impacts to more groups, and also complicates action, which can make developing causal models between government action and policy impact more difficult. Shorter policy chains make the connection between government action and the end result clearer.

There is another policy characteristic that influences clarity: the presence or absence of well-defined trade-offs. All policy decisions involve trade-offs: spending money on policy A means we have less money to spend on policy B. Doing activity A means we cannot do activity B. Sometimes the government is facing a trade-off, as with fiscal policy; other times, the government forces trade-offs upon its citizens: you either follow this regulation and gain X, or don't follow it and lose Y. Trade-offs may be obvious, such as when cities decide how to distribute a grant from the federal government, or they may be vague, such as when they decide to increase public safety funding without indicating the source of the funds.

When an obvious trade-off exists, such as in the allotment of a grant, the impact of various policy choices is clear: the City could fund a program that does X, or it could fund a program that does

Y. These types of direct trade-offs, however, are rare. Most trade-offs are not so clearly defined, and could be understood in different ways. If a city increases funding for the fire department, does it mean lower funding for some other department? For all other departments? Or perhaps it will mean higher taxes. The trade-off is not well defined, and leads to ambiguous and vague policy impact. In order to conceptualize the policy impact of an increase in funds for the fire department, we need to know what we are giving up for it. A vague and ill-defined trade-off prevents us from drawing out all the possible impacts that a policy has, and thus limits our ability to clearly identify policy impact.

Clarity and Participation in Santa Ana

Even though most policies have at least some vague and ambiguous impacts, policies vary significantly in the extent to which they have clear policy impacts, and policies that generated participation tended to have clearer impacts. Most policies in Table 3.4 presented officials with clear choices. Building a school, creating a mobile health clinic, and requiring students to wear uniforms are all relatively simple decisions that are easily understood. They have short policy chains and use direct and easily understood tools. The primary effects of these policies are also clear: jails and schools are built, barricades constructed, and funds distributed. Of course, these policies have secondary effects that may not be easily understood and may be highly contested. For example, some participants expressed concern that building a new jail would not reduce crime, whereas others debated the effects of school uniforms on the behavior of children. Even though participants disagreed over likely policy effects, the causal relationships were clear, and participants could easily reach an opinion as to likely effects.

A few examples will illustrate these points. Take the neighborhood traffic plans. The impact on traffic was not in question: both supporters and opponents agreed that putting in the mitigation measures would limit traffic on certain streets. All participants knew what the impact of the policy would be, but they disagreed over whether that impact would be beneficial. Similarly, with Measure C, the impacts (higher taxes for homeowners and new school construction) were clear, with the disagreement coming over whether the taxes were worth the benefit.[7] In some cases, the policy impacts were in dispute, but both sides *thought* that the impact was clear. For example, supporters and opponents of the space-saver school fundamentally disagreed over its likely impact on traffic and noise, but both sides had a clear vision as to what they perceived the impacts to be.

There were a couple of issues where such doubts did make their appearance. For example, some respondents were unclear as to the impact of the proposed light rail, the Centerline, on their neighborhood and noted that their neighborhood associations had meetings where residents struggled with likely impacts (although after discussion the impacts were perceived to be clear). The Centerline, however, is atypical: for most issues, respondents had a clear idea of the likely policy impact.[8] Noticeably absent from Tables 3.4 and 3.5 are policies that have a level of complexity that would prevent participants from understanding policy impacts.

Most of the policies in Table 3.4, as well as those mentioned by respondents, had well-defined trade-offs that were easily identifiable. For example, the trade-off of building new schools involved the competing values of maintaining neighborhood quality of life and relieving school overcrowding. Other land use issues, such as the closing of a swap meet and the placement of a drug rehabilitation center (both mentioned by interview respondents), exhibited a similar pattern of clear trade-offs between neighborhood quality-of-life issues and some other social good.

The CDBG distributions are a unique case of an extremely well-defined trade-off. As I mentioned above, most trade-offs are nebulous and are not clearly defined. But because the City is restricted in how it can distribute the grant (it can only use a certain percentage for social services), the funding decision becomes clearer: either fund nonprofit A or fund nonprofit B. This structure is the likely reason why CDBG funding decisions generated more participation than votes to approve the city budget. The City has some discretionary spending that it allocates in its budget, but the trade-offs here are numerous and complex; the City could use its discretionary funds for many different purposes, each of which means a lack of funds for other possible uses. Unlike CDBG, which presents a direct trade-off between competing nonprofit organizations, the city budget offers a less clear policy choice. Many of the nonprofits who spoke on the CDBG allotment could also speak at regular budget hearings to lobby for funds, but did not. Thus, although CDBG hearings consistently attract around twenty participants, most of the time city budget hearings only attracted a few participants, and sometimes none at all.

A few policies that generated some participation did not have well-defined trade-offs. The artists' village (discussed in Chapter 4) is an example. If the money was not spent on promoting the arts, it could have been used for a whole host of other programs or activities. Not only could the money be used for some other redevelopment project (e.g., improvements to the Fourth Street commercial district), it could have been used for transportation, public works, or public safety. The possibilities are endless. A few policies that generated participation had these types of vague trade-offs, but there is a definite bias on both Tables 3.4 and 3.5 toward policies that have clear trade-offs. This bias is notable because many local public policies do not have clear trade-offs. Budgets, administrative actions, and service provision all are decisions that entail many possible trade-offs, but these types of decisions are not well represented among those policies generating participation.

The Floral Park Traffic Plan

A detailed look at a couple of policies that generated high levels of participation can further illustrate the influence of directness and clarity on participation patterns. Floral Park is an upper-middle-class neighborhood on the north side of Santa Ana. The traffic issue came to the forefront in the early 1990s when construction was under way on a nearby freeway interchange notorious for its frequent traffic snarls. Because of traffic delays caused by construction, many commuters would exit the freeway and use surface streets to either reach their final destination or to connect to another freeway. This increased traffic on residential streets in Floral Park, leading some residents to propose measures to prevent commuters from using Floral Park as a shortcut around the construction.

A group called the Floral Park Traffic Committee, consisting of residents living on affected streets, drew up a plan to limit traffic by blocking certain streets, installing right-hand-turn-only signs, and reducing speed limits. Restricting access to through traffic on some streets was the central point of contention in the ensuing debate (supporters referred to the restricting structures as "diverters," whereas opponents called them "barricades"). The plan drew substantial criticism from residents who lived in adjacent neighborhoods fearing that the plan would push traffic onto their streets and limit their access to nearby shopping and business destinations. There were also accusations that Floral Park was trying to "barricade itself" off from the rest of the city and become an exclusionary neighborhood. Although there may be some merit to this contention, the critics of the plan were mostly homeowners who had similar socioeconomic characteristics, and unlike many other issues in Santa Ana politics, this one did not exhibit a rich-versus-poor dynamic.

The debate was quite emotional and generated high levels of participation. As indicated in Table 3.4, the city council hearings on the issue drew many speakers (and even more people who attended the meeting, but did not speak). There were also neighborhood meetings, petition drives, and other activities on this issue. Citizens were highly engaged, but the city council and mayor wanted little to do with the proposal. This issue was a no-win situation for them given the strong opinions on both sides. As one reporter put it, "No matter how the council members vote, they run the risk of alienating about half of the neighborhood residents" (Martinez 1991, B3). However, the council was forced to deal with the issue because of the high levels of citizen participation.

After some delays, the council approved the traffic mitigation measures in 1993. Initially, the measures were meant to be temporary; once the construction was finished on the freeway interchange they were to be removed. But in 1995, after another contentious debate, the city council made the measures permanent.

Residents in Floral Park as well as nearby neighborhoods viewed traffic as a critically important issue. The reason is that it directly affected them on a day-to-day basis in a direct and clear way. Street traffic influences noise levels in a neighborhood, a major concern for Floral Park residents. It also impacts safety, and some residents were concerned about accidents caused by speeding commuters. For people who did not live in the neighborhood but used the streets, the proposed barricades affected them by forcing them to alter their driving patterns. Traffic mitigation did not have a major financial impact[9] on either supporters or opponents, nor did it have much impact beyond Floral Park and a few surrounding neighborhoods. The future of Santa Ana (or Floral Park) did not hinge on traffic mitigation, but because it had such direct impact, citizens participated on the issue as if it did.

The Floral Park traffic plan had clear impact on residents. There was some debate over the precise impact it would have, particularly in terms of how commuters would respond to the barricades. Critics contended that commuters would simply shift to other residential streets, burdening Floral Park's neighbors. Proponents of the plan argued that commuters might just stay on the freeway or use one of the main thoroughfares rather than cutting across residential neighborhoods. There was also some debate over the actual amount of traffic there was (neither side trusted the numbers provided by the City's traffic engineers) and the inconvenience it would cause to nearby residents. Although there was disagreement over the impact of the mitigation efforts, it was not difficult for residents to come to a conclusion about the likely impact. All one needed to do was to assess how much traffic there was, arrive at a conclusion about how commuters would respond to the barricades, and how much longer trips would be for others who used the streets. Further, the policy choice facing the city council was clear: implement the traffic mitigation measures, do not implement them, or work out a compromise position that implements some of the measures. The issue did not involve complex and vague trade-offs nor did it involve long policy chains. Participants could easily grasp the ramifications of policy decisions, even though they often reached different conclusions.

The Floral Park traffic mitigation effort is typical of the type of issue that generated high levels of participation in Santa Ana. Residents attached high salience to this issue because of the nature of its impact on their daily lives. It was a relatively simple issue that presented clear choices to policy makers and had a direct impact on citizens. It may not have been "important" in a fiscal sense or in terms of the overall well-being of the city, but it was certainly important enough to residents for them to actively engage the issue and attempt to influence the city council's decisions.

The Space-Saver School

The space-saver school was one of the most, if not the most, contentious issues the school district faced in the 1990s and generated high levels of participation. The public hearing on the issue had sixty-seven speakers (Table 3.4), and seven of the fifty-three participants interviewed mentioned it as a policy with which they were personally involved (three opposed; four in favor). Why did this issue become the object of so much participatory activity?

The space-saver school was a proposed junior high school that would be built next to a strip mall, under the auspices of a state program that provided funds to urban school districts to build schools in unconventional places. Santa Ana desperately needed to build more schools; the city was experiencing rapid population growth and did not have enough schools to house all of their students. Further, there is scarce open space left in Santa Ana, justifying building schools in less-than-ideal places, such as next to a mall. Supporters saw major citywide benefits from building the school, particularly because the state government was paying for most of it. Opponents, primarily from surrounding neighborhoods, acknowledged that Santa Ana needed to build more schools but argued that this location was the wrong choice. The school was going to create enormous amounts of traffic, and noise from the children—both at the school and on their way to and from school—was going to disrupt the neighborhood. Opponents claimed that placing a junior high school next to a mall was a recipe for disaster, and that the cost of the land (which had to be bought from the mall owner) was going to cost too much.

Compared to other policies that the City and school district decide, building this school is fairly insignificant in terms of its total impact on the quality of life and financial well-being of the adjacent neighborhoods. There may be some negative impact to the neighborhood in terms of traffic and noise; however, a neutral observer could hardly claim that the impact has been the catastrophe that opponents claimed would happen (the school opened in early 2001). As for supporters, this school would help alleviate some overcrowding, but it was hardly essential, and the school district could have survived without it. Important though it may have been, it was not any more important than a host of other issues that the school district addressed during this time period.

The debate over the school was cast in terms of competing interests. Those opposed, mostly people living in adjacent neighborhoods without school-aged children, argued that building the school would ruin their neighborhood. Supporters, mostly parents with kids in Santa Ana schools, argued that the school was needed to improve education. The debate was about competing interests, but the reason this issue was so contentious was not because the participants were excessively self-interested. The interests of these two groups conflict over many issues that have greater impact on the quality of life and financial well-being of both groups (tax policy is one such issue that generated relatively little participation). Therefore, if we want to know why this issue generated so much participation, we need to move beyond a simple explanation of "they are being self-interested" and ask why this issue was seen as being so critical.

The space-saver school had all the policy characteristics that lead to direct and clear policy impact. The school board decision to build or not build the school had direct consequences on the participants' daily routines; supporters would have a new school for their kids, and opponents would have to deal with increased traffic and noise. There was much debate over the extent to which the school would impact traffic and noise, but participants did not need to have a degree in planning to make an estimate as to what the impact would be (even if they ended up being wrong). Further, the decision was clear (build or not build) and the school board had to make one up-or-down vote to decide the fate of the school. All of these characteristics made this issue one that citizens could identify what the impact was going to be and figure out how to participate.

The space-saver school generated so much participatory activity because of the nature of the issue itself. Citizens viewed this issue as being highly salient based on the clear and direct policy choice it represented. They could assess the impact of the policy and see how it could directly impact their own lives. Further, the decision to build the school was made in a few votes taken by the school district, presenting a clear focal point for participatory activity. If the issue was more complex and less direct, citizens may not have attached such importance to the issue and consequently not have participated as much.

Policy Impact and Participation

Policies generating participation in Santa Ana had direct and clear impacts on citizens, and policy impact is an important influence on participation patterns. This argument resembles Lowi's (1964, 1972) "policy determines politics" thesis, which states that the type of policy influences the type of politics associated with it (e.g., regulatory policy will lead to executive-centered politics because the nature of regulatory policy is conducive to executive action and poses obstacles to congressional action). My argument in this chapter makes an analogous causal connection: I contend that the extent of participation on any given policy is influenced by the nature of the policy's impact on citizens.

Two premises underlie Lowi's contention that policies act as an independent influence on politics (Lowi 1964, 688). First, political relationships are determined by the expectations of what people hope to accomplish when they relate to others. Second, expectations are determined by governmental outputs or policies: what people expect from government is a product of what the government does. Therefore, if political relationships are determined by expectations and expectations are determined by governmental policies, political relationships are determined by governmental policies. Political relationships structure the politics that occur on a policy, and thus, Lowi argues, we can best understand politics with a theory that describes how policy types influences political relationships.

For Lowi, policy characteristics matter because they determine individuals' orientations toward government and the policy process, and thus political behavior. We can develop a similar argument about how the policy characteristics I have identified (directness and clarity) influence participation. Policy impact determines how citizens experience the decisions that local governments make. The relationship of citizens to local government is mediated through the impact that local policies have on citizens; that is how governmental actions manifest themselves in citizens' lives. Because policy impact shapes the relationship between citizens and government, it influences how citizens define their preferences about local policies. In particular, for our purposes here, it influences how citizens assess issue salience. Policy impact has an influence on participation patterns because it is the means by which citizens determine the importance of a given policy, and thus whether it is worthwhile to try to influence.

Issue salience is fundamentally subjective: whether citizens find an issue to be important enough to try to influence it is a function of how citizens construct the nature of its impact. Although the process by which policy impact is translated into issue salience is subjective, policy characteristics lead citizens to consistently view some types of policies as more salient than others. The essence of my argument is as follows: those policies that exhibit more direct and clearer impacts on citizens will be seen as having greater salience. Policy impact, like issue salience, is socially constructed by citizens; neither can be measured objectively. However, this does not mean that it is a random process. The evidence from Santa Ana indicates that policies with certain characteristics, such as short policy chains or direct policy tools, will have a greater salience among citizens. This chapter has demonstrated that the issues that citizens find most salient, and thus generate high levels of participation, have clear and direct policy impact on their daily routines.

We can further clarify the relationship between issue salience and policy impact by drawing on the theories by Tiebout (1956), Wilson (1974), and Logan and Molotch (1987) discussed in Chapter 2. From these theories, I developed a few hypotheses concerning what issues are likely to generate the most participation. The shortcoming of these hypotheses is that they are all derivative of policy impact, and thus cannot explain how citizens arrive at judgments about issue salience. For example, citizens determine costs and benefits of public policies based on the impact that the policy has (or will have) on their lives. The same goes for measuring use and exchange values: The importance attached to specific use and exchange values is independent of policy impact, but the understanding of how policies are going to influence those values is not. Citizens use this understanding about costs-benefits and use-exchange values to determine the merits of the policy and its relative importance to their lives, which in turn will affect the policies they try to influence. These hypotheses are not wrong per se, but they fail to capture the dynamics of how citizens come to view some policies as more salient than others, and thus cannot explain participation patterns that we see.

4 Policy Entrepreneurs and the Opportunity to Participate

In Chapter 3, we explored the possibility that policy characteristics influence patterns of participation, that certain types of policies are more likely to generate participation than others. Another influence on participation patterns could be participants themselves: Some policies could generate a lot of participation because there are concerned citizens who promote it. The hypothesis is as follows: policy A will receive more participation than policy B because it was pushed by a citizen (or group of citizens) who was able to get it on the public's agenda and mobilize other participants. In this scenario, the characteristics of the policy itself are not the critical variable; rather, whether somebody takes it upon him or herself to mobilize participation is what shapes participation patterns.

Citizens who promote and mobilize participation on a particular issue are policy entrepreneurs. Following Mintrom (2000) and Schneider and Teske (1995), I define a policy entrepreneur as someone who promotes an innovative policy idea, "innovative" in the sense of being a departure from the status quo. Entrepreneurs differ from other political actors in that they reframe problems, offer different solutions, and actively promote their ideas through building coalitions and persuading others of the merits of their arguments. Policy entrepreneurs can significantly influence participation patterns. By developing an idea and actively promoting it, policy entrepreneurs can generate interest and participation among other citizens that would not have existed otherwise. If this situation occurs, then we can explain some of the variation in participation across policies by reference to policy entrepreneurs.

Measuring the influence of entrepreneurs on participation is problematic because of complex causal relationships; even with a correlation between participation levels and the existence of entrepreneurs, the causal relationship will be unclear. Policy entrepreneurs could take up an issue, causing there to be more participation, or extensive interest in an issue could be a catalyst for potential entrepreneurs. Further, certain issues could be more likely to generate both participation and entrepreneurs, making the correlation spurious. Thus, sorting out the impact that policy entrepreneurs have on participation is quite difficult.

Given this complexity, the data that I have from Santa Ana do not allow us to establish a firm causal relationship between policy entrepreneurs and participation patterns. My task in this chapter is less ambitious: I describe three examples of policy entrepreneurship from Santa Ana and identify how they relate to participation. This analysis will establish the processes by which policy entrepreneurs could have an impact on participation patterns. Although it will not identify the relative importance of entrepreneurs compared to other variables, it will present a compelling logic for how entrepreneurial activity influences participation patterns.

The conclusion I draw from my analysis of entrepreneurs in Santa Ana is that they influence participation patterns by altering the context in which citizens participate in local policy making. By putting an issue on the agenda, defining its boundaries, developing a strategy to address it, and mobilizing interested citizens, policy entrepreneurs change the barriers and incentives for participation on that issue. The importance of policy entrepreneurs lies not in their ability to persuade others of the merits of their arguments; I found few instances where entrepreneurs generated participation by altering others' policy preferences. Rather, their importance lies in their ability to structure opportunities for citizens to act on those preferences by formulating policy goals, putting issues on the agenda, and developing a strategy for participatory activity.

The literature on policy entrepreneurs has examined their role in setting the public agenda and their effectiveness at accomplishing political goals. Entrepreneurs work to get issues on the agenda by capitalizing on political and policy opportunities that arise (Mintrom 2000; Kingdon 1995). Most of the studies on entrepreneurs find that not only can they set the agenda, but they also have significant impact on policy outcomes. For example, Mintrom (1997, 738), in a study examining the adoption of charter school legislation, argues that the "the presence and actions of policy entrepreneurs were found to raise significantly the probability of legislative consideration and approval of school choice as a policy innovation." The three examples below support the findings in previous literature that policy entrepreneurs can be effective at setting the agenda and attaining policy objectives. My goal, however, is not to demonstrate the effectiveness of policy entrepreneurs. Rather, I am interested in exploring the impact that this activity has for participation.

Entrepreneurs at Work: Three Examples[1]

The Artists' Village

Santa Ana suffers from a poor image. Many residents in surrounding communities view Santa Ana as a blighted inner city with high crime rates and run-down neighborhoods. Santa Ana residents are keenly aware of the image problem. During interviews, many made comments similar to this one by a neighborhood activist: "what has affected the city now for so many years is the perception [of Santa Ana] is 100 times worse than the reality . . . [people say] 'you live in Santa Ana? Oh my god, is it safe?' You invite somebody over for dinner, 'Well, should I bring a flack jacket? Where should I park? Do I need to have a police escort?' I mean, it's just ridiculous." Since Santa Ana started to gain this reputation in the 1980s, city officials have been searching for a way to alter the city's image by revitalizing downtown and giving Santa Ana a reputation for something other than crime, gangs, and blight.

The person who supplied the answer was John Peters, a Santa Ana native involved in the arts scene in Los Angeles.[2] Peters proposed revitalizing downtown by fostering an "arts movement" in the city that would promote the flowering of culture and make Santa Ana the arts capital of Orange County. A central component of the plan would be an artists' village, located downtown, with a vibrant and energetic atmosphere where artists could live and work. Through the artists' village and other arts initiatives, Santa Ana would not only have a vibrant and rejuvenated downtown, but it would also shed its image as a crime and poverty mecca and replace it with one associated with arts and culture.

In 1988, Peters formed the Santa Ana Council of Arts and Culture (SACAC), an umbrella organization initially comprised of fourteen major arts organizations in the city. SACAC's mission is to develop goals and objectives, lobby the city for seed funding for arts initiatives, and provide support for initiatives once they were under way. After bringing together arts organizations, Peters identified others in the community who could contribute resources to this effort. They included neighborhood association leaders, many of whom had political clout with city officials, historical preservation activists, and various city officials. Bringing city officials on board was not always easy. At first, many officials ignored him, thinking his ideas lacked feasibility and practicality. Even some of those who may have been sympathetic to the arts movement idea were put off by his aggressive lobbying; Peters relates the comment of one official who said, "How big of a box do we need to build to control John Peters?"

Despite some skeptical politicians, Peters assembled an impressive coalition to push for the arts. The support of the historic preservationists and neighborhood leaders was critical because they had political clout. Arts organizations had many resources they could bring to the table, but their nonprofit status limited their political activities, and they generally did not have any political pull. Neighborhood activists, however, are a significant voting bloc and an important source of campaign volunteers; thus, many elected officials need their support for reelection. Using support from neighborhood leaders as leverage, by the mid-1990s Peters had two or three city council members who were vocal supporters of the arts, and could count on five or six votes on the seven-member council to support arts initiatives. The support of elected officials led to support among a skeptical city staff, who saw that whether they liked the idea or not, fostering an arts movement was fast becoming a centerpiece of the city's agenda. His ability to draw in the political resources of neighborhood associations to complement the substantive resources of arts organizations made for a powerful coalition, and was a primary reason why the artists' village was eventually supported by the city. He acknowledges as much: "The arts council could never have done anything without the neighborhood movement because that's where the political muscle is."

To get the issue on the agenda, Peters generated some buzz with special events, such as a party thrown for David Hockney, an internationally known artist. He also arranged for city officials to tour other cities with artist colonies, such as Pasadena, California, and Portland, Oregon. He created links between neighborhood associations and arts organizations by organizing joint events and offering free arts tickets to neighborhood activists. When in 1992 a proposed pawnshop in the area slated for the artists' village[3] generated neighborhood protests (organized by Peters, among others), it became clear to city leaders that the artists' village idea was on the minds of residents (or at least of active residents), and that they needed to consider the proposals seriously.

In the mid-1990s, the presence of many empty or near-empty early twentieth-century buildings marred the face of downtown Santa Ana. The idea behind the artists' village was to use these underutilized buildings for arts purposes. Using these buildings had two distinct advantages: They were inexpensive—a key ingredient for luring artists to the area—and they had the aesthetics conducive to an artistic environment. The cornerstone projects of the artists' village consisted of refurbishing these old buildings as artist studios or as apartments where occupants could both live and work— live-work studios. Starting in 1994, the City used Community Development Block Grant (CDBG) funds to renovate a few of these buildings, one of which was leased by the arts program at California State University, Fullerton. A private developer, with financial assistance from the City, renovated another building for use as studios and galleries. A construction permit for artist live-work studios was approved by the city council in November 2001.

The artists' village has its opponents. The primary opposition comes from officials and citizens who feel that the money could be better used for other purposes. The artists' village is not likely, they argue, to ever reach the heights that Peters and others claim it will. They are fighting an uphill battle, however, because the artists' village has been identified as *the* way to revitalize downtown. Despite some criticism, an organized opposition to the artists' village has yet to emerge, and there is minimal participatory activity to oppose the project.

Peters recruited a number of other citizens to be active participants in the arts movement, such as one of the cofounders of Commlink (an umbrella group of neighborhood associations) and various neighborhood association presidents. Instances of mass citizen participation were rare on the artists' village issue, however, a small group of activists spent significant amounts of time on working with the City to make the artists' village come to fruition. They were mostly citizens who were already active in local politics, and if they had not been involved with the arts movement, they probably would have shifted their efforts to other issues. This dynamic only applies to a handful of activists, but it is significant. Had Peters not pushed the idea, some citizens would have spent their time participating on issues other than the arts movement. In this way, his entrepreneurship influenced participation patterns.

The specific artists' village projects mentioned above did not generate much citizen participation outside of Peters and a handful of arts activists. City council hearings on artists' village proposals typically only attracted a handful of speakers, and there certainly was not a groundswell of public support for the initiative. By 1994, when the first of these projects was approved, the city council was supportive of the idea and thus the primary task was to work out the details, limiting participation to those (like Peters) who were willing to volunteer significant amounts of time to see the project come to fruition. That said, Peters' activity did have some (albeit modest) impact on participation patterns. I already mentioned one issue, the Main Street pawnshop, where Peters' entrepreneurship influenced participation. If it were not for the vision of the artists' village and the mobilization efforts of Peters, this issue would have generated less interest. Also, the artists' village was occasionally a topic of discussion at neighborhood association meetings and Commlink meetings. In the absence of Peters, conversations about revitalizing downtown and improving the image of Santa Ana may have focused on other alternatives, and participation may have shifted to other projects.

Observers have different opinions about whether or not the artists' village is a success. Supporters, including most city officials, see it as highly successful, and think that with one or two more additions (such as the artist live-work studios under construction) it will achieve its potential as a cultural center and revitalization force downtown. Others are less optimistic. There has been high turnover among artists, leading some to question whether the project can survive past its initial phase. Others note that most of the time the artists' village is void of visitors, and doubt that it will ever be the exciting and lively place billed by proponents. Its future remains uncertain, but there is no doubt that the City's creation of the artists' village as the centerpiece of downtown redevelopment was a function, in large part, of the tireless efforts of John Peters.

Antigang Efforts

In the early 1990s Santa Ana had a serious gang problem. Rapid population growth coupled with a large youth population had led to an explosion of gang activity that the City was unprepared to handle. Jose Miranda, a local lawyer and former president of the Santa Ana Hispanic Chamber of Commerce, decided to address the gang issue. Miranda, who says he was interested in the issue because, "I was at some point [in my youth] involved in some activities that one would consider gang activities," put together a fourteen-point plan that included establishing gang prevention programs and expanding recreational activities for youth. The focus of the pro gram was to develop alternatives to a gang lifestyle and to bring together resources from the community to address the issue.

A week after he presented his plan, a tragic gang shooting occurred in which a father of three was killed over a dispute concerning a cigarette. This murder received a significant amount of media attention, and the gang issue became the number-one priority (it was already high on the City's agenda, but the tragedy of this shooting increased the urgency with which the City dealt with the issue). This spotlight gave Miranda an opportunity (or what Kingdon [1995] refers to as a policy window) to make a case that his plan represented the best way to address Santa Ana's gang problem.

Miranda's approach to fighting gang activity revolved around providing help and support to at-risk youth to discourage them from joining gangs. Rather than approach gang activity as a crime control issue, he approached it as a problem of wayward youth. Miranda describes his understanding of the gang problem:

> And I will stand to the fact that those kids, they need to hang out
> with each other because they have no place to go, or they don't
> have the means to go anywhere else. Many times they have
> traditionally been earmarked or targeted as the gang members, and
> ultimately identified as criminal-street-gang members only because
> they grew up in [a low-income] neighborhood. So part of my

reasoning for getting involved is because I felt, as part of my role as an attorney, a criminal defense attorney, I found that many times many youngsters get caught in the system, the criminal system, with no choice. And that we do not have enough role models, we do not have enough leaders, we do not have individuals that will take the time to become big brother or big sister, and take one of these youngsters, even if it's one at a time, to help them out and become better members of our society. So my interest was because I felt it, I felt the problems, and because I grew up with it, I feel that I also have a little bit of a solution, and therefore I voiced my opinion, and submitted a number of proposals to the school district, to the city council, to the board of supervisors, as an attempt to make a dent in the understanding of this community.

The proposals Miranda made reflected his understanding of the problem; rather than hiring police officers or creating antigang units, Miranda focused his efforts on programs aimed at helping at-risk youth.

Miranda's strategy for getting his plan implemented was multi-faceted. Most visibly, he organized rallies and meetings to bring together community residents who were committed to addressing the issue. These activities generated some positive newspaper coverage, which in turn increased awareness in the community. At the same time he was generating broad interest in the community, Miranda identified allies, both within government and outside of it, who could help him achieve his goals. One group he reached out to were gang members themselves, successfully persuading them to agree to a truce between rival gangs. He helped them create an umbrella organization called United Gangs Council, whose mission was to promote nongang activities. He also contacted a variety of other players who had a role to play, from school officials to probation officers to community college officials to police departments. For each organization, he identified ways that they could contribute to a solution, and attempted to persuade them to take the recommended actions.

The fourteen-point plan that Miranda put together were actions that the city council could take to alleviate the gang problem. This plan was only one component of the antigang effort. Much of the work, as envisioned by Miranda, was to be done by citizens in the community themselves[4] or by other governmental bodies (such as community college districts or school districts). But the proposal to the council received the most attention in the media. To convince the city of the merits of his proposals, Miranda had a two-pronged approach. First, he attended city council meetings to apply pressure on officials to approve his plan. He also talked individually with council members and the mayor to present the argument in favor of his plan. Although officials were not opposed to the plan itself, they were hesitant to commit the funds that it required given a tight city budget. Thus, many of the meetings with officials revolved around what the city would be willing to spend and where those resources were going to come from.

The City formally adopted Miranda's fourteen-point plan, but most of it was never implemented for budgetary reasons. Over the next few years, the City experimented with a number of other approaches to the gang problem, including building a new city jail to house minor offenders and participation in the federal "weed and seed" program. By the late 1990s, gang activity had significantly decreased, which may be a function of these efforts or simply a reflection of a national trend toward less crime. Miranda feels that his participation was effective:

> I felt that a number of our recommendations were adopted and implemented. There were a number of recommendations that were modified to either meet a specific funding requirement or city plan, and there were other issues that were placed on the table that become the spring board to other activities that have essentially become productive to our society.

Even though the City did not fully implement his plan, Miranda had an impact on city policy, because without his efforts, the City's strategy for dealing with the gang issue would have been different, at least in some respects.

Miranda generated some participation on this issue. As mentioned above, he organized public meetings on the issue, one of which had about one hundred citizens in attendance. Others were prompted to participate in various activities relating to the antigang efforts, such as volunteering for recreational programs. The activity that Miranda's plan prompted was more along the lines of "public work" than of citizen efforts to lobby government, as there did not appear to be much participatory activity surrounding his efforts to persuade the city council to adopt his fourteen-point plan. Like John Peters' efforts to establish an artists' village, Miranda's plan did not generate a groundswell of participatory activity, and there did not appear to be significantly higher levels of participation on the gang issue as a result of his efforts.

Even so, Miranda made an impact on participation by channeling what participation there was on this issue into a focused outlet (support for his plan). It was already on the agenda and on people's minds; he did not have to convince anybody that gang activity was an issue that needed to be addressed. Further, there was consensus on what the results needed to be, as everyone wanted to see less gang activity. What Miranda did was provide a framework in which people could act to achieve common goals. By developing a strategy to address the gang issue, Miranda influenced participatory activity by presenting a clearer and more structured participatory opportunity. It made the task clearer, so that citizens interested in addressing the gang issue had clear outlets for their participation. If Miranda had not been involved, gang issues would still have been on the agenda, people would still have been concerned, and the desire to do something still would have been there. However, the opportunities to participate would have been different.

The Commercial Vehicles Code

Santa Ana, as an older suburb, suffers from visual blight. The neighborhoods built in the 1950s have seen better days, as the houses are starting to show the wear of time. Further, many of these houses are occupied by Santa Ana's large immigrant population who, for economic reasons, need to fit many people into these small houses.[5] These circumstances lead to outward signs of overcrowding, such as using porches for storage areas. Many neighborhood association leaders argue that addressing this visual blight should be a top priority, and promote enhanced code enforcement by the city as a solution. One particular code enforcement issue that was taken up by a group of citizens dealt with the parking of commercial vehicles (such as tow trucks, buses, and tractor trailers) on residential streets. Citizens complained about the number of commercial vehicles in residential neighborhoods (which they said looked ugly and posed safety hazards) and asked the city to address the issue.[6]

Mike Belliard, a neighborhood association president, led the fight. Initially, he got interested in this topic when he was informed by code enforcement that they could not act on his complaints about commercial vehicles parked in his neighborhood. Belliard found out that state laws invalidated parts of the old city ordinance regulating commercial vehicles, and these laws limit what the City could do in terms of restrictions. There were still some opportunities for the city council to address the issue, but they needed to adopt a new ordinance. Initially Belliard and other residents thought it was just a matter of getting city code enforcers to step up citation activity, but it quickly became apparent that serious action on this issue would require more. Thus began a push for the City to write and adopt a new ordinance.

Initially, Belliard took on the project by himself, but later brought in other citizens (mostly those active in neighborhood associations). He explains why:

> [W]hen I started this I was on my own. . . . It was getting to a point where some of my friends that had leadership in the city were telling me you'd better get together with other people. Have them come before [us], because what's going to be getting . . . they'll say, "Here comes that guy again." One person making noise, making noise. They never listen to one person.

He worked primarily through neighborhood associations and Commlink, gathering support and recruiting allies. Commlink held informational meetings on the issue, and invited city staff and elected officials to attend. Commlink also has a committee called Neighborhood Improvement and Code Enforcement (NICE) that stepped up its efforts on this issue. These meetings signaled to officials that this issue was of concern to more than just one person.

Belliard brought in a few other people to assist in the effort. Particularly valuable were some Commlink board members who agreed to help push for the new ordinance. If it were not for Belliard, many of these people would not have been active on the issue. For example, one of the people he recruited stated that it was a "supportive" issue for her. she offered to help Belliard because he was a frequent ally and felt that supporting him on this issue (which she supported but did not view as one of her top priorities) would strengthen her networks. A Commlink board member commented during an interview that he personally did not have a problem with commercial vehicles in his neighborhood, but he could understand why others would care about it, and participated based on that. All of the people that Belliard recruited agreed with his position on the issue; however, many of them did not have commercial vehicles as a top priority nor would they have participated had Belliard not prompted them to do so.

After some meetings and discussions, the city council instructed the city attorney to draft an ordinance. The drafting of the ordinance was a collaborative effort, with the city attorney and other city officials discussing the details of the ordinance with Belliard and his allies. The citizens who worked most on this issue indicated that they had many meetings and conversations with officials in the planning stages. When the council took up the ordinance for a vote, they were very careful and sensitive to the opposition (tow truck operators and others groups negatively affected by the ordinance were the primary opposition). They delayed the vote a few times to allow time for compromises, attempting to placate both opponents and supporters of the new ordinance. Belliard and his colleagues made a point of attending all the public hearings on the ordinance, and also made personal contact with various city council members to fend off attempts to weaken it. Council members added some amendments that altered the ordinance so supporters did not get exactly what they wanted. The council did eventually pass an ordinance, and thus it serves as an example of a victory by citizens in their attempt to influence government policy. The city council was predisposed to support such issues (they had passed similar code enforcement ordinances in the past), but would not have been likely to pass this one without some prodding.

In addition to opposition from tow truck operations, there was some opposition from individuals concerned that the new ordinance would create financial hardships for working-class Latinos. Most of the commercial vehicles—which included not just tow trucks but also buses and trucks used by landscapers—were driven by this group, who brought the trucks home because they had no other form of transportation to and from work. Critics contended that in the name of making neighborhoods look nice, working people would suffer economic hardship because they would have to find other means of transportation to and from work. Belliard dismissed this argument out of hand: "[They argued] this isn't going to be fair. I said, 'It's not fair to me. Why should I put up with the guy next door or across the street, big trucks, big tow trucks, that don't belong there and use my street for a parking lot?'" To Belliard, commercial vehicles represented a land use issue, not an economic one: the fact that commercial vehicles should not be parked in residential neighborhoods trumped any potential impact on the economic well-being of the people who drove them.

The appearance of residential neighborhoods is an important issue for many neighborhood leaders, and code enforcement is frequently a discussion topic at neighborhood meetings. Thus, when Mike Belliard came along asking for support in his efforts to get the City to adopt a new commercial vehicles ordinance, he received a favorable response. At the same time, the issue would not likely have surfaced without his efforts. For most neighborhood activists, though they cared about the issue, it was not a top priority, and they would not have gotten involved without Belliard's leadership. Belliard moved the issue up on their agenda. He accomplished this goal by doing the initial information gathering about why the old ordinance was not being enforced, what the state regulations were, and what the City needed to do to address the issue. In so doing, he was able to define what needed to be accomplished. Once the issue was framed as getting the City to write a new ordinance, the participatory task was made clearer, and citizens had a definable goal to accomplish. Without Belliard's efforts, there would not have been much participation on the issue of commercial vehicles, and thus we can conclude that he was able to alter participation patterns through his entrepreneurial activity.

Changing Participatory Opportunities

Policy entrepreneurs' influence on participation is derived from their ability to alter opportunities for citizens to participate on specific policy issues. For any given policy there are a set of contextual factors that shape the ways citizens can or are willing to participate. For example, whether a policy is decided by a vote of the city council or by a city administrator will impact whether citizens have an opportunity to comment on the policy at a public hearing. Another example: defining an issue narrowly so that it only affects one neighborhood provides a disincentive for citizens who live outside of that neighborhood to participate, even if the policy has wider implications. How an issue is defined, debated, and addressed by government will structure the ways in which citizens can attempt to participate on that issue. Policy entrepreneurs can alter these factors. Specifically, they can do three things: (1) define and frame policy issues, (2) create specific participatory occasions, and (3) develop strategies that organize individual participatory acts into a coherent whole. Each will be discussed in turn.

All three entrepreneurs defined and framed policy issues by taking a general issue and making it specific through identifying issue boundaries and feasible solutions. For example, Peters narrowed the quite expansive issue of "downtown redevelopment" to whether the city should promote an artists' village. He effectively shifted the discourse away from other potential options and focused debate on the arts. Even those who disagreed with his proposal were forced to engage in the debate over its merits. In Miranda's case, he broadened the scope of potential action on the gang issue beyond just police enforcement of laws. One way of viewing the gang problem was of crime control, which effectively limits policy action to the police and criminal justice system. Miranda defined the issue more broadly to include dealing with the problems faced by crime-prone youth more generally, opening up possibilities for different groups to take action.

How an issue is defined and framed alters the opportunities for citizen participation. Certain types of framings can either create roles for citizen participants or limit their involvement. It can also influence the type of activity that is best suited to accomplishing participants' goals. Belliard, by framing the issue of commercial vehicles as one where the City needed to write a new ordinance, created a role for citizens to lobby the city government to pass such an ordinance. Miranda's framing of the gang issue created a role for citizens where they could get directly involved in addressing the issue by working through nonprofits to help wayward youth. He also created opportunities for citizens to lobby the city council to pass his plan. The gang issue could have easily been framed to limit the role of citizens; for example, defining it as a problem of police effectiveness would have put the onus of action on police, not citizens.

In addition to framing an issue in a way that allows for participation, policy entrepreneurs generate specific occasions for participation. By "occasion" I mean that there was a defined activity
that citizens could engage in to influence a specific policy. Of course,
citizens always have opportunities to participate on any issue they
like. Even if governmental bodies refuse to take up an issue, citizens could at a minimum protest or organize community meetings
to discuss an issue. What policy entrepreneurs did in Santa Ana
was to make these opportunities concrete by creating a specific
occasion in which citizens could act to influence a policy. In some
cases it was obvious: for example, Miranda organized a public
meeting in which to discuss his antigang efforts. In other cases, the
process was indirect. By prompting the city council to consider a
new commercial vehicles ordinance, Belliard's efforts led to an
occasion for citizens to speak at a city council meeting to support
passage. The activities of policy entrepreneurs created specific and
concrete occasions where citizens could attempt to influence a particular policy issue, which can affect both how citizens participate
and which issues they attempt to influence.

Policy entrepreneurs can also alter participatory opportunities
by creating strategies to accomplish their political goals. Strategies
organize and coordinate participatory activities and change the
meaning and impact of specific participatory activity. For example,
opposition to the Main Street pawnshop was part of the larger
strategy to reserve an area downtown for arts-related uses. By
developing a strategy to accomplish this larger goal, Peters infused
additional meaning into this participation, so that rather that just
being opposition to an unwanted land use, it was part of an effort
to revitalize downtown. Miranda's antigang strategy also altered
participatory opportunities by tying together previously separate
efforts to deal with the problem. Developing a strategy to address
an issue not only changes the meaning of participation, but it can
also alter citizens' behavior by providing different incentives for
engaging in various participatory activities.

In all these ways, policy entrepreneurs alter the context in
which participatory activity occurs. The structure of the opportunity to participate can act as an incentive or disincentive to participate. In this chapter, we have examined three examples where
policy entrepreneurs altered participatory opportunities through

their ability to define and frame issues, create specific participatory occasions, and develop strategies to accomplish political goals. How they went about these tasks varied. Miranda was much more of a consensus builder than Peters or Belliard, who did not shy away from conflict if necessary to accomplish their goals. The three entrepreneurs also drew on different resources and engaged in different activities. Although the specifics of their efforts varied, they all had a common outcome: they structured opportunities for citizens to participate, creating focused outlets for their participatory efforts.

The mechanism by which policy entrepreneurs enhance participation on a given issue is by altering opportunities to participate. But how significant of an impact does entrepreneurial activity have on participation patterns? Does altering participatory opportunities on a particular issue lead to higher levels of participation? In all three cases we saw that activities of policy entrepreneurs generated some participation that would not have happened otherwise. We would be hard pressed to develop a scenario where the artists' village would have been on the agenda of neighborhood leaders absent of John Peters. Likewise, commercial vehicles probably would not have generated any participation were it not for Mike Belliard. Gangs would probably have generated some participation without Jose Miranda, but the focus and nature of citizen efforts would likely have been different.

Yet, in none of the three cases was there a groundswell of mass participation that extended beyond a handful of activists. When we see high levels of participation on an issue (such as with the Floral Park traffic plan or citywide redevelopment[7]), there are other factors (such as policy characteristics) that provide a more compelling explanation for why they generate so much participation. The evidence presented in this chapter does not support the argument that policy entrepreneurs are *the* driving force behind participation patterns or that mobilization by policy entrepreneurs is the critical factor in generating participation. What I have shown is that policy entrepreneurs can influence participation by structuring opportunities to participate and that some issues generated more participation than they would have otherwise because of entrepreneurial activity. We cannot, given the data that we have, draw firm conclusions about the importance of policy entrepreneurs compared to other factors that influence participation patterns. We can, however, conclude that the evidence supports the argument that policy entrepreneurs are a factor influencing participation patterns, but are not the dominant factor.

Policy Entrepreneurs as Citizen Lobbyists

Of the three policy entrepreneurs featured in this chapter, two (Peters and Belliard) engaged the policy-making process as lobbyists. Belliard is a prototypical citizen lobbyist: He identified a specific neighborhood issue that he felt was important and engaged in a series of activities to influence city policy concerning that issue. The manner in which he went about trying to realize that influence—finding allies, talking to officials, applying pressure when necessary—is standard lobbying activity. Peters took on a broader issue, but his approach to realizing his vision of an artists' village was very much a lobbying strategy. Miranda is best classified as a community problem solver, rather than a citizen lobbyist. He engaged in many of the same activities as citizen lobbyists, but his focus was on addressing a difficult social problem through engaging the community in a constructive dialogue. He had his fourteen-point plan to address the gang problem; however, he was more focused on fostering a constructive dialogue with other community members and governmental officials than in accomplishing his specific objectives. Miranda was unusual among citizen participants. Most focused on narrower neighborhood issues and were less concerned about developing a coordinated approach to a problem than in achieving specific policy goals. Miranda presents a strong contrast to the typical manner in which citizens engaged the policy-making process, and the fact that we saw few efforts similar to Miranda's is evidence that citizens generally engage the policy-making process as lobbyists, rather than as community problem solvers.

5 Local Newspapers and Participation

In this chapter, I explore newspapers' role in influencing participation patterns. Do newspapers increase citizen activity on the issues they cover? Did citizens participate on issue A rather than issue B because the former received extensive coverage while the latter did not?

We can delineate two plausible arguments concerning the influence of newspapers on participation patterns.[1] First, for many people, newspapers are the primary source of information on local politics: television gives short shrift to local affairs, and the sparse coverage it does provide is usually sensationalized. Newspapers, on the other hand, sometimes provide information to citizens that allows them to participate: they inform citizens about issues being addressed by city officials, announce when public meetings will occur, and give citizens pros and cons on the issues of the day. Newspaper coverage of a particular issue, therefore, should increase participation on that issue by enhancing citizen awareness and providing information needed to participate. If local papers do not cover an issue, citizens will have little knowledge of it, lack awareness that the issue is being decided, and consequently, will not participate. Thus, newspapers can enhance participation on the issues they cover by providing information that citizens need to participate, and these issues will generate more participation than those not receiving coverage.

An alternative argument downplays the role of local newspapers in generating participation. Newspaper coverage usually occurs after the fact, explaining what actions local authorities have taken and the politics surrounding those actions. This reactive coverage cannot foster participation because the opportunities to participate have already passed. Even when news stories occur before major decisions are made, they generally do not focus on opportunities for citizen participation. Newspaper stories may describe the actions of elected officials and explore the opinions of elected officials and citizens, but rarely do they focus on citizen attempts to influence public policy. Further, newspapers have a tendency to predict outcomes, and if citizens feel that outcomes are already determined, they will be less likely to participate. The reactive and predictive nature of news coverage makes local newspapers relatively unimportant for generating participation.

Based on the evidence from Santa Ana, I contend in this chapter that the second argument is closer to reality, and that newspaper coverage does not have a significant influence on participation patterns. First, newspapers do not provide the information that citizens need to participate. This failure is more than just a lack of local coverage: even when they report on local issues, the manner in which they do so does not foster citizen participation. Second, the core premise of the first argument—that citizens get most of their political information from newspapers—is not quite accurate. Whereas for the politically inactive, newspapers are the primary (and perhaps only) source of information on local politics, politically active citizens acquire substantial information through social networks. Newspapers may have an influence on the mass public, but they have much less of an influence on the portion of the population that is active in local politics. Because this latter group is most likely to participate, newspaper coverage will not have much of an impact on participation patterns.

The literature on local newspapers has focused on how they report the news. Local newspapers, as do many other news providers, rely heavily on official sources for their information (Taylor, Lee, and Davie 2000; Soloski 1989). Wong and Jain (1999), in a study of education reporting in Chicago, found that the two major dailies focused on the central administration in their reporting, and generally supported central administrators in conflicts with local school councils. Newspapers, they argue, usually did not present multiple conflicting viewpoints, and thus did not present a "pluralistic" viewpoint in their reporting. In addition to this bias toward official sources, newspapers also focus on symbolic issues. Because newspapers generally serve an entire region, not just one city, they try to report on issues that relate to the region as a whole, not just to a specific locality (Kaniss 1991). This task is best accomplished by focusing on symbolic issues, which can be of interest to even those readers who are not personally affected, and this priority explains the reluctance of newspapers to report on the details of public policy debates within a particular city.

There has also been some research on the agenda-setting effects of local newspapers, questioning whether newspapers influence public agendas (Wanta and Wu 1992; Gaziano 1985). These studies, however, usually do not take the analysis to the next step, asking what effect agenda setting has on political participation. Promoting thought and concern about an issue is qualitatively different than promoting action: newspapers may, in some instances, put an issue on the agenda, but can they motivate citizens to participate on it? A few studies have analyzed the media's role in fostering community participation. McLeod, Scheufele, and Moy (1999) found that communication, both interpersonal and through the mass media, fosters local political participation, based on an analysis of survey data from Madison, Wisconsin. Adkins-Covert et al. (2000), however, argue that the local media do not provide important political information to citizens, undermining democratic practices. Their study casts doubt on the conclusions of McLeod et al.: if newspapers do not provide adequate information on local issues, why would newspaper readership lead to greater participation?

This question highlights a general shortcoming of the local media literature. These studies have added to our knowledge of the connection between community involvement and local media, but they lack analyses of the precise dynamics of this relationship. The studies conducted by Adkins-Covert et al. and McLeod, Scheufele, and Moy are a start in this direction, but they leave many questions unanswered. Specifically, does the manner in which newspapers report on local issues influences participation patterns, and what types of information could newspapers provide that would prompt participation?

My analysis proceeds as follows. First, I describe newspaper coverage of Santa Ana politics and support my contention that there is a weak relationship between media coverage and patterns of citizen participation. The subsequent two sections provide an explanation for this conclusion; I explore why the current manner of local reporting is ill-suited to foster participation, and I explain why participants do not rely on newspapers as their primary source of information. I conclude by discussing the role that the media plays in local politics.

Media and Participation in Santa Ana

Santa Ana is a good city to study the effects of newspaper influence because of the minimal role that television news plays in covering events specific to the city. Santa Ana is in the Los Angeles media market, and local newscasts pay very little attention to Santa Ana outside of murders, fires, and the occasional sensational story (e.g., when a Santa Ana councilman was arrested by the FBI for extortion). Thus, newspapers are the primary source of information on local politics, and is the only media outlet that is likely to influence participation.

Santa Ana has two major English language newspapers, the *Orange County Register* and the *Los Angeles Times–Orange County Edition*, both of which cover local politics in all thirty or so cities in Orange County (Santa Ana is the largest city and the county seat). During participant interviews, respondents made many references to these papers, typically to criticize biased coverage, cite them as supporting evidence, or describe how they used the media in their participatory efforts. Although many (perhaps most) Santa Ana residents do not read newspapers on a regular basis, respondents clearly did read papers regularly, and thus examining whether the *Los Angeles Times* and *Orange County Register* influenced their participation is an important question.

For the eleven-year period of this study, the papers ran a combined total of 1,043 stories on city government activities and 374 stories on school district activities.[2] They ran 117 stories on local elections, and a host of other stories on Santa Ana that were not concerned with public policy decisions (these stories were not counted). The major daily Spanish-language paper is *La Opinion*, which is owned by the *Los Angeles Times*. *La Opinion* does not have an Orange County edition, (it has one edition for the entire Los Angeles metropolitan area), and thus does not cover Santa Ana politics as much as the two major English-language papers; it only ran eighty-three stories from 1992 to 2000 on Santa Ana politics.[3] There are also some weekly newspapers, such as the Spanish-language *Excelsior* which is owned by the *Orange County Register*, but these are not electronically indexed and thus determining the number of stories on Santa Ana was not feasible.

Does this coverage have any impact on citizen participation? We can begin our analysis by examining the relationship between public speakers and newspaper articles connected to our set of 730 controversial city council and school board votes. Does newspaper coverage of an issue increase the number of citizens who speak on the issue at a public meeting? For this analysis, I included only policies that had *either* a public speaker or a newspaper article. Of the 730 policies, 429 (59 percent) had neither a public speaker nor a related news story. These were deleted because having the majority of data points at "0, 0" would distort the analysis. Thus, we are left with 301 policies that had at least one public speaker or one newspaper story.

As described in Chapter 3, I collected data for the public speaking side by examining city council and school board minutes and counting the number of speakers on each issue. On the newspaper side, I culled articles from online databases (including both the *Los Angeles Times–Orange County Edition* and the *Orange County Register*). For the 301 policies in the analysis, I identified a total of 835 news stories, 462 from the *Los Angeles Times* and 373 from the *Orange County Register*.

The first statistic to note is that 496 of the 835 news stories (59 percent) appeared after the city council or school board made a decision on the issue.[4] Because almost all participation occurs before decisions are made, stories that appear after a decision is made will not have any effect on participation. To determine the effect of the stories occurring prior to decisions being made, I correlated them with the number of public speakers. Combining city and school district policies, there was an r of 0.437 (n = 301, p < .01). However, when analyzing city and school policies separately, the r for city policies was only 0.105 (n = 201), but it was 0.698 (n = 100) for school district policies.

Thus, we see a degree of correlation between the number of public speakers and newspaper coverage on an issue, at least for school district issues. This analysis, however, cannot speak to causality. We would expect, absent any causal effects, that they would be closely correlated: the most controversial issues are likely to attract both media coverage and speakers at public meetings.

Because we do not have an independent measure of controversiality on which our set of policies varies, we cannot sort out this relationship. We can note, however, that the correlation is not as close as we might expect given the propensity of the media to cover issues that would also generate participation, and thus we have reason to question whether any of this correlation is the result of media prompting participation.

The differences between the City and school district can shed some light on the media–participation relationship. For the school district, participation focused on a handful of "big" issues. School issues tend to either generate a lot of interest or none at all. Although the City had its share of big issues, participation was spread out over a larger number of relatively smaller issues (see Table 3.3 for the distribution of public speakers across issues). Media coverage was the same for both city and school district issues: They focused on a handful of big issues. Thus, many of the smaller city issues that generated some public speakers did not attract any media coverage, whereas a handful of school issues generated both high numbers of speakers and significant media coverage. One possible conclusion we could draw is that media may have more of an impact in increasing participation on issues already generating a lot of participation, but has little impact on other issues. Evidence presented later in this chapter provides some support for this conclusion.

We can also draw on the evidence from participant interviews to determine if media coverage has any impact on participation. As discussed in Chapter 3, respondents were asked why they decided to participate on the specific issues they identified. Table 3.6 summarizes the reasons given. Not one respondent identified reading newspaper articles as a prompt to participation nor did they say that they were initially informed about this issue through newspaper articles. If news coverage prompts participation, we would expect respondents to identify newspapers as a source of information that contributed to their decision to participate on a particular issue.

Further, if we look at the reasons that citizens offered for their participation, none are connected with media coverage. Of the five reasons given in Table 3.6, three have no relationship to media at all (personal experience, being asked by others, and participating through affiliated groups). The other two could possibly have a relationship. Perhaps participants believe that an issue is important or that a pending decision is misguided because of information they acquired from reading the newspaper: Citizens read about an issue in the newspaper, form an opinion about it, either in terms of its importance or its substance, and then participate. However, this possibility is unlikely for reasons that are discussed in greater detail below. Given that media coverage usually occurs late in the policy process and that politically active citizens had other sources of information about local policy, the possibility that citizens find certain issues important because of the media is remote.

When discussing their participatory activities, interview respondents rarely talked about the media. Of the fifty-five respondents, only twenty-one mentioned the media, and about half of these did so at the prompting of the interviewer. Most of comments fell into one of two categories: complaints about biased news coverage or comments about how they contacted reporters in an effort to generate coverage of issues they were trying to influence (discussed further below). When asked to describe their political activities or the influences behind their participatory decisions, respondents did not focus their attention on the media, indicating that it did not play a prominent role.

Newspaper coverage does not seem to have any significant influence on the patterns or extent of participation. This finding is somewhat counterintuitive: given the importance of newspapers in providing information about local politics to citizens, we would expect that they would have some role in fostering participation. Why does the newspaper's role of disseminating information not translate into a role in generating participation?

How the Media Reports Local News

In this section, I argue that the manner in which the media reports local news actually hinders participation. Specifically, newspaper stories exhibit four characteristics that undermine participation:

1. They report on stories late in the policy process.
2. They focus on outcomes rather than process.
3. They present issues as debates between opposing interests.
4. They present action as elite, not citizen driven.

Many interview respondents stressed the importance of early participation. By the time a decision reaches the city council or school board, it has already been in the works for quite some time, with advisory committees, staff, and interested parties providing input. Compromises may already be built into the policy, with the key players working out agreements among themselves. Further, supporters or opponents of a policy may be able to convince elected officials of the merits of their position well before it ever gets to a formal vote. Participation is most effective before positions harden, compromises are worked out, and advisory committees make recommendations; showing up at a city council or school board meeting on the day when a policy is scheduled to be approved is, in most cases, too late in the process to make an impact. Also, it takes time to organize opposition or support for an issue: phone trees need to be created, meetings need to be arranged, petitions circulated, and so forth. Such things cannot happen overnight, so the wheels need to be set in motion well before the issue is decided.

Because early participation is more effective, much participation occurs early in the policy process. To influence this early participation, newspaper stories would need to report on issues while they are still in the formative stages. Yet the majority of news stories occur toward the tail end of the process, either right before action is taken or after decisions are already made. As mentioned above, 59 percent of news stories on controversial city council and school board decisions occurred after the votes were taken. Further, of the 41 percent of policy issues that were published prior to decisions being made, many were published within a few days of the decision date. Because most newspaper coverage occurs after decisions are made or right before, it is unlikely to impact citizen participation, much of which occurs early in the policy process.

This pattern is partly a result of the nature of news reporting. The primary function of newspapers (as most journalists define it) is to report on actions that have been taken, and thus we would expect most stories to occur after the fact. Another reason for this trend, however, is the press usually does not report on issues until officials discuss them publicly. Although in some cases investigative reporting will produce stories about issues still in their formative stages, most of the time local reporters will rely heavily on official sources (Taylor, Lee, and Davie 2000; Wong and Jain 1999; Soloski 1989).

By the time officials are willing to talk publicly about an issue, compromises have probably been worked out and elected officials have
decided what actions they will take. Because newspapers frequently
take their cues from elected officials, many of their stories occur too
late in the process to allow for effective citizen participation.

One way newspapers could cover policies in their formative
stages is to pay attention to city advisory committees, where most
policies are discussed before they reach the council.[5] Yet coverage of
these committees is sparse. The City Planning Commission, the
most powerful of the city's standing committees, was only mentioned in sixty-three stories (twenty-nine mentions in the *Orange
County Register* and thirty-four mentions in the *Los Angeles Times*)
over the eleven-year period of this study, for an average of three
mentions per year, per paper. Further, most of these mentions were
brief, usually stating that the planning commission was to take up an
issue or that they had approved or denied a land use proposal. Rarely,
if ever, will newspapers explain the politics behind planning commission votes or solicit opinions from planning commissioners. In the
entire eleven-year period of this study, not one article was dedicated
to explaining in detail the workings of the planning commission.

Other committees are covered even less. The Environmental
and Transportation Advisory Committee (ETAC) deals with many
controversial issues before they reach the council, such as traffic
mitigation and street trees; thus, it is a significant player on many
issues of concern to residents. Citizens who want to influence the
types of issues addressed by ETAC are best served by going to
committee hearings: at the committee stage, there is likely to be
greater opportunity to sway opinions and make an impact than at
the council stage. Yet, only eleven news stories even mentioned
ETAC, and none of these stories described the operation of ETAC
in any detail. The inability or unwillingness to cover city advisory
committees limits coverage of issues early in the policy process, preventing newspapers from providing the type of early coverage that
could spark participation.

So the lack of coverage early in the process, when most participation occurs, is one explanation for newspapers' lack of influence
on participation. Another reason is the paucity of information
about the local decision-making process, which can be arcane and
difficult to understand. Even basic tasks like finding out what is on

the next council agenda can be rather difficult, as agenda items are often described in technical terms and convoluted language. Further, on many issues, multiple votes are taken over several meetings, and it is frequently unclear what is happening when. One role the media could play in facilitating participation is to translate jargon into language people can understand and to explain how the process works. Local newspapers, however, do a very poor job of illuminating the process by which local decisions are made. Instead of describing the process, newspapers focus on outcomes; they tell readers what decisions governmental bodies have made, not how those decisions were made. This consequence is a result of the paucity of local news coverage: given the limited space devoted to local issues, news sections lack space to discuss the details of local decision-making processes.

Scant coverage is dedicated to describing the nuances of the process so that people can understand what is happening, an essential ingredient to successful participation. Further, an outcome focus limits descriptions of ways that citizens can influence the process, which is important information that potential participants need to know. If newspapers covered and explained the governmental process in greater detail, they could perhaps have more of an impact on generating participation. Describing decision processes could have an impact on participation but stating outcomes will not: knowing what actions government bodies have taken is not of much use to citizen participants.

The tendency of newspapers to present local issues as debates between opposing interests also limits their ability to influence participation. The typical story on a local issue will first present a perceived problem by an individual or segment of the community. They will describe the problem and then have some quotes from those people who are promoting change. If it is a controversial issue, they then will present the other side with quotes from opponents. The story may end with a rebuttal from proponents, comment by city or school district staff, or comments from elected officials. Take, for example, an *Orange County Register* article on the artists' village.[6] The article starts with a description of the plan, actions taken so far, and the City's argument for why it is a wise investment of public funds. This opening is followed by some quotes from Ted Moreno, then a city councilman opposed to the artists' village, criticizing the village as a poor way to spend public money. After sections on the genesis of the artists' village and its successes so far, there are more quotes from opponents, and a brief rebuttal from supporters. Although it is just one example, most news stories in this study fall roughly into this pattern.

The problem with this format is its focus on an abstract, theoretical debate, rather than a description of the process by which the issue will be resolved. Presenting an issue as conflicting viewpoints does not give readers a sense of how participation by citizens may be able to influence the outcome. Rather than presenting local policies as issues that are amenable to discussion, change, and citizen influence, policies are presented as conflicts between groups within the community, with little mention of how the issue could be resolved or how ordinary citizens could influence the outcome. This format is not likely to foster citizen participation even if the article is written at a time when participation is still possible. These types of articles provide information about local issues, but they do not put this information in the procedural context that could allow citizens to use this knowledge to participate effectively.

A final characteristic of news reporting that dampens citizen participation is a tendency to describe policy actions as elite, not citizen, driven. Although newspapers provide column space for the *opinions* of nonelites, either through opinion polls or human-interest stories, policy *action* is usually understood in terms of elites. Citizens have opinions on policy issues, whereas elites take action on them. There are, of course, exceptions: at times, news stories will highlight actions taken by citizen participants. Most of the time, however, stories focus on city council and school board votes or actions taken by nonelected officials (such as the police chief or superintendent of schools). The discourse of elite action presents citizens as passive observers to the policy process and undermines participation because it does not offer citizens examples of how people like them can influence policy decisions. Citizens need to know how others are effective at influencing local policies, so that they, too, can be effective. Without this knowledge, citizens may simply decide to stay on the sidelines.

An example can illustrate these characteristics further. The example I will use is a series of articles done by the *Los Angeles Times–Orange County Edition* about pedestrian safety in Santa Ana.

Titled "Perilous Paths: Pedestrians at Risk on the Streets of Santa Ana," this series was prompted by a University of California, Irvine study that identified Santa Ana as having the highest pedestrian fatality rate in Southern California, and the third highest in all of California. The *Los Angeles Times* published twenty-four installments of "Perilous Paths" between May and December 1999. There were also fourteen other stories, letters to the editor, editorials, and columns on pedestrian safety between March and December 1999. This is a significant commitment of column space to a single issue, providing a valuable case to evaluate the link between media coverage and participation. Did all this media attention increase citizen participation on this issue?

Before this series, pedestrian safety was not a priority and was virtually ignored by elected officials. The *Los Angeles Times* series changed that, and for the next six months, pedestrian safety became a front-burner issue. The Santa Ana Police Department beefed up enforcement of jaywalking and speeding motorists, and the city and school district mounted an education campaign to teach pedestrians road safety. State officials also got into the act, with the local state assemblyman holding hearings to find solutions, and promoting legislation that provided additional funds for pedestrian safety projects. It is a clear example of the press exercising its agenda setting power: it effectively put an issue on elected officials' radar screen, and various public actions resulted from it.

Although it may be a classic case of media agenda setting, it is not a case where the media fostered significant citizen participation. None of the interview respondents identified pedestrian safety as an issue that they spent a great deal of time on,[7] and there was no indication in the newspaper articles that citizens were mobilized to act on this issue. There was a tremendous amount of official activity, but there did not seem to be a corresponding amount of citizen activity. How could this extensive series of articles on a local issue not translate into increased citizen involvement?

One striking aspect of this series is that only two articles (out of thirty-eight total) mentioned a future meeting where pedestrian safety will be discussed. Both of these articles made reference to a hearing (in Santa Ana) organized by State Assemblyman Lou Correa to find solutions to pedestrian safety problems. There were at least a few times during this period when the issue was discussed during city council or school board meetings, but the *Los Angeles Times* only mentioned these after the fact.

In addition to this dearth of information about public meetings, "Perilous Paths" also failed to explain to its readers how they could get involved. The stories provided readers with the various dimensions of the issue and the pros and cons of possible solutions. Significant and controversial policy choices needed to be made. For example, whether the police should crack down on jaywalkers or speeding motorists in order to reduce accidents. Also, whether the safety benefits of slowing traffic are worth the trade-off of requiring more time to travel from one part of the city to another. Whether pedestrian safety should be a higher priority among traffic engineers was another key issue. The news stories presented these issues, but they did not tell readers how they could have their voice heard. Not only were they not informed of public meetings, they were not given any indication of how citizens could influence pedestrian safety policy. The stories described a problem, offered possible solutions, and analyzed the pros and cons of those solutions, but they did not take the next step and describe how citizens can get involved. Unlike most news stories, the "Perilous Paths" series appeared before major decisions were made, so the series was in a position to foster participation. But because the stories did not provide the information necessary for citizens to choose to participate, the series did not take advantage of this potential.

The preoccupation of the "Perilous Paths" series was what officials were going to do about the problem of pedestrian safety and significant column space was dedicated to a description of various policy options facing officials. Yet, scant attention was given to the process by which these policy choices were going to be made. Reporters made the assumption that government officials were going to proceed in the manner that they chose, and whether officials decided on a course of action in a backroom smoking cigars or in an open public meeting after receiving input from citizens was a nonissue. Further, citizens were not presented as having an active role in the decision-making process; government officials made decisions and citizens followed them. There was no attempt on the part of the reporters to explore how citizens could influence the governmental process or how they could address the issue of pedestrian safety outside of formal governmental channels.

In general, the "Perilous Paths" series did not provide information to its readers about how they could participate, even though the series can be commended for providing a thorough and analytical presentation of the issue of pedestrian safety. Measuring the exact effect of this series on citizen participation is difficult because we do not have hard measures of all the ways citizens can participate. But we have no reason to expect that "Perilous Paths" had any significant impact on participation. Why would it? It did not give its readers any information that is crucial to participants nor did it present the issue as one that citizens could try to influence.

How Active Citizens Get Information

In this section, I delve deeper into the argument that personal experience and information received through social networks play a more important role than newspaper coverage in generating participation. Some literature on agenda setting has pointed out that media effects are much less for those people who engage in informal discussions with others over politics. For example, Erbring, Goldenberg, and Miller (1980, 41) point out that according to their survey data, "[p]eople involved in active social interaction networks evidently do not depend upon formal channels of communication [i.e., media coverage]." Participants in Santa Ana also depended more heavily on social networks than newspapers for information. My research identifies four reasons for why social networks played a more significant role.

First, coverage of issues salient to citizens in Santa Ana was scarce. One of the "big issues" for citizens was traffic mitigation, particularly reducing traffic on residential streets. The resulting neighborhood traffic plans were highly contentious, and generated high levels of participation: of the fifty-three respondents interviewed, thirteen (25 percent) mentioned a traffic issue as something that they have been personally involved with. Yet newspapers provided little coverage of these issues relative to the amount of participation.[8] On the other hand, one of the newspapers ran a series of lengthy articles on city funding of a local museum, yet this issue received no mentions from participants.

Second, newspapers lack extensive coverage of local politics. As most papers nationally, the two major dailies in Santa Ana cover a number of different cities, and thus can only dedicate so much column space to each city.[9] Further, even taking local coverage as a whole, newspapers dedicate relatively little space to local politics, and the coverage they do have is frequently of a human interest nature. The information gathered through social networks is bound to be much richer, informative, and greater in quantity than that received through newspapers.

Third, respondents probably have greater trust in their social networks. They were not asked specifically whether they trusted information from groups and individuals with whom they associate more than newspapers; however, we can hypothesize that it is the case. We know from national surveys that newspapers are not trusted, and that citizens are aware of editorial biases in newspaper coverage. This lack of trust in newspapers may mean that citizens are less likely to seek out information about their communities from newspapers and rely instead on their social networks.

Finally, the type of information that is communicated socially is likely to be more relevant for participants than what newspapers report. Social networks provide the "inside scoop" on issues that explain what is happening behind the scenes and can give a flavor for the nature of the politics and personalities surrounding an issue. Newspaper reports tend to either simply provide factual information or dwell on "fluff" that is not of much use to participants. In general, then, social networks are better situated to provide valuable information to participants about local issues.

The importance of social networks as an information source for participants, which I explore in greater detail in Chapter 9, explains why newspapers play a greater role in agenda setting than they do in generating participation. Newspapers are the primary source of political information for inactive citizens, as they are not likely to have the social networks that can provide information about local politics. Because most citizens are not active in local politics, newspapers play a significant role in setting the local agenda: the average citizen is susceptible to attempts by newspapers to set the agenda. Active citizens, however, do not rely on newspapers for their information, and thus their actions are much less influenced by newspapers. Newspapers can influence the agendas of the mass public, but they have much less influence over the activities of participants.

Conclusion: The Role of the Media

I have argued that newspapers do not influence participation patterns because of how they report the news and participants' reliance on social networks for information. Even though the literature has found that the media has some impact on making issues salient to the public, this saliency does not extend to politically active citizens. In short, a citizen's decision to participate on issue A rather than issue B is not influenced by media coverage of those issues.

There is scant evidence that media coverage influences participation patterns, but newspapers do have a role to play in local politics. Most interview respondents (83 percent) reported contacting the media at least once (Table 7.1), and a few listed attempts to receive media coverage as a component of their participatory activity (Table 7.4). Respondents had mixed responses about the importance of the media for accomplishing their political tasks. One, when asked if the media played a role in the outcome of space-saver school decision said, "No, I don't think it had anything to do with it." A former city councilman also downplayed newspaper influence: "I think it's short lived. Yesterday's ink is, you know . . . it's paper today and you wrap fish in it tomorrow." Others, however, put more stock in media coverage. One neighborhood leader referred to the media as an "absolute necessity," whereas another commented that the press helped in her efforts to preserve a historic building downtown. Thus, respondents disagreed on the importance of the media for achieving their political goals.

Respondents used the media for two purposes: to spread information and to pressure officials. As for the former, some respondents found newspapers to be an effective means of communicating their opinions. One person describes how she communicated her ideas: "I'll talk to my coworkers, and then I'll start writing letters to the newspapers. I think you would be surprised how many people read the opinion page. Yes, I was really surprised, because I get published quite a bit, and people have said, 'I've seen your letter.'" Others described how they contacted the media to prompt favorable news stories. Second, some respondents used the media to pressure officials. Officials read the newspaper, and some respondents felt that getting favorable news stories would pressure officials into conceding to their demands.

So local newspapers have an impact on local politics. This fact does not mean, however, that they generate citizen participation: newspaper coverage influences opinions and agendas, but it does not rouse people to participate. Given the way that newspaper cover local issues and the manner in which citizens participate, they do not generate participation on the issues they cover. If we want to understand why some issues generate participation and others do not, we need to look elsewhere.

The media's lack of value for participants has prompted some journalists and scholars to develop an alternative to current journalistic practices, commonly referred to as "public journalism" (Eksterowicz and Roberts 2000; Rosen 1999, 1996; Charity 1995). The central idea behind public journalism is that the role of the press is not just to report facts so that citizens know what is happening but to provide information to people to "make it as easy as possible for citizens to make intelligent decisions about public affairs" (Charity 1995, 2). Rather than as an objective purveyor of facts, public journalists see the media's role as that of democratic facilitator: The fundamental purpose of the media is to provide the tools that citizens need to be good democratic citizens. Toward that end, public journalists focus on helping to construct national debates about pressing policy issues, reducing the hurdles to participation by providing information that citizens need to participate, and assisting communities in solving their problems.

Widely implemented public journalism would lead to the media having a greater influence over participation patterns. Public journalism has the characteristics that I identified above that could facilitate participation—that is, reporting on issues early, describing political processes, constructing debates that are not just arguments between opposing interests, and identifying a role for citizens in the policy-making process. The type of reporting that we saw in Santa Ana is not inherent to the media industry or an immutable fact. Public journalism is a feasible alternative to current journalistic practices that could have a significant impact on the ability of the media to facilitate participation and influence patterns of participation.

6 Social Conflict and Participation

One possible explanation for participation patterns is that they reflect larger social conflicts. The policy issues that represent major social cleavages—the fault lines in society—are the ones that will generate the most participation, with citizens participating on those issues that serve as proxies for underlying conflicts. If this argument is true we should see the greatest level of participation in those issues that are representative of, or have implications for, major social conflicts.

In participant interviews, two social conflicts repeatedly emerged. The first is a debate over the appropriate function and organization of the city. What purpose do cities serve? Whose needs should they meet? What social goods should they prioritize? Participants fundamentally disagreed over these questions, and offered three distinct "urban visions," each a different conception of the ideal goals and aspirations for the city. Some envision the city as a cosmopolitan center, emphasizing high culture that provides a rich milieu for middle-class citizens fleeing from the banality of the suburbs. Others dream of a city that is simply a denser version of suburbia and strive toward making the city as much like a suburb as possible. Still others contend the city should focus on serving the needs of the working class, providing a safe and pleasant place to live for those unable to flee to the suburbs.

I argue that much of the participation in Santa Ana was geared toward promoting one vision over the others, and those policies that represented a trade-off between the visions generated more participation than those policies that were consistent with all three. Although not every issue generating participation was relevant to the debate over urban visions, enough of them were to lead me to conclude that policies relevant to this debate were more likely to generate participation than those that were not.

Local governments have to make choices regarding which vision to pursue, and policies that represent these choices generate citizen interest and participation. Thus, the participation patterns in Santa Ana are partially the result of the debate over competing urban visions.

Racial conflict was the other social cleavage appearing repeatedly in interviews. Many issues, regardless of their substantive content, had racial overtones, and for some race was a central issue. I contend, however, that racial conflict is not a significant influence on participation patterns. Most policy debates have a racial aspect; however, few of the issues that generated significant participation were directly about race. Racial conflict was evident in participant interviews not because the issues themselves were about race, but because race was used as a means to understand opponents' motives and behavior. Race was prominent in local policy debates, but it did not influence participation patterns.

One reason race was so prominent in policy debates was because participants did not always recognize the trade-offs between urban visions, instead casting issues in terms of racial conflict. Participants consistently attributed racial motivations to their opponents, failing to consider that their actions and attitudes were derivative of a particular urban vision, not race. It is not that race is unimportant or does not influence attitudes on policy issues, but the core debate was about urban visions. This debate, however, was frequently transformed into racial conflict.

Three Urban Visions

Three competing visions of the "good city" dominated policy debates in Santa Ana. The first vision, which I call the "cosmopolitan city" vision, sees the city as a cultural center that provides uniquely urban amenities that cannot be found in suburban or rural areas. Proponents of this view see the city as a unique entity that has positive attributes lacking in suburbs. Unlike the banal, bland, and culturally void suburbs, city neighborhoods and shopping districts have character, providing a rich and stimulating milieu for its residents. Proponents of the cosmopolitan city vision want to create an alternative to the "gated community lifestyle" found in other Orange County suburbs. This comment is representative:

You can just see all those upper-middle-class families from Irvine and Mission Viejo and Aliso Viejo [suburbs near Santa Ana] all down there holding the mirror in front of their face, everyone [asking], "Who's the fairest of them all?" Santa Ana never showed up. But as we divorced ourselves from a suburban mentality or a suburban model and became increasingly urban, we became the ones that said, "We aren't you." They were saying before that, "We don't want to be like you," but now we were saying, "We don't want to be like you. We're different." And that was important for the city staff to get over because they were trying to adopt all these suburban models as what we needed to do to reinvigorate the urban experience.

Energy and diversity are key components of the cosmopolitan city vision. Creative energy and cultural dynamism are the holy grails for cosmopolitans because they make the city an enriching and fulfilling place to live. A good place to live, as defined by adherents to this view, is an intellectually and culturally stimulating environment.

City policy, according to cosmopolitans, should be geared toward creating this unique urban milieu, which includes promoting culturally enriching experiences, redeveloping aging downtowns to make them more visually appealing, reducing dependency on the automobile (a suburban vice) by developing mass transit, facilitating pedestrian traffic, and implementing other policies geared toward creating an appealing urban environment. To make these goals economically feasible, cities need to be attractive places for middle-class residents who can afford to patronize the arts and downtown businesses. As one respondent put it, "If you are going to get people like me who have discretionary income to want to live in Santa Ana and spend their money in Santa Ana, you have to give them lifestyle options. You have to give them amenities that they want to go to." According to the cosmopolitan city vision, providing these "lifestyle options" and amenities should be a key goal of city policy.

Diversity is welcomed because it can add to urban stimulation, but large numbers of one minority group is shunned because it can homogenize the culture and limit urban possibilities. Also unwelcome are large numbers of the poor, who generally cannot afford to use urban amenities and cannot provide the tax base to support them. Cosmopolitans are not, in principle, exclusionary, but their focus on creating urban amenities and intellectual and cultural experiences means that large numbers of poor people are a barrier to progress. Typical of cosmopolitans is this comment, made by a respondent after extolling the virtues of diversity: "We have enough low-income housing and affordable housing in the city. What we don't have is the other housing. The housing for the CEO or the executive that is going to hire the gardener, the maid, the pool boy."

The second view is the "city-as-suburb" vision, whose basic goal is to make the city (as much as possible) like the suburbs. People flee from the city to the suburbs for a reason: suburbs provide people with the convenience and high-quality services that they cannot get in the city. Therefore, to retain businesses and residents, the city should strive to provide the type of lifestyle that people can get in the suburbs. The role of the city is not to provide a culturally and intellectually stimulating environment, but to create a context in which people can go about their routines of work and play with maximum convenience. Rather than creating enlightening experiences for its residents, proponents of this vision argue that the city, first and foremost, should provide a pleasant place where people can conduct their business and personal activities.

For the city-as-suburb vision, the goal of city policy is to provide the amenities available in suburbs, such as affordable single-family homes, free parking, and good schools, in an urban context. In Santa Ana, the focus was on creating quiet and clean residential neighborhoods through traffic mitigation and code enforcement. The opposition to new schools was also derivative of this vision, as schools were seen as generators of traffic and noise that could detract from the suburban character of neighborhoods. Throughout the 1990s, a spate of city ordinances restricted everything from street vendors to garage sales to clutter on peoples' balconies, all of which were meant to create a suburban environment within the city (Table 6.1).

The city-as-suburb vision was evident in many comments by respondents justifying their policy positions. For example, a respondent explained her support of a neighborhood traffic mitigation plan by saying, "Santa Ana is perceived as not being a desirable place to live, and part of the reason is because we don't have neighborhoods such as Irvine and the other south county cities . . . what do the neighborhoods that are considered more desirable have? They have limited [traffic] access." In another neighborhood, a basketball court was ripped out to limit the noise from teenagers playing basketball, prompting one respondent to say, "So, a lot of people are being deprived of playing full-court basketball, but the neighborhood is quiet." These quotes represent the feelings of many respondents who supported city actions that promoted suburban values and moved Santa Ana closer to a suburban environment.

The third urban vision focuses on the needs of the working class. Cities are the repository of those people who cannot afford to live in suburbs: the poor, working class, and recently arrived immigrants. Others may live in the city, but they do so by choice not by necessity. Because the working classes have to live there, the city's role is to create a context where the lower echelons of society can meet their daily needs. The "good" city, therefore, is one that provides basic services and provides an environment that allows the working classes to survive economically and go about their daily routines of work and play.

City policy, according to the working-class vision, should focus on the basics. The working classes need well-maintained infrastructure—roads, parks, public buildings—that allows them to pursue their daily routines most efficiently. Further, public services such as schools and libraries are critical because most residents lack the ability to buy these services in the private market. The "extras," such as cultural amenities and shopping experiences, are not as important because the poor lack the disposable income to take advantage of them. The inconveniences of city life—the noise, poor aesthetics, and traffic—are only minor problems; although nobody enjoys such characteristics, they are not of major concern to the poor and working class, who have more pressing issues (e.g., making a living, supporting a family) to address.

The working-class city vision inspired many of the critiques offered of past and current city policies. Some complained that the City was trying to force out poor Latinos, such as this respondent from the Santa Anita neighborhood, a poor area on the west side of the city:

> The city wants to see this neighborhood to look like Newport,
> Irvine, Mission Viejo [wealthy suburbs south of Santa Ana], and
> that area in reality tomorrow. And if they can get [rid of] most
> of these illegal [immigrants] with the overcrowding that we have
> in this neighborhood. . . . And if they had their own way to do
> it, to disband this whole neighborhood, they would. Mow it
> down to put new housing in here or new businesses, just so they
> can beautify it.

Others criticized the City for putting too much money into such
projects as the artists' village and not enough into basic infrastructure. One neighborhood leader, commenting on the poor condition of city streets, said, "They put stuff in the arts. I think the arts
are great, but don't put all our money into it. And a lot of people
are not into arts and they see all this stuff going on and when they
go to my [neighborhood association] meeting they're angry."
Another echoed this concern, stating that "nobody from this
neighborhood is going down there [to the artists' village], it's not
a priority."

Trade-Offs and Urban Visions

The three urban visions prioritize different values and present alternative goals that cities can pursue. The values and goals of each
vision are not mutually exclusive: for example, supporters of the
working-class city do not oppose cultural amenities, cosmopolitans
do not oppose suburban amenities, and city-as-suburb proponents do
not oppose infrastructure improvements. There are some policy
decisions that are consistent with all three, for example, a decision
to enhance public safety by implementing community policing.
Though not polar opposites, the three visions differ in the value
placed upon social goods and the desirability of goals, requiring
policy makers to make trade-offs among the values and goals presented by the three visions.

Trade-offs between the visions are of two basic types: spending
priorities and conflicting goals. With limited budgets, cities need to
decide whether they will spend money on such things as cultural
amenities, repairing infrastructure, building schools, or planting
street trees. These activities are consistent with all three visions but
each prioritizes them differently. Decisions by policy makers to

prioritize one over the others will favor one of the urban visions. Further, some of the goals of the three visions overlap, but they also contain conflicting goals. For example, cosmopolitans favor aesthetics over convenience, whereas proponents of the other two visions consider convenience to be more important. Also, city-as-suburb adherents prefer regulations on social behavior to limit what they perceive as negative influences, whereas working-class city proponents desire fewer regulations that could interfere with the lives of working-class people. When goals conflict, policy makers need to decide which goals they will favor. Inevitably, policy makers will be in a position where they will have to decide which values and goals they will prioritize, and in the process support one of the three visions.

Two arguments can be made against the contention that the three urban visions are in conflict and entail trade-offs for cities. First, if a city is successful in attracting wealthy residents and businesses, it can enhance its tax base, leading to more money for high-quality services, infrastructure, and cultural amenities. With a healthy tax base, cities can meet the needs of all classes, and can have the best of all worlds. In other words, pursuing wealthy residents and businesses will generate tax revenues that can be used to meet other goals. Paul Peterson (1981) has elucidated this theory most forcefully, arguing that this logic essentially drives urban policy. In Santa Ana, this dynamic has manifested itself in the City's dedication of significant resources to promoting the arts, which supporters say will revitalize the city, enhance the tax base, and allow the City to pursue other goals, such as improving the schools and making infrastructure improvements.

This logic is compelling, but it does not eliminate the trade-offs described above. Cities will always have budget constraints, even if they are successful at attracting wealthy residents and businesses, and the need to prioritize goals and values will always be present. Further, they will still have to deal with conflicting goals when making policy decisions. Generating additional tax revenues does not resolve these conflicts. Peterson (1981) may be correct that cities try to generate additional tax revenues to enhance services, but this strategy does not resolve any of the conflicts between the three urban visions.

The second argument is that cities can serve all three visions at once, and currently do. In many cities, there is a downtown area that provides cultural amenities, residential housing tracts that resemble the suburbs, and other neighborhoods that serve the needs of the working class. Cities can be all things to all people because there is a geographic division of labor among areas of the city. Cities do not have to be of "one type" or another; they can encompass all three visions at the same time.

There are two flaws in this argument. First, cities do not equally distribute funds across different areas of the city: city governments use greater resources on some areas at the expense of others. There are still trade-offs here; it just takes a geographic form. Goals still need to be prioritized and choices made. Second, areas of the city interact with each other, and at times may cause conflicts. Residents favoring a city-as-suburb vision may not want a poor, working-class neighborhood next door, and may want to see it transformed. Similarly, those desiring more cultural amenities may want to limit suburban-like development and working-class neighborhoods, for fear that they will not patronize cultural amenities (thus reducing their viability). Even though cities may encompass all three visions in various neighborhoods, they still must make trade-offs and prioritize goals.

Rosy scenarios where trade-offs are not part of policy making and goals never conflict work well as political rhetoric, but do not represent the reality of urban politics. Local policy makers have to choose between competing goals and prioritize a myriad of social goods. These decisions inevitably generate policy conflict.

Urban Visions and Participation in Santa Ana

Many of the policy decisions generating participation in Santa Ana required local officials to make trade-offs between urban visions, even though decisions were rarely cast in these terms. Below I discuss some issues where these trade-offs are evident, and explore how much of the participation in Santa Ana is focused on promoting urban visions.

The Artists' Village

No issue better captures the tensions between the visions than the artists' village, the City's effort to revitalize downtown by promoting the arts, which was discussed in Chapter 4. The primary supporters of the artists' village were cosmopolitans,[1] who saw the project as a means to enhance the cultural environment of the city. The logic supporting the artists' village mirrors that underlying the cosmopolitan city vision. Developing the arts provides a culturally enriching environment, making Santa Ana a more desirable place to live and work. Here's one respondent discussing the benefits of the artists' village:

> Many years ago, the *Register* reported [downtown] was a ghost town. Well, today it's starting to come back alive. It wouldn't be coming back alive I think if it hadn't been for the arts movement. . . . In order to rejuvenate the downtown, and I really believe, that you need more of a diversity. . . . There was a time where you could come in here and anybody outside of a Latin culture really didn't feel welcome. . . . You saw something happening in downtown Santa Ana that hasn't happened in years. All of a sudden, you started seeing an influx of every culture showing up downtown. Black, Asian, White, whatever. Latino. Every culture I could think of started showing up. And you started seeing young people coming back downtown again. And I think that's something that this county is striving for, is some kind of identity or real hub. And young people can be creative and be free to express themselves. . . . [A business owner] came to our neighborhood with a vision and asked for our help because the city was fighting him because he wanted to open a house for kids. No alcohol or drugs, just a place where kids could express themselves with poetry, drums, beating of the drums, and dancing. Graffiti art. Get kids off the street. It could serve two purposes. It gave young people in the community, not from just Santa Ana but from all over Orange County, a place to go. But it also served another purpose for the city. The prostitutes and the drug dealers were off the street. . . . Boarded buildings bring riff-raff. But when you have activity going on, you don't have riff-raff.

Further, investment in the arts will reap economic benefits for the city because it will prompt business investment downtown and spark a revitalization of business activity, leading to a stronger tax base. Thus, not only will the artists' village provide a socially desirable amenity, it will also yield economic rewards.

As already mentioned, critics argued that spending over $10 million to develop the artists' village while streets were in disrepair and essential city services were lacking is an indication that the city has fundamentally skewed priorities. Rather than being a benefit to all of society, they saw it as a perk for a wealthy few, as most people in Santa Ana will not patronize the village and its benefits will not trickle down to the average Santa Ana resident. There was also a perception that an underlying goal of the project was to push Latinos and Latino-owned businesses out of downtown (one respondent referred to it as the "delatinization" of downtown). The gist of these criticisms aligns with the working-class city vision. If the primary function of the city is to provide a place for the working classes to live, the artists' village should not be a priority, as it does not assist in meeting their needs.

The debate over the artists' village illustrates the tension between the cosmopolitan city vision and the working-class city vision. Even though supporters claimed the artists' village would increase tax revenues that could be used for other purposes, they essentially argued that promoting the arts was more important than spending money on infrastructure and services, at least in the short term. Arts and culture is worth the money. Opponents disagreed, prioritizing other social goods over developing the arts. Although there are many aspects to this debate,[2] fundamentally the debate was about whether the city should focus on providing a culturally rich environment or on maintaining infrastructure and basic services.

Traffic Mitigation

The artists' village was a pet project for cosmopolitans, whereas adherents of the city-as-suburb vision pushed neighborhood traffic plans. Respondents discussed plans in four different neighborhoods: Floral Park (discussed in Chapter 3), French Park, Washington Square, and Wilshire Square. In all four neighborhoods, the proposals attempted to reduce traffic by barricading streets, installing stop signs, or restricting left-hand turns. The justification for these measures generally rested on the contention that they would improve neighborhood quality of life by reducing noise and improving safety. Supporters desired traffic mitigation in the hope that it would result in quieter, more peaceful neighborhoods that resemble those found in the suburbs. Here's one respondent describing why she supported a traffic mitigation plan for French Park:

Because Santa Ana is perceived as not being a desirable place to live, and part of the reason is because we don't have neighborhoods such as Irvine and the other south county cities, what do the neighborhoods that are considered more desirable have? They have limited access. They're not through [streets], they're cul-de-sacs and when traffic is allowed to flow unimpeded through neighborhoods, as an alternate to arterials, there's no respect for the quality of life in those neighborhoods. Those cars behind you you hear whizzing by, and you're going to hear more in a few minutes, are not coming home here to French Park. They're on their way up to Washington [Street], and from Washington to the freeway. And the more congested Main Street gets, the worse it's going to get on French [Street]. And then on our east–west streets. So we're standing there saying, "Hey wait a minute. We live here just as much as people in Irvine, Mission Viejo, Aliso Viejo, Rancho Santa Margarita [wealthy south county suburbs]. And there's no more reason that we should have to put up with commuter traffic than they should have to put up with commuter traffic."

Opponents, many of whom lived within the neighborhoods with proposed traffic plans, saw these plans as exclusionary and accused proponents of trying to block themselves off from the rest of the city. They also argued that traffic mitigation inconveniences those in adjacent neighborhoods by making people take alternative routes. Opponents were not necessarily motivated by urban visions. Some just thought that limiting access was a bad idea, either because it was exclusionary or because it would inconvenience them. Others just did not see the perceived problems caused by traffic. Here's a comment by an opponent to the traffic mitigation plan in Wilshire Square that critiques the vision underlying the traffic mitigation proposal:

Just those who knew that "Gee, I want my street to be traffic free so my kids can play basketball." Well, that's great. That's ideal and I think maybe forty, fifty years ago we could do that. But when you're living in probably one of the most highly condensed cities in the county, what did you expect when you moved here? And not only that, we have the highest concentration of youth. Which are going to be potential drivers, which the whole situation is that we have a lot of cars, we have a lot of traffic. . . . That was the other thing. Shouldn't they play in the back yard? "Well, they should be free to play in the front yard." Well, this is managing your children. What's more important? And that was the concept, you started to feel, that children should be able to play in the street. They wanted it to be like Mayberry USA. Which I think would be great. But we have over 300,000 people in this city and it's not going to happen.

Traffic mitigation was an important issue for city-as-suburb adherents: traffic plans allow residential neighborhoods in dense urban environments to maintain a suburban feel by limiting the noise and inconvenience created by traffic. Neighborhood traffic plans were a vehicle by which the suburb-as-city vision could be promoted. Although opponents had various reasons for their dislike of traffic plans, supporters were clearly motivated by their desire to see their residential neighborhoods mimic suburban ones.

Code Enforcement

Throughout the 1990s, Santa Ana enacted a series of ordinances aimed at "cleaning up" the city, some of which are listed in Table 6.1.[3] Additionally, the City beefed up its enforcement of existing codes. All of these actions were meant to change the appearance of the city to make it look less like a city populated by working-class immigrants and more like a suburb. Support for these actions was derivative of the vision one held for the city. City-as-suburb adherents were the most vocal in support of these measures, with some support from cosmopolitans, who believed that these policies would make the city more aesthetically pleasing. The working-class city vision is hostile to such regulations because in most cases the people being regulated are the working classes and in some cases impose real hardships on them.

These issues varied in how much participation they generated. As already discussed in Chapter 4, the commercial vehicles code was initiated by a neighborhood leader, and many others involved with Commlink participated in support. Several of the other issues generated some participation as well. A few respondents mentioned efforts to get the city to enhance residential code enforcement, and others raised the issue of attempting to institute permit-only street parking. Some respondents also talked about their opposition to

Table 6.1. Selected city regulatory ordinances, 1990–2000

Ordinance	Date	Description
Commercial vehicles ordinance	12/18/00	Restricts the parking of commercial vehicles on residential streets
Front yard fence moratorium	9/1/99	Placed a moratorium on the construction of front yard fences (until a new ordinance could be passed regulating their size and appearance)
Pushcart ban	8/3/98	Banned all pushcarts/street vendors in the city (ordinance was modified after a lawsuit settlement in November, 2000)
Garage sale limitations	5/16/94	Limits garage sales to four weekends a year
Property maintenance standards ("clutter law")	1/18/94	Prevents clotheslines in public view, trashcans left on curbs, and other "untidy" practices
Anticamping ordinance	5/18/92	Banned "camping" by homeless on public property
Swap meet ban	2/19/91	Banned all outdoor swap meets

Source: Santa Ana City Council minutes.

the street vendor regulations, a highly controversial issue. Other issues in Table 6.1 generated less interest, but the fact that so much participation in Santa Ana was geared toward these issues indicates the importance that urban visions play in generating participation. The goal of all of these policies is to create a city that resembles a suburb, and these policies were another way that city-as-suburb proponents tried to make their vision come to fruition.

Land Use

Some of the land use debates were also related to contested urban visions. In 1995, a proposed supermarket sparked a major political battle between cosmopolitans and working-class activists. The Northgate Supermarket, which caters primarily to working-class Hispanics, was slated to be located downtown, adjacent to the middle-class French Park neighborhood. The neighborhood opposed the supermarket, saying that it was too big, ugly, and would be a blight on their community. One French Park resident explains her opposition as follows:

> My neighbors were talking and they called me and said there was going to be a huge supermarket right there on that corner, and there is going to be a warehouse and huge trucks rumbling in and out, and they asked if I would like to come and speak [at a city council meeting]. Because I've studied architecture and urban planning, I've thought a lot about what has made the urban centers that I have lived in really livable and enjoyable. . . . I really believe that in order to create this sense of neighborhood and community in a downtown, that a small mom-and-pop supermarket was a lovely and integral part of the culture. So in my speech I described my vision of what that market could be, knowing that it was going to be Hispanic, but the smell of the cilantro and the tomatoes, and you go and pick up your six pack to have your porch party in French Park.

Supporters of the supermarket argued that there was adequate demand from nearby communities to justify its size and that it was a needed service for many residents in Santa Ana. At the core of the conflict was a debate over whether the aesthetic and traffic concerns of the neighbors should take precedence over the shopping needs of the working class. Again, we see support or opposition breaking down according to urban visions, with cosmopolitans and city-as-suburb adherents prioritizing aesthetics and neighborhood quality of life, and working-class city proponents emphasizing the needs of the lower classes.[4]

The space-saver school debate (described in Chapter 3) also exhibits the influence of urban visions. Although all recognized the need to build more schools, opponents of the space-saver school argued that despite the need, the school should not be built if it was going to negatively influence the neighborhood. Supporters prioritized the need of the school district to build more schools for the primarily working-class youth in the city. There was more to the debate than just this issue: People disagreed over whether there would be, in fact, any negative effect on the surrounding neighborhood, and there was also concern about the cost of the school.

But one point of contention in this multifaceted debate was whether the needs of the working classes should take precedence over maintaining the suburban qualities of nearby neighborhoods.

Summary

Not every issue that generated participation in Santa Ana centered on a debate over urban visions; some controversial issues, such as school uniforms and Measure C, had absolutely no relationship to them. But enough issues were implicated in the visions debate to conclude that this connection is relevant for our understanding of participation patterns. In this section I demonstrated that much participation in Santa Ana was sparked by a desire to promote an urban vision and a corresponding set of priorities. The examples offered above illustrate the trade-offs that exist between urban visions, and that at times local officials need to decide whether they are going to prioritize the values of one vision over the other two. These types of decisions frequently generate significant levels of participation, and thus I conclude that the urban visions debate is a factor that can help explain participation patterns: policies that represent trade-offs between urban visions are more likely to generate participation than those that do not.

Race, Participation, and Urban Visions

A social conflict that is an obvious candidate for influencing patterns of participation is racial tension. The logic is simple. Racial tensions are a central problem in American society, and one on which citizens hold deep and strong opinions. When a local issue deals with race, citizens will be more likely to participate because it is connected to this larger social conflict. Thus, we should see more participation in issues that concern race than those not pertaining to racial issues.

Many of the issues generating participation had a racial dimension to them. The space-saver school is a good example. Supporters of the school accused opponents of being racially motivated, as demonstrated by this quote from a school supporter explaining why the opposition was so strong:

It's the issue that you are going to have "those" children going through "their" neighborhood. It's [the surrounding neighborhood] essentially an Anglo area with Hispanic children going through it. They said our crime rate is going to go up. We kept hearing, we have all these delinquents going in and out of our streets. . . . And it really became the old thing of "not in my backyard." It's okay to educate "those children" but not in my backyard. It became very much we are the white families who have the money and influence in this city, don't cross white boundaries. It was basically anything north of 17th [Street] was, this is our area, everything south is, you can have it, we really don't care what happens to it. . . . I think it [neighborhood concerns about traffic and noise] was window dressing. I think it was the whole prejudice issue; it was easier to remain prejudice and ignorant than to find out what these children really are like.

Another supporter commented that he was "still upset about the whole issue. I can understand their concerns for vandalism and safety, but they upset me because they see a brown face and they want to keep us out." Opponents not only denied their position was racially motivated, but also accused supporters of using the race issue to divert attention away from their legitimate concerns about traffic, noise, and neighborhood quality of life.

The city's downtown policy was also criticized as racist in nature. Here's one respondent's take on the artists' village:

[A] few years ago I heard that there was going to be an area that was earmarked for the arts. I said, "Wonderful." Oh, man this will be great. I can see glass blowers, leather work, kind of like Olvera Street [in downtown Los Angeles]. All this [sounded] great. . . . Guess what? The plan didn't include the Hispanic community. . . . This is what the city is doing: They're trying to change the face of downtown. . . . So, hey, we better grab these buildings before it gets to be another Hispanic business area, and we're going to pour some money in there, make it a success.

Defenders of the city's downtown policy counter that a racialized view of the issue is not called for: "I think that people who say things like that are racist. Those kinds of thoughts are a knee-jerk reaction. I understand the roots of those beliefs, and somebody who views themselves as an underclass feels that they are going to be stripped of any future in the city. But I think it's total bunk."

Many respondents complained about race being brought into policy debates. A neighborhood leader, in discussing the commercial vehicles ordinance, commented that "[t]here were some discrimination factors brought up by certain city council people too, which I didn't like. I hate that card being played all the time." Another, complaining about how every issue has racial overtones, asked rhetorically, "But I honestly feel like, why do we have to talk race all the time?" Most issues were not overtly about race; however, these comments illustrate that many had some racial aspect to them.

The prevalence of racial overtones to policy debates could lead us to conclude that race, and not urban visions, is the key fault line that organizes political debates and influences participation patterns. If race were the central issue in political debates, however, we would expect issues that were more centrally about race to generate participation. Issues directly about race—for example, affirmative action, redlining, and racial profiling—were not represented among high-participation issues. Why is it that so many issues generating participation had racial overtones, yet issues directly about race did not generate much participation at all?

New schools, downtown redevelopment, and code enforcement are not inherently racial in character, even though all were framed as such. As is evidenced by the quotes above, many participants used race to understand policy debates, either attributing racist attitudes to their opponents or accusing them of using race as a debating tool (i.e., "playing the race card"). Many issues, regardless of their subject matter, were cast in racial terms because participants used race to explain their opponents' behavior. Thus, race was a common feature of policy debates not because racial conflict generated participation but because it was used to explain others' behavior. Race was a fallback position that citizens used to understand political conflict, not a generator of the conflict itself.

One reason race was often used to understand political debates was that the conflict and trade-offs among urban visions were not recognized. Often, citizens did not acknowledge that others have a different conception of the good city or believed that their urban vision did not have any negatives. Although tensions among urban visions were central to policy debates, respondents usually did not explicitly discuss them or even acknowledge their existence. Respondents rarely framed policy issues in terms of trade-offs, and the debate over urban visions is no exception. Failing to recognize trade-offs, they relied on race to understand disagreement with their position. Rather than engage in discussion about how to resolve the trade-offs between urban visions, respondents assumed there were no trade-offs and chalked up opposition to their position as racially motivated.

A debate over a liquor license for a downtown restaurant illustrates this dynamic. Shelley's Restaurant is located on Fourth Street in an Hispanic shopping district, but caters primarily to a middle-class clientele (such as professionals who work in the courthouse across the street). Shelley's has about five or six tables on the sidewalk, and its owner applied for a permit to serve alcohol outside (it already had a permit for alcohol inside). Opponents to granting the liquor license argued that the City's long-standing policy of limiting bars downtown to keep out bad elements should be continued. Supporters, however, saw Shelley's, with its sidewalk dining and an occasional three-piece jazz ensemble for entertainment, as contributing to a cosmopolitan environment downtown. Here's one respondent talking about why she supported Shelley's:

> Well, it's just so interesting because here's Shelley's Bistro on Fourth Street. She's a white woman. She's got this great restaurant. You would love it. Great food, fine dining. . . . And she's got this patio now, this area that comes out. It's like a Pasadena thing. She's got a nice little fence. . . . Inside the restaurant, she's got this beautiful bar that's wooden and carved and the bartender is there. Very elegant and upscale. Typical. We all think, no brainer. It's a good thing.

Here's another supporter:

> I thought Shelley's was a step up for Santa Ana. Being across from the courthouse, those people are high up, people that work there, attorneys, FBI. They're used to going into nice places and having lunch or dinner or just a drink. And Shelley's was providing that [with] outdoor dining. In fact, one of my things when I spoke, I think it was at the planning commission, I had been a couple of

days before I spoke I had drinks at [unclear]. And there was a restaurant, and how they were showing how their city, which was Monrovia, has changed and evolved, they showed outdoor dining. It was exactly like Shelley's. This is how they are showing how nice their city is and how walkable their city is and how inviting.

The Shelley's issue developed a strong racial undertone. Fourth Street, where Shelley's is located, is a thriving commercial district that caters primarily to working-class Latinos. Supporters viewed opposition as an attempt to keep white-owned businesses (and whites generally) out of the area. One supporter claimed that "Hispanics on Fourth Street don't want any of the Caucasians in and having businesses down there." For their part, opponents saw discriminatory practices on the part of the City: they believed that Hispanic-owned restaurants would not be allowed to serve alcohol outside if they applied for permits. Shelley's, in their view, was receiving special treatment (an exception to the standing city policy limiting bars downtown) because it was a white-owned business that caters to well-to-do professionals.[5]

The debate over Shelley's, at its core, has little to do with race and everything to do with urban visions. Supporters saw Shelley's as a positive contribution to the downtown environment because it added a cosmopolitan element with its outdoor dining and live entertainment. Opponents did not see the benefits of such a restaurant to the working-class clientele of other Fourth Street establishments. Both sides failed to see this disagreement and transformed the debate into one of racism, discrimination, and exclusion.

We also see this dynamic of using race as a way to explain conflict caused by urban visions in the issues described above. The artists' village offers a typical example. Many opponents saw the artists' village as a way for the city to reduce the influence of the Hispanic community downtown. Because they failed to see the trade-offs between their vision of a downtown catering to the working classes and a cosmopolitan vision, opponents used a racial explanation to account for the push to create the artists' village. Supporters made the same mistake. Not seeing how anybody could oppose the arts, they chalked up the opposition to an antiwhite bias among Hispanics. The artists' village, a downtown redevelopment project, became a racial issue, not because it inherently has something to do with race, but because participants did not recognize the conflict over urban visions, and consequently relied on race to understand opposing arguments.

In sum, race became an issue in many political debates because trade-offs between urban visions were not acknowledged. Race was frequently a point of contention, but the core conflict centered on urban visions; and because this conflict was not articulated, participants used race as a means to understand their adversaries' positions. For some issues the city and school district address, race really is the central point of contention; however, racial overtones in many instances are derivative of conflicts over urban visions, a fallback position that is used to understand disagreements when trade-offs are not recognized. Thus, although many of the issues generating participation had a racial component, it is not likely that race was the factor prompting participation.

Conclusion

My goal in this chapter was to explore whether social conflicts have explanatory value for patterns of participation; does issue A generate more participation than issue B because it serves as a proxy for an emotional or contentious social conflict? To answer this question, I analyzed the dynamics involving two social conflicts that repeatedly emerged in participant interviews: competing urban visions and racial conflict. As for competing urban visions, I outlined three different visions of how citizens define the "good city," each of which contains a different set of policy goals. The evidence presented supports the hypothesis that issues encompassing trade-offs between urban visions will generate more participation than those that do not, that is, this social conflict does have some explanatory value for understanding participation patterns. Policies that require trade-offs between urban visions often generate participation, acting as a proxy for the larger battle over the direction of city policy regarding the nature of the urban environment. Citizens do not always recognize the trade-offs in their visions, but they participate to promote the values underlying their vision and try to persuade the City to make choices conducive to it. Much citizen participation in Santa Ana revolved around issues that are significant from the perspective of urban visions. Not all issues generating participation were relevant in this regard, however, enough were to conclude that urban visions can influence what types of issues generate participation.

The evidence that racial conflict influenced participation patterns is less compelling. Although most controversial issues in Santa Ana had a racial aspect to them, this situation had less to do with the power of racial conflict to generate participation than the tendency of participants to use race to explain their opponents' behavior and make sense of policy debates. Of course, it is not that in other cities racial conflict will not generate significant levels of participation; clearly, there are cities that exhibit this dynamic. The point here is that the existence of a racial discourse in local policy debates does not necessarily mean that it has explanatory value for participation patterns. More generally, the contention that urban visions, rather than racial conflict, was the social cleavage with the greatest influence on participation in Santa Ana is meant to illustrate how social conflicts can influence participation patterns, not claim that competing urban visions is *the* social conflict that matters for understanding participation patterns. In other cities, there may be a social conflict other than urban visions that serves the same purpose. The goal of this chapter was to illustrate the dynamics of how social conflicts can act as a prompt for participation, which I did using the conflict (the debate over competing urban visions) that was most prominent in Santa Ana.

The analysis in this chapter supports the citizen-as-lobbyist model of policy engagement by providing evidence against two of the alternative models. First, the issues that are connected with urban visions such as traffic mitigation and the artists' village— are not connected with core ideological debates in American society. If citizen were engaging the policy-making process as ideologues, they would not focus on these types of issues. The fact that these issues generated participation indicates that citizens were more interested in addressing issues that directly affect them rather than contributing to a larger ideological debate. This chapter also provides evidence against viewing participants as collaborative problem solvers. If citizens had engaged the policy-making process in this manner, there would have been a greater effort to develop a coherent plan to pursue one of the urban visions through policy, and a more conscious recognition of what type of vision the community wants to pursue. Instead, participants lobbied on specific issues without paying much attention to the overall direction of city policy or the cumulative effects of their efforts. Thus, the fact that participants often focused on specific issues related to the urban visions debate presents evidence against viewing participants as either ideologues or collaborative problem solvers. In the next three chapters, I will present evidence that makes a positive case for why the citizen-as-lobbyist role is the best explanation for how citizens engage the policy-making process.

PART III

How Citizens Participate

7 Participatory Strategies and Tactics

In this chapter and the following two, I explore how citizens attempted to accomplish their political goals through participation. Up until this point, I have examined why citizens participate on one issue rather than another. Here, I set aside that question in favor of looking more closely at the ways citizens participated. Citizens have many options when deciding how to influence policy, and the choices they make can illuminate the nature of citizens' engagement with the local policy-making process. This analysis shows how the manner in which they participate resembles that of lobbyists.

At the beginning of the participant interviews, I asked respondents a few general questions about how they participate. I first presented them with a list of activities and asked if they have engaged in that activity during the last ten years.[1] As Table 7.1 indicates, respondents engaged in most of the activities listed (which is not surprising because a criterion for inclusion was prior participatory activity). Hiring a lobbyist was the only activity with few affirmative responses (6 percent); most respondents did not stand to gain financially from their political activity, and thus spending money on a lobbyist represented a significant monetary investment with the promise of little or no return. A sizable majority stated they engaged in a protest, but it was the only activity other than hiring a lobbyist below 80 percent (78 percent).[2] Every respondent at one point or another had spoken to (or encouraged others to speak to) an elected official, and almost all had spoken at a public meeting.

After interviewees addressed these closed-ended questions, I posed an open-ended question about whether they commonly engaged in any other activities not already listed. Thirty-one of fifty three respondents offered an additional activity, but some of these responses were just restatements of activities already mentioned. Table 7.2 summarizes additional activities not covered by the previous

Table 7.1. Frequency of political activity

Activity	Yes (%)	No (%)
Speak at a public meeting	98	2
Organize/join a protest	74	26
Write a letter to an elected official	96	4
Speak with an elected official	100	0
Write a letter to a non-elected official	87	13
Speak with a non-elected official	98	2
Encourage others to contact officials	100	0
Hire a lobbyist	6	94
Contact the media or write press releases	83	17
Circulate a petition or organize a letter-writing campaign	92	8
Organize a meeting to discuss an issue	93	7
Issue a report, study, or list of recommendations	85	15

Table 7.2. Other activities

Activity	Times mentioned*
Gather/disseminate information	6
Join organizations/committees	6
Attend/organize community meetings	5
Networking	4
Organize other citizens	3
Other	4

*Respondents were allowed to offer more than one response. The number of responses ranged from 0 to 3.

list. Unlike those listed in Table 7.1, most of these activities are not meant to influence elected officials directly. Rather, they contribute to an overall lobbying strategy by helping citizens accomplish political tasks, such as collecting information about local policies and finding other citizens to join their efforts. As I discuss in the next section, these activities play a prominent role in citizens' attempts to influence policy.

I also asked respondents to identify the activity that they engage in the most and the activity that they find most effective at achieving their goals. Results are in Table 7.3. Interviewees perceived communicating with officials (whether it be directly speaking to them or writing letters) as the most effective way to participate, and this was also the most common form of participation. Public meetings and

Table 7.3. Most common and most effective activities

Activity	Engage in the most*	Most effective*
Contacting officials (both writing and speaking)	21	28
Organize other citizens	7	4
Speak/attend public meetings	6	11
Join organizations/committees	5	0
Attend/organize community meetings	4	1
Networking	3	3
Contact media	2	1
Petition	0	2
Protest	0	1
All/combination of many	6	2
Other	1	1
Don't know	8	10

*Some respondents offered more than one activity, and each activity was included (thus, the entries are total mentions by respondents).

organizing activity also received some mentions, although significantly fewer than contacting officials. Petitions, protests, and letter-writing campaigns tend to be practiced infrequently, and were rarely mentioned as the most effective participatory activity.

Citizen Attempts to Influence Local Policy

The data above are limited in that they are based on top-of-the-head responses about how the respondents generally participate, which leads to two shortcomings. First, we know from past research that respondents have a tendency to overreport political activity, such as voting (Anderson and Silver 1986). Even though it is impossible to confirm overreporting of many acts of participation, there will likely be overreporting when respondents are asked whether they have ever engaged in a particular activity. Second, the questions take participatory activity out of the context in which it occurs, treating participation as a series of isolated acts rather than as an effort to influence actions taken by government. If our goal is to understand how citizens try to influence local policy, then we need to know how specific participatory activities, such as contacting officials and attending public meetings, combine to form a lobbying strategy and how these activities are used by citizens to accomplish their political goals. General queries about whether a respondent engaged in a particular activity, such as the ones described above and those typically found in public opinion surveys (e.g., Verba, Schlozman, and Brady 1995), cannot provide the information needed to address these issues.

In order to overcome these limitations, I asked respondents to identify and discuss two to three policies they tried to influence. The result was a series of rich, extensive descriptions of how respondents lobbied local officials, including not only an identification of specific acts in which they engaged, but also an explanation as to why they participated in those acts and how they fit together into an overall lobbying strategy. This evidence ameliorates the overreporting problem because it is much more difficult to fabricate activities within the context of responding to a specific policy than it is to claim to have voted in the last election, for example; the former requires much more imagination and intent to deceive. It is possible that some respondents claimed to have done things that they did not do; but because they were discussing participation in the context of a specific issue, the chances of doing so are less. Furthermore, asking respondents to describe their participation on specific issues places their activity in a context that allows us to analyze participation as part of an effort to accomplish political goals and influence policy, not simply as a series of isolated activities.

The interviews proceeded by asking respondents to list two to three issues that they personally tried to influence over the last ten years, then by asking follow-up questions on each issue, including queries about their strategy and activities (all of these questions were open ended). The fifty-three respondents offered 121 policies total (see the Appendix for a complete list of policies). For each policy, the respondent's activities were coded into fourteen categories,[3] which are shown in Table 7.4.

Attending Public Meetings

Attending and speaking at public meetings—primarily city council or school board meetings—were the most common participatory activities. Despite the fact that officials are unlikely to change their opinions based on public comments at meetings, respondents identified other functions that this activity serves. For example, a show

Table 7.4. Activities: Number of mentions

Activity	Number of mentions
Attend/speak at public meetings*	61
Contact elected officials	52
Organize other citizens/network	45
Attend/organize community meetings	44
Collect/disseminate information	43
Contact nonelected officials	35
Use media	16
Join committees or organizations	14
Circulate petitions/letter-writing campaigns	13
Use federal strategy	10
Make proposals	7
Protest	7
Take legal action	5
General public acting**	4
Total number of activities	356

*This category includes only public meetings of governmental bodies, such as the city council, school board, and planning commission.

**Defined as attempts to solve community problems without appeals to officials for help.

of force at a city council meeting can demonstrate to officials that citizens care about an issue, or can pressure them to put an issue on the agenda. Respondents used the opportunity to speak at public meetings to accomplish a range of political goals, such as embarrassing elected officials, persuading them on the merits, agenda setting, and delaying decisions. The many functions that public meetings serve and the relative ease of the activity account for its common occurrence. The function and role of public meetings are discussed in greater detail in Chapter 8.

Contacting

Contacting elected officials (fifty-two mentions) and nonelected officials (thirty-five mentions) were also very common activities. The majority of these contacts were face to face or phone conversations. For many respondents, their preferred method of participation was to have private conversations with their elected representatives, city manager, or school superintendent. Letter-writing was also common, although less so than one-on-one conversations.[4] On some occasions, private meetings that brought together a small group of citizens and government officials were arranged. Although there were complaints among respondents that some officials were not accessible,[5] there was extensive contact between citizens and elected and nonelected officials.

Respondents offered three reasons for why they contacted officials. First, they frequently talked or wrote to officials to persuade them of the merits of a particular policy position by presenting arguments and evidence to support their desired policy outcome. Much of this activity involved just calling an elected official and expressing an opinion. Below is a typical exchange about efforts by a respondent to get the City to condemn and tear down a blighted apartment complex:

> The [local news]paper wrote this article about Mayor Pulido and about the positive image that Santa Ana had. And he gave this glowing explanation, and this was almost ten years ago, when he had just first got elected, and about how the image of Santa Ana was changing. And I read that article and I just came unglued. So I wrote him [Mayor Pulido] a letter, and I made copies of the article, and I fired out to him that I thought he was wrong, how can he say that Santa Ana has a positive image in the county when the people get off the freeway and see this terrible situation [a blighted apartment complex] over there. And I wrote him the letter, and a couple days later, he gave me a call, "I want to talk to you." So my wife and I went down and met with the mayor, the [city] attorney, and the city manager. Just my wife and me. And he said, "You just don't understand what we are doing. The city attorney has done this, this and this." And I said, "Well, we appreciate that, but those of us in the north end of Santa Ana, near *that* place, cannot think positive about Santa Ana because it has gone on so long," and at that time we were considering moving. And we said we are going to get out of Santa Ana just as quick as we can. And other people are thinking about it as well, because you just have let that go to those terrible conditions. So it wasn't too long after that that he gave me another call and said we got the OK, we are going to tear it down.

Most attempts to persuade were targeted toward elected officials, but sometimes respondents also found it valuable to work on city or school district staff, which can be seen in various efforts to obtain upgrades to neighborhood parks. The Parks and Recreation Department prioritize (subject to city council approval) which parks are first in line to receive funds, and many respondents discussed their efforts to get their project moved up the list. One commented that "we're right now in the process. . . . We have a group that just writes letters to the city council, and also to the director of Park and Rec, saying that we don't want to be put at the bottom [of the list of priorities], we want to be up." Note that here the respondent also mentioned contacting city council members—rarely did respondents deal with just staff.

A second reason for contacting officials was to gather information. Here, the contact is not meant to persuade officials but to gain information that the respondent needed to participate more effectively. For example, after the Environment and Transportation Advisory Committee (ETAC) voted against a traffic mitigation plan that a respondent supported, he commented that he "got in touch with [Councilwoman] Lisa Bist that night and basically asked her [about] her perception of what had occurred, and then I started to get in touch with some of the ETAC commissioners that I knew to get information about that public meeting and what transpired." Here, a participant is drawing on relationships with officials to find out what happened at a meeting that he was unable to attend. Another example is when a neighborhood wanted to convert an empty lot into a small park. There was some confusion over who owned the land, so the neighborhood association leaders contacted city officials to clarify the situation. As the neighborhood president relates it, he "sent a letter [asking], 'Well, what's going on? We don't understand this.' And that's when Dave Ream, [the] city manager, called back and he did a title search."

Sometimes officials initiate the contacts. For example, one parent–teacher association (PTA) activist had the following to say about contacts concerning the battle over the space-saver school:

> So I have to say we took a lot of direction from Mike [Vail, facilities director for Santa Ana Unified School District (SAUSD)]. He would come in and say, even though we were there every week, he would say, "This is an important one. We need people at this meeting." And we would go out and get people to show up. Or he

would say, "Some rocky stuff is happening in Sacramento. We need some phone calls." So we'd make phone calls and call some other people to make phone calls.

Here, we see a case where officials are initiating contact with citizens to prompt participation that they desire (there were two school board members opposed to the school, and staff wanted parents to counteract that opposition). Regardless of the motivations of staff in this instance, citizens were able to use these channels of communication to gather information about what was happening and what they needed to do to participate effectively.

In addition to gathering information, many respondents contacted officials to give them information, frequently to inform them that a group that they represent (such as a neighborhood association or PTA) felt a particular way on an issue. Some neighborhood presidents would write letters to officials to inform them of votes that their association has taken. Below is how one neighborhood president described the process:

> Well, we as a board did it [write a letter to the city council] in response to what we heard from our neighbors. We talked to the neighbors, and we brought it up to them and said, "You know, these are some of the things that are going on that could affect our neighborhood," and we got their input, and based on their input, we said, "Okay, this is the way the neighborhood has requested to go," and we, on behalf of the entire neighborhood, wrote the letter. And we put in the letters on behalf of the Morrison Park Neighborhood Association.

Another respondent discussed how she met with city officials in an attempt to gain support for a downtown festival:

> Basically, the initial phone call was made to their [city council members'] office and a luncheon was set up. And we met with them individually . . . and we both sat for an hour, and we just discussed all the positive things and changes that were going to happen in this particular event. And we just wanted to know if they were in favor of it and if they would support it.

Here, we see persuasion by presentation: the idea was that by explaining to elected officials the positive aspects of the festival, they would have the necessary information to support it.

The types of contacts that I have been discussing are what the literature refers to as "general referent" contacts (Hirlinger 1992), which are efforts to change policy. They were not about getting the City or school district to assist in an individual problem—such as a problem with trash pickup or unfair treatment by a teacher—which are labeled "particularized contacting" in the literature. Citizens in Santa Ana probably made many of these requests, but. the interviews were focused on how citizens engaged the policy-making process, and none of the questions asked about contacts dealing with particularized benefits. Although help with a personal problem may be a very common reason for contacting officials, the structure of the interview precluded respondents from discussing those contacts.

Organizing Other Citizens and Networking

The "organize other citizens and networking" category includes activity aimed at getting others in the community to participate, building coalitions, and finding allies. Typically, respondents drew on social networks and previous relationships to enlist the support of others, which is why organizing and networking were put in the same category.[6] With forty-five mentions, organizing was a very common activity, reflecting the fact that most respondents were heavily involved in politics and frequently spearheaded organizing efforts.

Respondents organized other citizens by communicating with them in the hope that it would spark participation and support. For example, a PTA president explains how the association organized support for a new school: "We networked with a lot of the parents in the neighborhoods close to where the school was going to be built. And also the fundamental school [a type of charter school] parents because this was going to be a fundamental intermediate school. Also, just networking with people that lived in the neighborhood." Here's a description of organizing attempts by a respondent who opposed a new sports arena in his neighborhood:

We would have the meetings in my living room. We would sit down and we would assign tasks to each person. And we would decide what a good battle plan would be. We never went off on knee-jerk reactions. We always made an entire plan as to how we were going to get this accomplished. So we would assign different tasks to different members, committee members. They would go out and get their tasks accomplished, and the next meeting they would report on how it was going and so on and so forth.

Measure C, the bond measure for building new schools, also exhibited a coherent effort to organize citizens (in this case, to mobilize the vote). A Commlink board member (one of the few to support the measure) explains his organizing efforts this way:

Grassroots, getting on the phone, I had a list of all the principals, vice principals, and I wish I would have had a better list of the PTA presidents, just getting on the phone and talking to them personally. Encouraging their support, which most of them welcomed our support, welcomed my involvement. Trying to get the media behind it as much as possible, my influence there. Just speaking with as many concerned parents and families as I could, really working in a strong attendance there at the forums that we [Commlink] had on Measure C, making sure the press was there to hear the concerns and see how the vote was leaning, how the discussions were leanings. Just the old-fashioned hit the streets, hit the brakes, knock on doors, get on the phone, eyeball to eyeball. Whatever it took to see people, greet people, meet people, educate people and get them on board.

Others active on Measure C, both for and against, describe similar activities in their effort to get out the vote on this issue.[7]

Organizing attempts varied in their sophistication. Some, such as the Measure C campaign, were very organized and targeted groups that were most likely to respond favorably. Others were more haphazard. A parent who sat on an ad hoc committee on school uniforms said that she was "frantically looking for other parents" to support her position before a school board meeting. Organizing efforts also varied in the means used to communicate with others. Some used face-to-face conversations at community meetings, whereas others relied on flyers, phone banks, or e-mail lists. The method for communicating may have varied, but the basic goal of all these efforts was the same: to enlist support for their position and improve their chances of success.

Attend or Organize Community Meetings

"Community meetings" include neighborhood association meetings, PTA meetings, meetings called on a specific issue, and meetings of community organizations such as the Downtown Santa Ana Business Association. The forty-four responses in this category refer to instances where respondents used community meetings as a platform to discuss an issue that they were trying to influence. These meetings serve functions beyond the obvious ones concerning the functioning of the organization itself. Sometimes the meetings were used to mobilize others or to persuade them of the merits of a particular policy position. Other times community meetings were used to figure out what to do. Given the many purposes of these meetings, they were often a central participatory activity. Even though respondents complained about attending endless meetings, they serve important functions by providing a setting where citizens exchange information and ideas about public problems, as well as decide on a course of action. A few examples will illustrate this.

When Orange County officials proposed a light rail system that would run through the city, known as the "Centerline," many neighborhoods held meetings to decide whether they would support or oppose the plan. Below is a description of how one neighborhood handled it:

> The first thing we did was we had the representatives for the light rail come to a neighborhood association meeting. We called them in and [they] let us know what their plans were. And we also called the City because the City was involved also. . . . So we had them come in and we looked at what they were doing, and once we saw it, it was clear to us that it wasn't going to benefit us. So once that happened, through our neighborhood association, we as a group voted as to whether this was something we wanted or didn't want. We voted against it, the majority of the people were against it, there were some people there that were for it.

Here, the neighborhood association meeting is used to learn about a particularly policy issue and to decide what position the neighborhood would take. Based on the information they received and the subsequent neighborhood vote against the light rail, the neighborhood proceeded with circulating petitions and speaking against the proposal at city council meetings.

Another participant described how his neighborhood association found out about SAUSD's plans for a new school in their neighborhood: "He [the councilman for the area] informed us [the neighborhood association] they were leaving the site and the school board was looking at the site, and also another developer was looking at that site. So that's where we found out about it, at one of our meetings." Inviting officials to meetings, as is the case here, was a common activity, and one that many participants found to be valuable. Sometimes it can lead to positive change, as related by a respondent trying to get the City to install a stoplight in front of a neighborhood school: "One time we invited a politician to meet us, it was a neighborhood association meeting, and he had just had knee surgery, but he came. He was wonderful, he spoke with such optimism and spoke with such eagerness to help. And he has kept his word. We mentioned the problem that we had with the light, and lo and behold, the City is hopping to get that light."

The "join committees or organizations" category (fourteen mentions) is similar to the community meeting category in that the basic activity is attending and participating in meetings. The difference is that the respondents here use their committee or organizational membership to have a direct impact on public policies. Most community organizations have little formal power, and thus are used to just gather information or express a policy position. A few boards or commissions, however, have some authority, and joining them allowed respondents to work through those bodies to influence local policy. For example, four of the fourteen responses were for individuals who sit on the Santa Ana Empowerment Zone Board, which has the authority to administer federal grants. This type of authority, however, is relatively rare. Despite the fact that respondents joined many organizations and committees (Table 1.1), most of them do not have any power to influence policy outside of making recommendations.

Collecting or Disseminating Information

The "collect or disseminate information" category overlaps with the previous categories: collecting and disseminating information can be done through community meetings, and is often a critical part of organizing. This category includes instances where citizens did research on policy issues or disseminated that research outside of community meetings or organizing efforts. Most research involved talking to other people, such as knowledgeable citizens and government officials on both the local and state levels. Many respondents considered research to be a critical part of their participatory activity, however, it rarely took the form of reading government documents, library work, or utilizing formal channels of communication. For the most part, information was gathered and disseminated through face-to-face conversations and meetings.

With forty-three mentions, collecting and disseminating information was quite a common activity, and for some respondents it was a central activity. One respondent, when asked how his organization went about getting a new park approved for a low-income neighborhood, said that "one of the things that we did was our families went into a research mode. . . . They basically came up with a needs assessment . . . that really painted a picture of a need for the whole city of more resources." A respondent trying to procure park upgrades for a different park also spoke of significant amounts of research that she did, such as exploring possible funding sources and understanding city budget processes.

Sometimes the research efforts took the form of knocking on people's doors to find out what they wanted. A respondent promoting the revitalization of Minnie Street (a poor immigrant neighborhood) decided she needed to know what the community wanted and needed. Below is how she describes her activities:

> In order for a neighborhood to buy in to any project or program, it has to be from their perspective. They're the user. Are we going to create a car just for show or are we going to be able to create a car that they can use? We can have a whole lot full of those great cars but nobody will buy them. We began to focus in on their needs. I knocked on every door, and number one was security and safety because we didn't have it. . . . We took on another project. I went

out knocking on doors again, with a handful of neighbors, and we asked. We thought it would be the redevelopment of Minnie Street, it needed to be the redevelopment of Minnie Street. But that's not what they said they wanted. They wanted a homework center where they could send their children, where they would have the benefit of catching up, and not always lagging behind.

Here we see research efforts by a citizen to find out what the community wants so that her participatory efforts will have direction. Many respondents, when trying to get the city to do something, did not just express opinions or demand action; they also did research to find out what their goals should be and how they could be accomplished.

Once citizens collected information, they also undertook efforts to disseminate it throughout the community. The two most common ways of doing so were through meetings and face-to-face discussions. Occasionally citizens would organize events to get out a particular message. For example, one neighborhood association organized a "neighborhood awareness gathering" where they passed out fliers to parents dropping their kids off at school, letting them know about traffic problems at a neighborhood school. Another example was when proponents of the artists' village took officials on trips to other cities with similar projects to let them see the potential benefits of an artists' village in Santa Ana. More common, however, was raising an issue at a neighborhood meeting or passing along information through informal conversations.

Petitions, Protest, and the Media

Petitions were not that common, but those who used them found them to be effective. One neighborhood leader presented a petition to the city council opposing the light rail, and had the following to say about its effectiveness:

> I think it is important because most of the people on the city council . . . have been involved in the neighborhood association, and they seem to be intelligent enough to know how things really work down here in the neighborhoods. Because it's not enough for one person to call and complain about something. . . . When it comes to making calls or one person going up, most of the city

council members know they are really only speaking for themselves or for a couple or three people. I think the petition means a lot because a petition means votes.

Letter-writing campaigns, like petitions, were also used infrequently but were generally found to be effective. The point of engaging in both activities was to put electoral pressure on officials by demonstrating widespread support for a policy position. Given how effective they were at this task, it is noteworthy that they were not done more often.

Protests were quite rare, which could be a reflection of the types of people interviewed (neighborhood leaders and PTA members are not typically protesting types) or a reflection of the types of issues that residents cared about (e.g., it's difficult to imagine protests over park improvements). A review of newspaper articles for the eleven-year period under study revealed very few mentions of protests on local issues (although quite a few protests happened in Santa Ana on other issues, such as statewide initiatives). In the 1980s, there were many protests over redevelopment and housing (Haas 1991), but these had ceased by the 1990s. The few protests that were mentioned by respondents included a candlelight vigil in support of the space-saver school and a rally in opposition to a new sports arena.

As we saw in Chapter 5, most participants do not use the media as a source of information, relying instead on social networks and personal experience. They do, however, use the media to apply pressure on elected officials and to generate public support. Particularly common were attempts to use the media to get the attention of elected officials, which appears to be a very effective strategy. For example, on one occasion, the school superintendent made a thirty-minute presentation at a school board meeting to refute an article in the *Los Angeles Times* concerning the expenditure of school bond funds. Participants know that critical articles receive a response from officials, and thus they do their best to get newspapers to write them. Further, participants try to get favorable newspaper coverage to enhance their public support. For example, citizens on both sides of the Measure C campaign mentioned media as a key strategy. This only occurred in regard to the most controversial issues, as newspapers are unlikely to give much coverage to lesser controversies and people are even less likely to read stories about them. On most issues, therefore, the media did not play a very large role.

Public Acting

The public acting category encompasses attempts by respondents to address community problems themselves, bypassing formal governmental channels. For example, one respondent, frustrated by a lack of funds from the City, decided to improve his neighborhood park by assembling private and nonprofit resources to realize park improvements. There is probably much more of this type of activity (particularly through nonprofit organizations) than is represented here. Because the questions asked specifically about influencing local policy, however, respondents were led away from talking about public acting.

The "make proposal" category is a form of public acting because it involves doing the work that typically is done by local governments. In this case, citizens put together a detailed plan of action and present it to government. A good example was the antigang strategy developed by Jose Miranda, as described in Chapter 4. Note that making proposals is more than just making demands: citizens here are actively researching and developing strategies for addressing community problems, not just telling government that they need to "do something."

Going Outside the System

If citizens are unable to influence local policy by working within the local political system, they have a couple of options for influencing it from without. Legal action is one strategy. The few cases where this occurred involved citizens who, after repeated attempts to lobby government failed, decided to bring the matter to court. The other option is to appeal to either the state or federal government, which I call a "federal strategy." There were two scenarios under which citizens pursued a federal strategy. First, if local officials were unresponsive, some citizens went to their state legislators for help either in directly solving the problem or pressuring local officials to do something. For example, when the City balked at funding a community center for Delhi Park, supporters went to their state legislative representatives, who helped them secure state funding and put pressure on local officials to contribute funds as well. The second scenario occurred when local authority was overridden by state laws, which happened with the overcrowding issue: a city ordinance limiting the number of residents per household was struck down by the courts as conflicting with state law (which set higher limits). Given the limited power of local officials, some respondents went to state legislative representatives for help, even though housing ordinances are traditionally a "local" issue. Most instances of resorting to the state government occurred when the state already had a clear role to play; rarely did citizens try to bring the state into a policy area where they did not have an obvious role.

Lobbying Strategies: Three Examples

Below are three examples of how lobbying activities fit together into an overall strategy to influence local policy. These cases are typical in that the activities that citizens engaged in to influence these policies are the avenues of participation most frequently chosen—those that appear at the top of Table 7.4. Collectively, they present an overview of the tactics and strategies that citizens employed in trying to influence local policy.

Space-Saver School

In previous chapters I explained the controversy over the space-saver school, SAUSD's proposal to build a school on a small lot adjacent to an outdoor shopping center. My focus here is on how both supporters and opponents tried to influence this issue. The school district staff, including the superintendent, wanted the school, and when opposition emerged, they asked parents active in the PTA to provide some support. The parents worked with school district staff to make a case for the proposal. Parents talked to school board members, lobbied state officials (who needed to approve the project), and showed up at public hearings to counter opponents' claims. The five-member school board had two members strongly in favor of the school, two adamantly opposed, and one who was leaning toward support but slightly wavered. The primary goal of the supporters, knowing they had a sympathetic district staff and a (tenuous) majority of the board, was to make the case for the school so as to maintain and increase public support. One of the parents leading the fight for the school said that if it were not for the participation of the parents, "There were some things that wouldn't have gotten done. We would not have been able to have plopped 800 signatures on the school board's desk and say, 'Look, these are just average citizens of the school district who say they want the school.' There wouldn't have been as many people showing up to school board meetings to keep that public pressure going." Maintaining public support was critical for ensuring they had the third vote on the school board and that the state legislature would approve their plans.

Opponents, led by councilwoman Lisa Mills, had a multi-pronged strategy. They made a few trips to Sacramento (the state capital) to convince the state not to fund the project. They also tried to work over school board members, one of whom characterized their efforts this way: "There were lots of phone calls from people pleading, accusing, you know, the threats came later, but they were more disguised. They were much more racist in tone. Then there were threats to my political position." Opponents frequently criticized the school district for being closed to influence, restricting their ability to apply pressure in private. Of course, this may simply be the result of the fact that they disagreed with district officials and that they knew attempts to persuade officials of the merits of their views were likely to fail.

Opponents tried to pressure officials through one-on-one conversations, but the primary strategy was to apply pressure through the media and public hearings. The space-saver school issue was the type of issue that interests local newspapers, replete with controversy, racial overtones, and strong feelings on both sides. Opponents capitalized on this situation by using the press to make their case that the school was a bad idea (including a leak by an opposing school board member concerning the price the school district paid for the land). The public hearing where the school board was to decide the issue attracted hundreds of citizens and had sixty-seven speakers (both supporters and opponents were represented among the speakers). The school board delayed their decision two weeks, and opponents claimed that the public opposition at the hearing pressured the board to put off the vote. Regardless, two weeks later they approved the school, which later received approval from the state. The school was completed in early 2001.

Participants on both sides of the space-saver school debate used multiple avenues to influence decisions. Opponents tended toward more pressure tactics, primarily because they knew that school officials were committed to the school, although supporters also applied pressure to maintain their school board majority. We have another interesting dynamic here: both sides brought in state officials to buttress their position. State officials, of course, played a major role because they controlled the funding; but we can easily imagine participants on both sides keeping it a local issue, because the decision to build was made by the school district. Yet, there was a channel here—particularly for the opponents—to influence the outcome of the school decision by appealing to the state, and they did not fail to utilize that channel.

Playground and Park Improvements

The next set of issues is much less controversial than the space-saver school; in fact, we would be hard pressed to find anyone opposed to increased spending for parks and playgrounds. Five respondents talked about their efforts to secure improvements for their neighborhood park (three different parks were discussed).

The issue with park improvement is always one of budget priorities: how much money should the City dedicate to park improvements, and which parks should be the first to receive funding? Thus, the primary goal of citizens lobbying for park improvements was to convince the City that their project should be prioritized and that it was worth the money. Generally, the strategy was to discuss the matter with the Parks and Recreation Department and elected officials, in an effort to demonstrate the value of the project. They also took a proactive approach in working out project details in terms of equipment to buy, landscaping, and so forth. Finally, they were all active—some successful, others not—in trying to secure grants from entities outside the city.

Conspicuously absent, except in one instance, were attempts to apply public pressure on officials. Rather, the strategy was a private one: work with Parks and Recreation officials to develop a plan for park improvements, and contact elected officials to persuade them to fund their projects. Citizens did not go to city council meetings to raise the issue, did not try to use the media to apply pressure, and did not sign petitions or start letter-writing campaigns. The strategy consisted of nudging and prodding officials to prioritize their park and attempting to privately persuade officials to fund their projects.

As mentioned, there was one exception: Delhi Park, a proposed park and recreation center for the Delhi neighborhood, a working-class Latino community. The proposal was significantly larger and more expensive than the projects discussed by other participants: rather than just improvements to an existing park, it entailed the expansion of a park along with the construction of a community center. After trying to work privately with city officials and failing to secure funding, supporters of Delhi Park went public, including appearing en masse at city council meetings, signing petitions, and appealing to state legislators for help. The difference here is that the Delhi Park supporters felt that they were not being listened to and needed to go public to apply pressure on city officials. Further, the size of the project and the supporters' unwillingness to compromise (they rejected a number of city proposals to scale down the project) made private prodding of officials less effective.

The Commercial Vehicles Code

In Chapter 4, I discussed efforts by some neighborhood associations, led by Mike Belliard, to develop a new ordinance regulating the parking of commercial vehicles in residential areas. The battle over the commercial vehicles code highlights two themes concerning how citizens participate. First, the importance of the social network created by the neighborhood associations was evident. The ability of Belliard to recruit allies from other parts of the city and make this particular concern a citywide issue—not just a neighborhood issue—was critical, as it got the ear of officials and put it on the political agenda. Commlink, and the neighborhood associations in general, provided an excellent vehicle to do so, and even though they have no formal power and receive no funding from the City, they can assist citizens by providing a platform to raise and discuss an issue. Second, supporters used a combination of formal and informal methods for achieving their goals. On the formal side, they attended public hearings and worked through Commlink and its Neighborhood Improvement and Code Enforcement (NICE) committee. Informally, they engaged in discussions with the city attorney, other city staff, and city council members to sway their opinions. This multipronged approach was typical of how respondents lobbied government.

Some General Observations about How Citizens Participate

Given this description of respondents' political activities, what generalizations can we make about how citizens lobby local government? Below are some general observations about the tactics and strategies citizens in Santa Ana use when they participate.

The Importance of Interpersonal Relationships

We saw above that citizens spend a lot of time networking, building relationships, and communicating with other citizens and officials. On one level, it should not be surprising that people prioritize using their social networks. Politics is fundamentally a group activity and any expectation that participation is individual centered is a likely result of overemphasizing voting, one of the few participatory acts that citizens do alone. But the extent to which citizens' activity revolved around personal relationships is noteworthy. Thinking about the activities listed in Table 7.4, some require or utilize personal relationships more than others. For example, circulating a petition or attending a public meeting does not rely heavily on personal relationships, whereas organizing, contacting, and research do to a much greater extent. Although not all of the common activities rely on interpersonal relationships, many do, and participants who lack these relationships are limited in the range of activities that they can engage in.

Participants' social networks are an important political resource because participants can use their networks to help them accomplish political tasks. I will discuss the political value of social networks in Chapter 9.

Persuasion versus Pressure

Citizens can influence policy decisions by persuading officials to change their views on an issue or by applying pressure to force them to take desired actions. Most citizens interviewed believed in the power of persuasion; as mentioned above, many of the contacts between citizens and officials were attempts to persuade officials of the merits of a particular argument. Attempts at persuasion usually occurred in private conversations or meetings with officials, although public hearings were sometimes used for persuasion purposes.

Citizens also resorted to pressure tactics—such as petitions, letter-writing campaigns, and protests—to achieve their political goals. Attendance at public hearings could also be considered a pressure tactic if the goal was to intimidate officials into voting a certain way, not to persuade them on the merits. Officials can feel pressure for two reasons. First, there is electoral pressure. If elected officials receive a petition with a thousand signatures, they may decide that opposing the signatories' wishes could have negative electoral implications. Or citizens screaming and yelling at a public hearing could have unwanted electoral repercussions, as it paints elected officials in a negative light. There is also pressure that may reduce the capacity of officials to govern. If citizens are angry enough and willing to be obstructionist, they could, under some circumstances, pressure officials to give in simply because officials fear that fighting will be too costly. Citizens can make officials' lives difficult through participation meant to obstruct and delay, and can force officials to use more time and energy on a policy issue than they would otherwise.

Overall, citizens directed their efforts more toward persuasion than they did toward applying pressure. Of course, the focus varied depending on citizens' views of the receptiveness of officials. Some respondents thought officials were completely unresponsive, making persuasion unattractive as a strategy. Most respondents, however, thought that at least some officials were responsive, and thus attempted to sell them on the merits of an argument. Further, respondents generally felt more comfortable with persuasion than with pressure tactics. Most citizens who participated did not seem to define their roles in terms of applying pressure on officials;

rather, they saw themselves as people with good ideas, and conceptualized their strategy as convincing others that their proposals should be considered.

Public and Private Activity

Participation can be either public or private. Public participation—attending hearings, circulating petitions, attending informational meetings—are all ways to participate that are visible to outsiders and are conducted in groups. Private forms of participation include such things as talking to officials and some forms of research and networking. Citizens varied in their preference for each. Some preferred the more public forms of participation because they like the grandstanding aspects and found that officials will listen more if citizens complain in public. Others preferred private conversations with officials. The fact that so much participation occurred in private explains why it often goes unnoticed by the press and nonactive citizens. When most people think of citizen participation, they think of public activities, such as going to meetings or protests, and they ignore the significant portions that occur behind closed doors.

Working within the System

Most citizens interviewed for this study prefer to work through the system (defined here as the local policy-making process) rather than trying to bring pressure from the outside: street protests, sit-ins, and similar tactics were infrequently mentioned. This is partly a result of the people I interviewed. Neighborhood leaders, PTA members, and others involved in civic organizations are likely to work through existing channels of influence, as their very membership in these organizations indicate their willingness to accept existing political arrangements. When asked why they work inside of the established policy system, participants commented that it is more effective because the best way to accomplish political goals is to form relationships with other citizens and officials, relationships that may be jeopardized by engaging in street protests and similar tactics. Other participants mentioned that street protests and other such forms of participation were now frowned upon: one respondent commented that she does not "want to get really radical because these days people are really not into the 'sixties kind of thing.'"

Another explanation for the dearth of protests is that they are most likely on emotional, "hot-button" issues that are usually not dealt with by the City or school district. Most of what local governments do is less emotional, dealing with mundane issues that will not stir citizens enough to prompt them to take to the streets. The few times we did see protests in Santa Ana were on issues that typically generate a highly emotional response (e.g., a police shooting of an unarmed Hispanic man). In the 1980s, there was much more protest activity in Santa Ana, led by Alinsky-style groups organized by Jesuits (Haas 1991). These protests over issues such as slum clearance and a perceived anti-Hispanic bias among city leaders have since died down, and its leaders (some of whom I interviewed for this study) have taken to more traditional methods of participation.

Given the information gathered by my research, I am not in a position to make a conclusive determination regarding why there are fewer protests and sit-ins now than in the 1980s, nor why most citizens interviewed were not engaged in these activities. Suffice to say that most participation in Santa Ana is well within the boundaries of traditional policy-making structures, and that protests and other similar activity is relatively rare.

Participants as Citizen Lobbyists

This description of how citizens participate supports the citizen lobbyist model as the best representation of how participants engage the policy-making process. The types of activities that citizens engage in are the same ones that traditional lobbyists perform. Citizen participation was largely geared toward forming relationships with other participants and government officials. These relationships are formed in many ways: through organization membership, direct contacts, and a variety of networking techniques. The general mode of participation is to talk to people, build alliances and social networks, and use them to achieve policy ends. Less common pressure tactics, such as letter-writing campaigns, protests, and petitions, were used but the emphasis was on relationships among citizens and between citizens and officials.

Respondents saw building bridges between themselves and others as a key to success and, consequently, relationship building constituted a central part of their participatory activity, which is exactly how lobbyists go about accomplishing their political goals.

We can contrast how citizens participated with other potential forms of engagement in the policy-making process. One possibility is that citizens act as pawns, taking direction from elites. There were a few instances where citizens did what elites told them to do (for example, sometimes citizens were asked to appear at a public meeting by officials), but it was not that common. For the most part, citizens determined on their own (or with other citizens) how they would participate. The description of citizens' political activity in this chapter also does not support the citizen-as-watchdog model. At times participants did try to obstruct government action, but much of their activity was proactive and focused on promoting desired policy. Watchdogs would also engage in less relationship building and more pressure tactics, which are better suited to blocking policy that government officials desire. Further, the tendency to focus on persuasion rather than pressure and the frequent use of private forms of participation are counter to what we would expect from citizens participating as ideologues. Ideological debates are typically very public and confrontational, and participants' tendency away from this mode of participation indicates that their focus was on accomplishing specific policy objectives rather than participating in a larger ideological debate.

The citizen-as-lobbyist model best captures the essence of citizens' engagement in the policy-making process because it highlights the use of interpersonal relationships, the emphasis on persuasion rather then pressure, the extensive use of private forms of participation, and the bias toward working within the system. It also illustrates that citizens did not just perform isolated participatory activities but also developed strategies to accomplish their political goals similar to the strategizing of lobbyists. Although citizens did not always act as lobbyists, for the most part, they did.

8 Public Meetings and the Democratic Process

Most local governments hold regularly scheduled meetings to discuss and decide public issues. Opportunities for citizens to voice their opinions are usually part of these meetings. Public input could either take the form of comments on specific issues before the governmental body or it could be general comments on any issue citizens care about. In either case, citizens are given a specified period of time (typically two to three minutes) to state their opinions and are usually prohibited from engaging other citizens or officials in dialogue.

As we saw in Chapter 7, attending public meetings is a common form of participation. In this chapter, I ask what role public meetings can have in contributing to a participatory policy process. Can they play a constructive role by allowing citizens to voice their concerns and influence policy decisions, or are they a hollow ritual that merely provides a facade of legitimacy? If we want to incorporate greater public participation into the policy process, is there a place for public meetings? I add to the literature that examines the role of public participation in policy analysis (Walters, Aydelotte, and Miller 2000; Thomas 1990) by exploring what functions public meetings serve and how they can fit into a larger institutional context for citizen input into the policy process.

I argue that public meetings serve important democratic functions by providing citizens the opportunity to convey information to officials, influence public opinion, attract media attention, set future agendas, delay decisions, and communicate with other citizens. Meetings are a tool that citizen lobbyists can use to achieve political objectives. This tool is ill-suited to fostering policy deliberations or persuading officials to change a vote on a specific issue. But meetings serve another purpose: by giving citizens a venue where they can achieve political goals, public meetings enhance the political power of citizens and, consequently, improve governmental responsiveness to citizens.

If we keep in mind the functions that public meetings can and cannot serve, their role in a participatory policy process becomes clearer. Public meetings can serve as a complement to structures that foster citizen deliberation (such as citizen panels, forums, and roundtables) by providing citizens the opportunity to engage in the political process before deliberations commence and after citizens have developed a set of recommendations or a consensus policy position. Although public meetings themselves are not deliberative, they can facilitate citizen participation and the development of good policy by assisting citizens in achieving their political goals. I hope to show in this chapter the purposes that public meetings serve and how they can fit into a larger scheme of citizen input in policy making.

This chapter also provides support for the citizen lobbyist model by illustrating how public meetings were used as a venue to help participants achieve specific goals. Citizens typically did not use meetings as a platform to engage in partisan debates, which we would expect from ideologues. We also did not see appearances at meetings being coordinated by elites (except on one or two occasions). Public meetings were a tool that citizen lobbyists used to accomplish political goals, and their use of meetings are indicative of how citizens engaged in both tactical and strategic maneuverings in their efforts to influence policy.

Institutional Design and Citizen Participation

In recent years, many scholars have argued for an enhancement of the extent and quality of citizen participation in policy making (e.g., King, Feltey, and Susel 1998; Roberts 1997; Schneider and Ingram 1997; deLeon 1997; 1995; Fischer 1993; Dryzek 1990). They contend that we need to develop structures and institutions to provide citizens with the opportunities to participate effectively. But how do you design institutions for allowing citizen input into the policy process? Citizens can be brought into the policy process in many ways: public hearings, citizen juries, roundtables, and electronic town meetings are examples of institutions meant to create opportunities for citizen participation.

One of the most common methods of citizen participation is the public hearing. A survey of city managers and chief administrative officers found that over 97 percent of cities use it as a strategy for dealing with citizens (Berman 1997, 107). Public hearings, which are usually required by law, allow citizens to comment on a specific issue or proposal before a governmental entity makes a decision. Despite their widespread use, public hearings are not held in high esteem. The most common critique, made by participants, academics, and governmental officials alike, is that citizen comments do not influence policy outcomes (Cole and Caputo 1984; Checkoway 1981). Citizens march up to the podium, give their two-minute speech, the presiding official says, "Thank you very much," and then officials proceed with their business irrespective of the arguments made by citizens. Citizens may speak their mind, but officials do not listen and usually have their minds made up before the public hearing. Hearings, in this view, are mere democratic rituals that provide a false sense of legitimacy to legislative outcomes: officials can say that they received input from the public, and it can give their decisions the respect afforded to democratic processes, even though citizen input has no impact. Rather than being a means for citizen input, hearings allow officials to deflect criticism and proceed with decisions they have already made (Rowe and Frewer 2000; Kemp 1985; Checkoway 1981).

A second critique of public hearings is that they are a poor mechanism for deliberation (King, Feltey, and Susel 1998; Kemmis 1990, 51–53; Checkoway 1981). Citizens go to the podium, speak their piece, and then sit down. There is rarely dialogue between citizens and officials; even when officials respond to citizen comments, it is usually in the form of a question-and-answer session, not a true dialogue. Although citizens have a chance to state their position and support it with a reasoned argument, public hearings do not allow them to engage elected officials or other participants in a dialogue to try to persuade them to change their opinions. Public hearings do not afford citizens a venue where they can engage in public discussions about common problems and try to reach understanding with their fellow citizens and elected officials. Further, public hearings frequently degenerate into the worst sort of debate: rather than citizens stating their opinions and offering supporting argumentation, they will employ sound bites, hyperbole, and falsehoods to criticize and demonize opponents—hardly a model of citizen deliberation.

Hearings are also criticized for attracting an unrepresentative sample of the population (McComas 2001a; Gastil and Kelshaw 2000). People who show up to meetings are more likely to be extremists on the issue being discussed, since they have greater personal incentives to participate. Hearings may be dominated by those with very strong views on the subject being discussed, crowding out moderate voices that represent large segments of the community. This dynamic has two repercussions: It undermines the legitimacy of the hearing as a venue for assessing public opinion, and it provides officials with an excuse to ignore public comments ("they're not representative of what the public really thinks").

While even defenders of public hearings acknowledge they are a poor venue for deliberation, some research indicates that hearings can be an effective form of citizen participation and citizens can, at times, be representative of the public at large. Mazmanian and Sabatier (1980) and Rosener (1982), in studies of the California Coastal Commission, found that citizen participation at public hearings had an impact on the denial rate of permits under consideration by the board. Others have argued that under the right conditions (e.g., meetings held at a convenient time and advertised extensively), hearings can be effective at influencing policy and at attracting a representative sample of the citizenry (McComas 2001b; Chess and Purcell 1999; Gundry and Heberlein 1984; Gormley 1986).

Dissatisfaction with public hearings as an outlet for participation has led many scholars and practitioners to develop alternative methods for involving the public in policy making. One alternative has been to modify the format of public meetings, discarding the structured and non-deliberative hearing format in favor of a roundtable or small-group setting. These settings differ from traditional public hearings in that citizens have an opportunity to discuss the issue at hand, and engage in deliberation with fellow citizens and with officials. Roberts (1997) argues that the public deliberation that can occur at these meetings should be the foundation of an alternative way to solicit public input, and Weeks (2000) describes successful attempts to integrate meetings into a deliberative policy process.

National Issues Forums (NIF), a nationwide network committed to enhancing civic life and public involvement in politics, has
experimented with alternatives to the traditional public hearing for
almost twenty years. Here, citizens deliberate over public problems
with the goal of developing a plan of action to address the issue (for
descriptions of the type of deliberation fostered in NIF forums, see
Mathews 1999; Doble Research Associates 2001; 2000a; 2000b).
America Speaks, a nonprofit organization, promotes and organizes
electronic town hall meetings that allow citizens to deliberate over
policy issues. Using a mix of face-to-face deliberation and communication through technology, America Speaks attempts to empower
citizens to voice their opinions and inform governmental action
(America Speaks 2002; Moynihan 2003).

One common obstacle to public meetings concerns size: the
more people show up at the meeting, the more difficult it is to have
the type of face-to-face interaction and discussion that deliberation
proponents desire. America Speaks and other organizations have
addressed some of the logistical problems caused by size, but fostering deliberation in large groups is still a challenge. One response
has been to convene "citizens panels" or "citizens juries" to deliberate over issues (Crosby, Kelly, and Schaefer 1986; Kathlene and
Martin 1991; Haight and Ginger 2000). These panels are representative samples of the public, and thus can act as a proxy for deliberation among the entire public; because it is not feasible for
everyone to deliberate over an issue, selecting a representative sample to do it for them is the next best thing. Fishkin's (1991, 1995)
deliberative opinion polls are a variation on this theme: select a random sample of the public to deliberate on an issue (or an election),
and their recommendations will be reflective of what the public at
large would have decided if they had deliberated themselves.

Finally, surveys and focus groups are often considered to be a
form of "participation," although a qualitatively different form
than those listed previously. Surveys do not allow for any deliberation, nor do they even allow for citizens to express their individual
voice, as hearings do. Although focus groups allow for greater voice
and deliberation, they are still limited by a structure that is meant
to solicit opinions, not form them. Even though surveys and
focus groups by themselves do not offer much of an opportunity for

citizens to participate in policy making, they can be used to enhance other participation tools, such as the ones described above, making for a more meaningful and rich participatory structure (see for example, Weeks 2000; Kathlene and Martin 1991).

I have described various mechanisms by which citizens can provide input into the policy process. Where in this landscape of meetings, panels, surveys, and forums does the local city council and school board meeting fit? What role can they play?

The Functions of Public Meetings

Attending city council and school board meetings is a very common form of participation (Tables 7.1 and 7.4). Even though almost all interviewees stated that they went to public meetings, there was some disagreement about the effectiveness of attending a meeting. A few respondents said that attending meetings was the most effective form of participation, however, most did not. Many echoed the common complaint that elected officials already have their mind made up before the meeting. Despite this widespread belief, many respondents offered other reasons for why attendance at public meetings is effective. These explanations form the basis for the findings that follow. They are not meant as a characterization of the aggregate opinion of respondents, as opinion was too varied to reach any firm conclusion about the attitude of respondents toward public meetings. Rather, the findings below describe some functions that public meetings perform and offer reasons for why we should maintain this institution.

Public meetings of local governments in California are governed by the Ralph M. Brown Act, which requires that all meetings be open to the public and allow for public participation. The Brown Act gives the public the right to comment on items before the legislative body, and also stipulates that "time must be set aside for the public to comment on any other matters under the body's jurisdiction" (California Attorney General's Office 2002, vii). Thus, citizens have an opportunity to speak on agenda items as well as any other local issues they feel are important. Below are six ways that citizens use these opportunities to accomplish their political goals.

1. Provide Information

Public meetings can be an effective way to convey information about public opinion to officials. One piece of information that needs to be communicated is interest in a particular issue: letting officials know that you "are out there" is a necessary first step to participation. One respondent stated that attending public meetings was important because "it seems like if you don't show up at the council meetings, the council says, 'Well, maybe this is a non-issue.'" Another participant made a similar point, arguing that getting a lot of people to a council meeting was critical to showing that people cared about an issue (in this case, a traffic issue). There are, of course, other ways to let officials know that a particular issue is important to citizens: They could circulate petitions, write letters, or call officials directly. In some circumstances, however, attending meetings can be the most effective way of indicating interest. Gathering a group of citizens to go to a meeting is not only relatively easy, but it also clearly communicates to officials that there is interest in an issue.

Some respondents also felt attendance at meetings was important to counterbalance opposing views and to get out their message. A common theme among respondents was that there was power in numbers, and turning out the masses at city council or school board meetings provided a political advantage by adding force to their message. This dynamic was evident on both sides of the space-saver school debate. A supporter of the school stated that "we wanted to have a lot of parents with school children there [at the public meeting] because otherwise you were going to have an imbalance." School opponents also noted their attempts to bring out large numbers to meetings, and both sides claimed they outnumbered their opponents. Having numbers turn out for meetings is important because one common discourse in local politics concerns which side in a debate has more popular support. Absent scientific polls, actual levels of support are not known, leaving participants free to convince elected officials that they, in fact, have more support. Turnout at public meetings may be seen by officials as evidence of popular support (although frequently weak support, given the unrepresentativeness of those who attend), and thus can be used as a debating point. Lacking other information sources, elected officials may rely on turnout at public meetings, however unrepresentative, to gauge public support or opposition on a given policy.

Comments by two of the former elected officials interviewed indicate that they use public meetings as a source of information. One former school trustee said she kept tallies of supporters and opponents on an issue to get a feel for what the community thought. A former city councilman, talking about a proposal for a permit-parking district in a residential neighborhood, told this story:

> We were told that this was going on and the neighborhood is
> happy with it and the staff was happy with it, and they worked it
> out and it was all ready to go. Then it came before us to vote on it,
> all of the sudden we had a swarm of people who were against it.
> . . . I was prepared to go ahead and vote with it from the
> information I had, but then when this large constituent [sic] of
> business owners came out I said this is something I hadn't planned
> on. I can't vote on it. We need to sit down and work this through
> to see if we can't make both sides a little bit happier. Those groups
> of people got to me. . . . I would do my homework, and my
> colleagues—we did our homework. . . . We may have had our
> minds made up with the facts that we had been given, but when we
> would have a group come and speak against it, I wouldn't ram it
> on through, but make a motion to continue it. Let's hear more of
> what the people are trying to say and sit down and talk to them,
> again get that dialogue going so we can really find out what their
> concerns are and what we can do to alleviate it.

For this city councilman, a public hearing provided information about where his constituents stood on an issue. Note that he did not state that public comments persuaded him to change his thinking on an issue by offering new ideas or new interpretations. He did not say that the citizens appearing at the hearing changed his mind or persuaded him that he was mistaken in his support for the proposal. He did, however, change his actions based on the opposition to the proposal that was evident at the public hearing. The public hearing provided new information that altered the actions he took, even if it did not persuade him that his views were mistaken. Rather than acting as a deliberative forum where ideas are exchanged and people's opinions change based on rational persuasion, the view of meetings that emerges here is of a forum where constituents provide their elected officials with new information about their views on an issue, prompting altered behavior on the part of officials.

Officials, of course, may have other sources of information about public opinion, such as surveys, focus groups, forums, letters and phone calls from constituents, conversations with others, and media reports. Some of these, such as surveys and focus groups, are a more accurate reflection of public opinion because the participants will be more representative of the population as a whole. Despite this shortcoming, public meetings have some benefits as a vehicle for voicing public opinion. First, public meetings are useful in measuring the strength of opinion on a particular issue. Officials know that citizens who take the time to come to a meeting care about the issue under discussion, whereas surveys make no such indication. Further, meetings are open to anyone who wishes to speak, whereas surveys, focus groups, and advisory panels have restricted participation. Although not having restrictions may introduce bias into the opinions presented, the open meeting has an advantage in terms of legitimacy: citizens who may feel their voice is not being represented in survey results or panel recommendations have an opportunity to express views that may be a bit off the beaten path. By providing a venue for citizens wishing to present alternative opinions than those from other formats, meetings can add to legitimacy to the policy process. By themselves, public meetings do not provide an accurate picture of public opinion on local issues; but they can act as a valuable and important supplement to other forms of public opinion, providing both additional information and legitimacy.

2. A Show of Support

One recurring theme among respondents was the importance of supporting friendly elected officials taking controversial policy stands and expressing displeasure with officials taking stands with which they disagree. On controversial issues, elected officials are forced to take a position that will alienate some constituents, which is not a desirable position for politicians who prefer to please everyone. When an elected official is taking a position unpopular with some, his or her supporters will frequently make a point of coming to a meeting to express agreement with the stand taken, in a show of support for a politician in an uncomfortable situation. For example, one participant made this comment about his support for the space-saver school: "We certainly gave Rob and Audrey [two school board members] counter high ground to stand on. They could say, 'Look. These people, our constituents, the parents of the children, they are here to support.' This gave them a public high ground to stand on to shape the argument. . . . It didn't change anybody's mind, but it certainly helped to direct the flow of discussion."

Sometimes, officials need political cover for taking unpopular stands, which can be provided by supporters at a public meeting. If a politician is supporting the view of a small minority (e.g., one particular neighborhood) that is highly unpopular, they could take a major public relations hit; they could be characterized as out of step with the majority, catering to "special interests," and the like. These characterizations can be even more potent if they are out there all alone, without any support, while opponents are banging away. Citizens at public meetings, however, can provide some cover by showing public support for an unpopular position. For example, one participant explained why he attended a meeting in support of the liquor license for Shelley's restaurant (discussed in Chapter 6): "It makes it easier for them [the city council] to make a decision if they have support, rather than you making that decision on your own because you know it's right and its best for the community. It takes some of that burden, some of that responsibility, from the council if there's public support." Although the politicians supporting the liquor license might still take some political heat, at least they can point to a group of citizens and say, "I have some support in the community for my position." A show of support from a public relations standpoint can be critical, providing cover for a politician in a tight spot and diffusing some of the criticism. Public meetings are an excellent venue to provide this support because they are usually televised and sometimes covered by local newspapers, allowing supporters to get out their message.

Supporting sympathetic officials does not affect votes on issues nor is it meant to. But it does have an impact. First, it strengthens the relationship between a politician and his or her supporters and creates channels of communication. Elected officials, seeing who supports them during the tough times, will be more likely to return phone calls, arrange face-to-face meetings, and listen to those constituents. Politicians appreciate support on controversial issues, and as a consequence, will be more willing to listen to their constituents on other issues. In other words, public meetings allow citizens to identify themselves as supporters, giving them an opportunity to create a relationship with officials. Second, it provides an avenue by which citizens can help those officials they want to remain in office. As mentioned, popular support for a controversial vote is important political cover: without it, elected officials are susceptible to accusations during the next election that they are out of touch with their constituents and out of step with public opinion. Public meetings provide a means by which citizens can provide political cover for supportive politicians, thus reducing their exposure during the next election.

3. Shaming

Most citizens at public meetings are not there to support but rather to criticize. Elected officials frequently complain about citizens who are silent until they want to vent about a decision they disagree with. At first blush, this type of behavior may seem futile. Yelling and screaming at a meeting is not likely to change the votes of elected officials, so why do citizens go to meetings to complain? One function it serves is to shame elected officials for disagreeable actions. As explained above, support at a meeting can provide political cover for officials; the converse is also true. Criticizing officials in a public forum can create the perception that they are out of touch with the community, which is particularly important from a media perspective: the local newspaper or TV newscast is likely to report the fact that officials were criticized by their constituents at a meeting, particularly if it is a highly controversial issue. Even if the citizens at the meeting are not representative of the community at large, the image of an official being hammered by his or her constituents is a powerful one, and one that may have important electoral implications.

One example of the shaming dynamic was when a group of parents went to a city council meeting to criticize Councilwoman Lisa Mills for her opposition to the space-saver school. The decision to build or not to build was a school district decision (which is a separate entity from the City), but Councilwoman Mills was at the forefront of the opposition to the school (the school was located in her district). A group of school supporters went to a city council meeting to complain about her activities on the issue. One leader of the group explained why it was necessary: "[Lisa Mills] was very divisive. . . . It was really a lot of lies that were coming down the pipe. A lot of people that weren't involved with the school district, that's all they were getting. So it was very important to counterbalance that. And you had to do it with numbers, you had to do that with a lot of people." Another leader of the group made this comment: "When [Mayor] Dan Young said after the meeting that he'd never ever seen anything like that before in his life, it was like 'OK, we got our message across.' To get up there and publicly censure Lisa Mills for her activities. That was something that . . . it was a distraction and a lot of energy that we didn't need to continue to fight that so we went in and we hit hard and she wasn't really heard from much on that issue after that."

Because the council had no authority over the issue, school supporters were not trying to change the outcome of any policy decision: Their only aim was to shame Councilwoman Mills, which served two purposes. First, it altered the terms of the debate and perceptions among the public by indicating the amount of support that the school had. Also, it gave Councilwoman Mills a political black eye, which could have been a liability during the next election (she decided not to run for a second term).

Another example illustrates the effectiveness of shaming officials at public meetings. The issue was the proposed park and community center for Delhi discussed in the last chapter. The City had been promising to build the park for years but never provided the funding. After repeated stonewalling and delays by the City, supporters decided to force the issue by going to a city council meeting. A supporter relates the following account of what happened:

> So we organized a meeting at city council, we took about 150 people to that meeting. . . . And the questions were very simple. They were like, why haven't you kept your promises? And I think in many ways, we sort of shamed people, we shamed them because, you know, why haven't you kept your promises? . . . And so what happened was that was aired on Comcast [the local cable company]

throughout Santa Ana. . . . [S]o before you know it, I had people
calling [me] . . . they were saying, "They can't do this to you guys.
They can't just put all the money into north Santa Ana. They have
to pay attention to all these neighborhoods." People starting
coming out of the woodwork, you know, they said they have to
make this project for this community. So I think they [the city
council] were probably receiving those kind of calls. And the day
after the meeting . . . at the meeting, the Mayor and the rest of the
council, they were kind of cool about things, very evasive, didn't
act like they were disturbed in any way. But I'll tell you, the next
morning, the mayor was begging me to meet with him. He said,
"Please, let's sit down and let's try to work something out."

The value of this shaming strategy does not lie in its capacity to persuade the council that the park was a good idea; accusing the council of lying and breaking promises is hardly the way to accomplish
that goal. Rather, by embarrassing the council, they forced them to
pay attention to the issue and take action (the council did, eventually, provide some funds for the park, although not as much as
requested). A public meeting was the ideal venue to carry out this
shaming strategy. It was televised, and thus many people in the
community heard the park supporters' message, placing additional
pressure on the city council.[1] For council members, having to sit
through a meeting where 150 angry residents accuse you of lying
and breaking promises, while other constituents watch on TV, is
hardly an enticing prospect. We should not be surprised that this
strategy bore fruit and got the City to move on the park project.

The capacity to attack officials in public is an important aspect
of democratic governance: citizens need a venue where they can
counter what their elected officials are doing or saying. Public
meetings provide that venue. It gives citizens the ability to gather
in one place and express opinions that run counter to what officials
are saying. Citizens have other venues in which they can criticize
officials, such as by writing letters to the editor, staging street
protests, or voting against them in the next election; however, public meetings present a unique opportunity because they are public,
easily accessible, and allow any citizen to speak his or her mind.
Elected officials never look good when they are being yelled at, and
thus venting at public meetings can serve to undermine and weaken
the positions of elected officials. Much of the criticism that officials

receive may be unjustified and unfair, and I certainly do not mean to imply that citizens are always correct or that elected officials always deserve derision. Fair or not, the ability to criticize elected officials is a cornerstone of democratic politics, and public meetings provide an excellent opportunity for citizens to do so.

4. Agenda Setting

The power of elites to set the agenda is well documented in the urban power literature (Gaventa 1980; Crenson 1971; Bachrach and Baratz 1962; see Polsby 1980 for a critique). Much less studied is how and under what conditions citizens can influence the agenda. We generally think of public meetings as venues where policy decisions are made, not where agendas are formulated. Although true in most cases, meetings do provide opportunities for agenda setting by citizens. In Santa Ana, both the city council and school board allow for public comments on nonagenda items, allowing citizens to discuss issues that have not yet been formally taken up by officials (as required by state law). Some participants, when asked whether speaking at public meetings was effective, stated that attending a meeting the day an issue was going to be decided was useless, but going earlier in the process was effective as an agenda-setting device. One respondent, who was both president of her neighborhood association and president of the Library Board (a city advisory board), has the following to say about whether meetings were valuable:

> You have to be smart when you do it. Like we started speaking a while ago about the library budget because they won't make their decision, they're starting to make their decisions now [March], but they'll make final decisions in June and July. I think they're thinking, too, if you speak on the agenda items, well no, it's totally done before it comes to the committee. So you have to speak now about . . . like we spoke about Centerline [the light rail proposal]. . . . We spoke about Centerline before it even came up at all. And they said, "Why are you talking about this today?" and we said, "Because we know you are going to make a decision on it soon. We know you are. We've heard the buzz. So we are going to get a voice now, even though it's not an agenda item or anything." I think that's where you have to be smart.

The respondent is making two interrelated points about the value of speaking at public meetings on nonagenda items. First, she is highlighting the importance of early participation. By the time a decision reaches the city council or school board, it has already been in the works for quite some time, with advisory committees, staff, and interested parties providing input. Compromises may already be built into the policy, with the key players working out agreements among themselves. Further, supporters or opponents of a policy may be able to convince elected officials of the merits of their position well before it ever gets to a formal vote. Participation, therefore, is most effective before positions harden, compromises are worked out, and advisory committees make recommendations; showing up at a city council or school board meeting on the day when a policy is scheduled to be approved is, in many cases, too late in the process to make an impact. However, by speaking early in the process, citizens are able to get their opinions heard while officials are still deciding how they want to resolve the issue. This is why it was "smart" to comment on the Centerline proposal well before it came up to a formal vote (at the time, it was unclear how the city council was going to vote).

Speaking at public meetings can also influence the agenda by making officials pay attention to issues they ordinarily would not. The respondent quoted above illustrates this point with her comment about the library budget. Usually, the City does not pay much attention to the library budget and rarely provides additional funding. By speaking up early at a public meeting, citizens can establish an issue (in this case, library funding) as one that needs to be addressed. Another respondent, when asked why speaking at budget hearings was effective, said that it has some impact because "even though they've already made up their minds, it could stay up in their minds for the next budget meeting."

Agenda setting effects tie back into my first point about public meetings sending information to officials: the reason why speaking at meetings may help set the agenda is because elected officials may use it as a measure of citizen interest in a topic. If citizens are coming to meetings to talk about the Centerline proposal months before a decision is due, officials may conclude that it is a highly controversial issue that deserves more attention than they are giving it.

Conversely, if no one raises the library budget as an issue, it will likely be ignored by officials (as it usually is). Not only could officials use public comments at meetings to gauge where their constituents stand on the issues of the day, but they can also use them to determine what issues are important, and thus deserve their attention. With limited time at their disposal (elected officials in Santa Ana are part time), they need to pick and choose the issues that get on their agenda, and citizens showing up to discuss an issue at a meeting may influence those decisions.

That said, public meetings are not the most effective way to influence government agendas. Motivating a group of citizens to attend a meeting to discuss an issue that will be decided far in advance is difficult. Further, elected officials may forget about public comments by the time decisions need to be made. Other forms of participation, such as writing letters, circulating petitions, or speaking directly to officials, may be more effective at getting them to pay attention to certain issues. Public meetings, however, can be used in conjunction with these other methods and can further advance the agenda setting goals of citizens. They are particularly useful in making public a group's demands on officials. More private forms of participation, such as letter-writing and speaking directly to officials, may get some attention, but they are likely to get more attention if they are coupled with a public display. As mentioned above, one chief virtue of public meetings is that they are public, and thus capable of reaching a larger audience than just officials and a small group of participants. They may not be a very effective method by themselves, but they can serve an important agenda setting purpose if used along with other methods.

Many of the other participatory structures discussed above, such as panels, forums, and roundtables, already assume an agenda that is decided by officials. Sometimes, officials use these structures to define agendas (e.g., Weeks 2000), but usually the issue to be discussed is identified and framed by officials beforehand. Citizen comments at public meetings can play a role in deciding for what issues panels or roundtables will be convened, and how those issues will be framed. Public meetings can provide the raw opinions and ideas that can start more deliberative and, ultimately, constructive processes to address public issues.

5. Delay

It is rare for elected officials to change their votes based on citizen comments at a public meeting, but it is more common for votes to be delayed due to a public outcry, especially if it is unexpected. In some cases, officials may delay to avoid making unpopular decisions with people present, hoping that at the next meeting fewer people will be there. In other instances, citizens may desire a delay. One respondent tells of a planning commission meeting where a development mitigation plan was being discussed. A neighborhood resident, seeing that the planning commission was prepared to vote against them, stated that "we told them we need to know what our rights are, and we asked them for a thirty-day extension, and they granted it to us." This extension gave the neighborhood residents time to develop a strategy for accomplishing their goals. In some cases, citizens may not find out about an issue until the last minute, and thus they may not have time to take actions that can apply pressure on officials, such as circulating petitions or organizing a letter-writing campaign. A delay may create time to work over officials or to gather more support in the community.

Public meetings are an excellent venue for asking for a delay: Elected officials might find it difficult to ignore citizens who are merely asking for more time to study an issue, try to reach a compromise, or (as in the example above) figure out what actions they can take. Asking for a delay is not an unreasonable request, increasing the pressure on elected officials to accommodate it. The ability of citizens to ask for a delay publicly, and to provide reasons for why a delay is necessary adds to the force of the request. Privately requesting a delay (such as in a letter or in a phone conversation) does not allow citizens to publicly state their argument in favor of a delay, and thus is not as politically forceful. Public meetings provide the best opportunity for citizens to ask elected officials to delay a decision because they can publicly present arguments that attest to the reasonableness and wisdom of the request.

6. Networking

The primary channel of communication at public meetings is from citizens to elected officials, but citizens can also use meetings to communicate to each other. Communication among citizens is not easy because they usually lack the money to send out mailings and frequently lack the time to knock on doors or organize phone trees (although on occasion citizens do engage in these activities). Public meetings allow citizens to get their message out to other citizens relatively cheaply and without a significant time commitment. Usually, only citizens active in local politics are in attendance or watch the meeting on TV, so they are not a good venue for communication to the citizenry at large. But they are good for communicating with other citizens who are active. Public meetings can serve to create and maintain social networks among active citizens by allowing them to let others know what they are doing. We saw an example above, with the citizen who was advocating a new park for the Delhi neighborhood. She mentioned that after the public meeting, people from other parts of the City called her about the park issue, fostering networks between her group and other neighborhoods and organizations. Of course, citizens have other ways to communicate with each other, and I do not mean to imply that public meetings are a primary or an effective means by which to build networks. But they can help citizens get their message out and reach out to other citizens in the community.

Influencing Votes

Public meetings can serve functions in addition to the explicit function of trying to influence the votes of officials. The six functions listed above are examples of how citizens can use meetings to achieve political goals, which may indirectly influence votes by altering the political context in which the votes are taken, but they do not directly change a specific vote. Whether public meetings are effective at the latter is a point of contention in the literature. To round out my picture of the role and place of public meetings, rather than claim that meetings are either effective or not effective (which is how the question is usually posed in the literature), I will explore under what conditions meetings might be influential, and why.

My research uncovered one case where a public meeting unequivocally changed the outcome of a city council decision. The issue was a proposed citywide redevelopment project that came before the city council in 1993. The State of California allows cities to create redevelopment zones in areas deemed "blighted," a vague term that can mean anything from rundown buildings to high levels of unemployment. Redevelopment areas use a tax-increment financing scheme where additional tax revenues generated by new development are channeled back into the redevelopment area to further development efforts. Redevelopment areas also facilitate the use of eminent domain powers by city government. The City wanted to create one large redevelopment area that would cover over one-half of the city, excluding the wealthy neighborhoods in north Santa Ana and a few areas in south Santa Ana. Supporters claimed it was needed to raise money for infrastructure projects such as parks and schools. The central area of the city was very run down and in desperate need of schools, and the hope was that new development would provide the funds to meet these demands.

Opposition to the proposal swelled when the City sent out a notice (as required by law) to residents within the proposed area explaining that the City considered their neighborhood to be "blighted" and that the redevelopment area was needed to fund infrastructure improvements. Most people do not consider their neighborhood to be blighted (even if it does meet the criteria) and were concerned that the City might use eminent domain powers to take away their home or business. A few community activists opposed to the plan spread word about the potential for residents to lose their homes and the possibility that the redevelopment plan could fundamentally disrupt their lives. The fear over the impact of citywide redevelopment was exacerbated by the fact that many residents did not trust city officials, particularly true in the context of the early 1990s when the city council was rife with infighting and petty disputes. Also, the long history of animosity between the City and school district made it unlikely that any revenue generated by the redevelopment area would be used for new schools. Many residents saw the plan as a ruse aimed at eliminating working-class Latino neighborhoods and replacing them with white middle-class neighborhoods.

A meeting was scheduled for May 1993 at which the council would vote to move forward with the plan. Going into the meeting, most observers expected it to pass. In the weeks before the meeting, a few opponents rallied citizens to go to the meeting to voice their opposition. Their efforts worked better than they had hoped:

according to newspaper accounts, over 2,000 citizens showed up to protest. After a handful of irate speakers, the city council voted unanimously to table the item, and it was never brought up again. According to all sources, the redevelopment plan would have passed if it were not for the outpouring of opposition at the meeting.

This incident illuminates some conditions that can lead to public meetings effectively changing votes. First, elected officials were surprised at the turnout and the opposition.[2] If they had known that it would generate so much opposition, they would have likely postponed the decision until they could marshal more support. Or if they had the resolve, they may have just voted for it despite the opposition. Here, we have a case where meetings conveyed new information to officials (the amount of opposition in the community) that had a direct impact on a vote taken. The reason it had such a profound impact was because officials did not have the luxury of a public opinion poll to gauge opposition, and thus were blindsided at the meeting. The conclusion I draw is that if elected officials misjudge public support or opposition, meetings may change votes because they provide new information that changes officials' political calculations.

There were two other conditions that contributed to the vote being changed by the public meeting: the sheer numbers of people to appear and the absence of supporters. Attendance of 2,000 at a public hearing is phenomenal, particularly in a city with a total population of 320,000. This unusual show of force must have indicated to officials that this vote could have serious political ramifications, and thus prompted them to change their votes on the spot. Further, the fact that all present were opposed made a "yes" vote politically dangerous. Having support provides political cover, but none was present here,[3] making an affirmative vote more difficult.

There is one more condition that may contribute to a public meeting changing a vote that was not present during the redevelopment incident: ambivalence of elected officials. Some issues may be more important to citizens than to elected officials, and the latter may be willing to change their votes based on comments at a hearing because they do not have strong feelings either way. But a last-minute change of mind is not likely because elected officials are usually in tune with the wishes and demands of their constituents. Still, it may happen on occasion.

Whether public meetings are more effective than other forms of participation at influencing the votes of elected officials is a research question beyond the scope of this chapter. My point is not that attending meetings is the most effective strategy for changing legislative decisions, but that under some circumstances, meetings can be used to accomplish this goal. Adding this argument to the previous section's description of other functions that meetings can serve illustrates the usefulness of meetings for citizens. They may not be the best tools for accomplishing political goals, but they do add a weapon to the citizen's political arsenal that can be marshaled to enhance the effectiveness of citizen participation.

Conclusion

At the core of democracy is citizen deliberation and rational persuasion: citizens deliberate over pressing public issues and make arguments to persuade officials and each other to take desired actions. Public meetings do not contribute to either of these goals: neither are they deliberative, nor are they an effective vehicle for rational persuasion. Public meetings, however, have a role to play in maintaining a democratic system. Around the core of deliberation and rational persuasion is a democratic periphery of political maneuvering and pressure tactics that are essential parts of a democratic process, and this periphery is where public meetings come into play. Meetings are a tool in the citizen's participatory toolbox that can help them accomplish political objectives—such as supporting allies, embarrassing enemies, setting the agenda, getting their voice heard—that can add to their influence and effectiveness. Citizen lobbyists find public meetings valuable because they can contribute to their efforts to influence local policy. The findings from Santa Ana demonstrate some ways that meetings can be used to citizens' advantage.

How do public meetings fit into the overall scheme of citizen participation and policy making? Public meetings do not directly contribute to the process of formulating effective policy solutions to public problems; other devices, such as roundtables, forums and panels are more effective at this task. Citizens acting as collaborative problem solvers would find little value in them because of the lack of deliberative qualities. But meetings, by helping citizens be more effective, can enhance the responsiveness and accountability of government. Citizen deliberation and discussion on tough policy choices may lead to the formulation of better policy, but by itself, does not make government any more responsive to citizens. If citizen recommendations go unheeded, then the whole process is for naught. This situation is where public meetings fit: they provide a venue where citizens can carry out a political struggle to have their voices heard and recommendations heeded. In other words, public meetings are valuable when citizens are lobbying governments to adopt specific policies. Ideally, after citizens deliberate on an issue, weigh policy choices, and make recommendations, they can go to a public meeting to make the case that they should be listened to. Meetings do not currently play this role, inasmuch as most speakers at public meetings argue for their personal opinions, not collective opinions derived through deliberation. But if additional deliberation structures are put into place, then public meetings could have a valuable role by enhancing the political power of citizens and, consequently, increasing the chances that government will be responsive to their recommendations.

As we saw above, public meetings can also assist citizens at the front end of the policy process by providing a venue for citizens to set the agenda and frame policy issues. In many participatory venues, the issues to be discussed are identified beforehand and a framework for discussing the issue is set. Although this planning may be necessary to foster constructive deliberation, it does limit the voice of citizens, preventing them from altering the structure of the conversation or changing how an issue is framed. At public meetings, citizens are free to identify different issues that need to be discussed and offer new frames to understand issues already under discussion. Before deliberation in forums, panels, or round-tables commence, citizens should have the opportunity to propose what issues need to be discussed, how the issue should be understood, and the manner in which the process should work. Public meetings could give citizens the opportunity to influence the way citizens participate, rather than having government officials decide for them.

Thus, public meetings have a role to play at the beginning and the end of participatory processes. Designing institutions that allow for citizen participation in the policy process requires that we create deliberative and constructive outlets for citizen input. But this "positive" political power needs to be supplemented by other forms of participation that allow citizens to flex their political muscle (see Rimmerman [1997] for a description of different forms of political participation). Both types of power are needed for a healthy democratic policy process. A process that lacks opportunities for constructive citizen deliberation will lead to disillusionment among citizens and reinforce the disconnect between citizens and their government. On the other hand, a process that allows citizens constructive input but limits their capacity to fight political battles, influence legislative votes, or criticize officials will serve to reduce governmental responsiveness. Without the political power to back up citizen input, much of that input will be duly filed, never to see the light of day again. The power to pressure, lobby, and cajole government officials is an essential complement to positive power, as constructive citizen deliberation is only valuable if officials pay attention to it. Thus, public meetings, as a venue where this can occur, cannot be replaced by more deliberative or constructive venues.

In this chapter, I have explored the value that public meetings have for citizens. But why would local officials want to hold them? By giving citizens an opportunity to accomplish their political goals, public meetings reduce the power and control exercised by officials. There are, however, two reasons why officials would desire to keep public meetings. First, as mentioned above, they can provide information to officials about public opinion, particularly concerning what issues citizens feel are important and the strength of their opinions. Second, because public meetings are an open forum where any citizen can speak, they provide a measure of legitimacy to the policy process. As many scholars have noted, citizens are cynical about politics and government (Rimmerman 1997; Berman 1997; Harwood Group 1991), and thus are likely to approach a roundtable, forum, or other project with a wary eye. By providing an open forum for citizens to express their opinions, public meetings enhance the legitimacy of the policy process, a desired commodity for public officials. Public meetings benefit citizens more than they do officials, but the latter group do derive some benefit, and would be wise to maintain the institution.

9 The Political Value of Social Networks

Scholars who study the resources used by citizens participating in politics have found that three are critically important: time, money, and civic skills (e.g., Verba, Schlozman, and Brady 1995, 270–72). In this chapter, I propose to add a fourth resource to that list: social networks. Although scholars recognize the importance of networks for mobilization and recruitment, few have seen networks as a political resource that citizens can draw upon once they have decided to participate. Like money in the bank or spare time, social networks are a resource that citizens can use to accomplish political objectives.

I argue that social networks are used extensively by citizens when they participate, and these networks are a resource as important as time, money, and civic skills. This chapter explores the role and functions of social networks in aiding citizen attempts to influence local public policy. Although social networks are not a required resource for citizens, they facilitate participation by helping citizens accomplish specific political tasks. In the same way that campaign contributions enhance access to officials, free time increases the capacity to circulate petitions, and oratory skills help citizens make persuasive arguments at public meetings, social networks assist citizens in gathering information, mobilizing allies, pooling resources, and other political activities. Neglecting the role of social networks as a political resource results in a distorted view of how citizens participate and their effectiveness at influencing public policy.

To conclude the chapter, I make the case that citizens' ability to use social networks as a political resource distinguishes local and national participation. On a national level, citizens' personal social networks are not extensive enough to be of much value politically, but in local politics they do serve as an important political resource.

The smaller scale of local governance allows citizens to use their networks as a political resource, which in turn allows them to engage the policy-making process as citizen lobbyists, using their networks to accomplish a variety of political tasks.

Social Networks and Political Participation

Social networks are the personal relationships between individuals within a community. These relationships could be formed through many channels: organizational membership, political activity, recreational activity, and so forth. They are "social" in the sense that they are interpersonal relations between people, but they are not necessarily derived from social (as opposed to political or economic) activity. Even though the networks themselves could be derived from social, political, or economic activities, I focus on the political implications of these networks, not their effects on other spheres. Specifically, I explore how citizens use interpersonal relationships to facilitate their political participation.

Social networks are a unique resource that is not encompassed by the other three (time, money and civic skills) identified by Sidney Verba and his colleagues (Verba, Schlozman, and Brady 1995). Of course, all four resources are interrelated. For example, having monetary resources can influence the extent of free time one has, or certain civic skills can enhance the extent of one's social networks. What creates the analytical distinction between them, however, is not their independence but their nature. Social networks are a fundamentally different type of resource than the other three because they are constituted by the relationships between individuals, not by attributes or resources held by individual participants. The resource that citizens draw upon when they participate is their relationship with others, which is distinct from the other resources (time, money, and civic skills) that are not derivative of social relationships.

We should also note the difference between social networks, a political resource, and the civic skill commonly referred to as "networking." Networking is the activity by which citizens develop relationships with other people, and is a civic skill that varies among individuals. Good networking skills can enhance one's social networks, however, the process of building networks is distinct from using those networks as a resource to accomplish political goals. One can build networks and not use them for political purposes, or use networks that were not the result of intentional networking (e.g., family networks). Thus, we can maintain an analytic distinction between networking, a civic skill, and social networks, a resource that may or may not be derivative of networking activity.

The literature analyzing the political impact of social networks has focused on the role of social networks in mobilizing citizens to participate. The literature has identified three possible ways that social networks can mobilize citizens:

1. Social networks create opportunities for others to mobilize citizens.
2. Social networks foster democratic norms and civic virtues.
3. Social networks help citizens develop political skills.

First, social networks can mobilize citizens by providing a means for others to communicate with them. In this sense, social networks are a tool that political leaders can use to increase participation: social networks open up lines of communication for those desiring to mobilize others to participate. For example, citizens who are members of voluntary associations are susceptible to group leaders who want to encourage them to participate. Rosenstone and Hansen (1993, 84) argue that "involvement in associations promotes political activism," because political leaders target association members for mobilization. Leighley (1996) found evidence of this type of intentional mobilization, although its extent is dependent upon the goals and motivations of the members. Others exploring variation in mobilization across different groups generally conclude that variation is greatest in organizations that are explicitly political (Fuchs, Minnite, and Shapiro 2000; Booth and Richard 1998; Pollock 1982).

Social networks can also create political participation indirectly by fostering democratic norms and civic virtue. Associations and social networks can "instill in their members habits of cooperation and public spiritedness" (Putnam 2000, 338) and other civic virtues, such as trustworthiness, tolerance of the views of others, and respect for the rule of law (M. E. Warren 2001, 73). Citizens who have these civic virtues are more likely to participate, the hypothesis goes, because they will be more accepting of democratic norms, the democratic process, and the political system generally. Studies analyzing whether citizens exhibiting these civic virtues participate more have analyzed one civic virtue in particular: interpersonal trust. Lake and Huckfeldt (1998) found that informal social networks among citizens (not necessarily those created through joining organizations) can lead to politically relevant social capital, which in turn leads to greater political involvement. But this relationship could work the other way: political involvement could lead to greater levels of social capital. Brehm and Rahn (1997, 1017), using data from the General Social Survey, contend that trust and civic engagement are in a reciprocal relationship, "where the effect of civic engagement on interpersonal trust was much stronger than the reverse effect."

Social networks can also develop skills that citizens need to participate in political life. The hypothesis here is that citizens with greater political skills will be more likely to participate because they will be more comfortable when engaging in political activities. Brady, Verba, and Schlozman's (1995) study of citizen participation illustrates the importance of civic skills for political involvement: public speaking skills, organizing skills, and other attributes are needed to engage in a variety of different political activities. Brady, Verba, and Schlozman argue that these skills are acquired from formal education, from the workplace, and from activity in various civic organizations, and the lack of opportunities to develop political skills is a powerful explanatory variable for political inactivity. Leighley (1996) also concludes that skill-building activities within organizations can lead to more political participation, and Marschall (2001) found involvement in community organizations to be a strong predictor of political participation. Berry, Portney, and Thomson (1993), however, conclude that the existence of strong neighborhood associations do not increase the overall level of citizen participation in city politics. Despite this negative finding, on balance the research has found that activity in civic organizations—a particular type of social network—can lead to the development of political skills, and consequently a greater probability of political activity.

These three social network-participation links deal with the extent of citizen participation: all posit ways that the existence of social networks can mobilize citizens to engage politically. Social networks, however, can play another participatory role in addition to being a mobilizing force. Once citizens are mobilized and decide to participate, they can use their social networks as a tool in their efforts to influence governmental decisions. Like some of the mobilization hypotheses, social networks here also build capacity but to a different end: rather than providing the motivation to participate, it provides the means. In other words, in addition to being a mobilizing force, social networks can also act as a resource for citizens once they decide to participate.[1]

In this chapter, I undertake two tasks that have not been adequately addressed in the literature. First, I systematically describe the different ways that participants use social networks. Past research provides examples of citizens using networks as a resource, but it does not pull back from the specific examples and develop a general typology of how social networks are used as a political resource. Second, I explore the implications of these dynamics for our understanding of how citizens engage the local policy-making process.

The Role of Social Networks in Participatory Efforts

Once citizens have decided to participate, they need to use their political resources to accomplish political tasks. We know how time, money, and civic skills are used by citizens to achieve their political objectives: money can be given as campaign contributions, time can be used to organize protests, and so forth. But how are social networks used? What are they good for? Below, I discuss five political activities for which social networks are a valuable resource: 1) mobilizing citizens, 2) pooling resources, 3) gathering information, 4) disseminating information to citizens, and 5) communicating with officials.

1. Mobilizing Citizens

Many political activities require large groups of citizens to be effective: community forums need attendees, petitions need signature gatherers, protests need protesters, and so forth. Social networks can assist in assembling these groups by identifying others in the community who would be interested in a particular issue and by acting as a communication channel between organizers and potential supporters. As mentioned above, the literature has found that associational links are used to mobilize citizens (Rosenstone and

Hansen 1993; Leighley 1996). Social networks—whether they are formed through associations or other means—are a political resource that citizens can draw upon when they need to find allies or assemble a large group.

Social networks, by fostering personal relationships among community members, facilitate mobilization efforts. The importance of relationships for mobilizing citizens was perhaps best put by an organizer for a faith-based community group: "Our expectations of who we get to a public meeting are based on our relationships with those specific people. If we expect 500 people, we've got a relationship with 500 people." The relationships do not always have to be that strong to be effective. For example, one parent–teacher association (PTA) organizer described how they used a phone tree list to generate support for the space-saver school. Whether the ties are "strong" or "weak" (Granovetter 1973), they serve the same purpose: acting as a means by which mobilization efforts can occur.

Mobilizing through social networks is effective because when citizens are asked to participate, who is asking them may matter as much (if not more) than the issue on which they are asked to participate. A request to participate will more likely get a favorable response if it comes from a friend than from a stranger, which is why alternative means of mobilization, such as using the mass media or passing out fliers, will not be as effective as recruiting through networks. Citizens are unlikely to attend a forum, join a protest, or engage in other activities based on a flier or news story alone because they lack the background information that will make them feel comfortable participating. The trust and reciprocity (i.e., social capital) that is formed through social networks can increase the effectiveness of mobilization. Many participants did pass out fliers or canvass door to door as a means to spread information and gain support. For example, some PTA members passed out fliers in front of schools as parents picked up their kids to inform them of various political activities. This approach works well for spreading information, but is less likely to prompt parents to become actively involved in political activities, as the information presented is too thin and the relationship too weak to prompt participation.

In many cases, the process of mobilization occurs simultaneously with network building: attempts to recruit others to join in political actions may lead to new relationships and stronger networks. For example, a neighborhood leader who wanted to mobilize other neighborhood activists to support his plan to rid the city of inoperable vehicles ("physical graffiti" he called them), said that he attended other neighborhood association meetings to present his case. He also attended social functions where he passed out literature and asked other activists to sign a petition. So, in the process of gaining support for his proposal, he also strengthened his social networks by talking to other neighborhood leaders and discussing their mutual concerns. Another community activist engaged in similar activities in his fight to stop citywide redevelopment (discussed in Chapter 8). In an effort to mobilize opposition, he went to meetings of various organizations in the city and talked to them about the problems with the redevelopment plan. He also said that many people called him to ask about what the redevelopment plan would mean for their neighborhood, and often invited him to speak to small groups of concerned citizens. While he drew on his social networks to mobilize opposition, he also enhanced his networks by developing new relationships in the process.

Mobilizing others is critical for effective participation because when it comes to political pressure, numbers count. A former elected officials when asked whether a large group of people was more effective than just one person with a good idea, responded, "The numbers worked for me." This sentiment was echoed by many of the other respondents who often stressed how important it was to represent a group when talking to officials. For example, one neighborhood leader commented that "we were really diligent in our neighborhood about making sure when we took a position that it was representative of the neighborhood." Another said that if you try to do something by yourself, "they'll [city officials] say, 'Here comes that guy again.' One person. Making noise, making noise. They never listen to one person." To represent people, however, you need to talk to them, solicit opinions, have them come to meetings, and interact, all of which require some network connections. An organization—whether it be a PTA, neighborhood association, or other group—would have a very difficult time representing individuals without having networks with them. Further, representation is best demonstrated through acts of mobilization: if a group is able to assemble large numbers to go to a meeting, sign a petition, or send letters, it demonstrates to officials and community members that they do, in fact, represent a large group.

2. Pooling Resources

In addition to mobilizing others, social networks build bridges between groups and individuals within a community who are addressing the same issues. These links are critical because they allow citizens to combine their time, money, and civic skills into a collective effort. Most citizens (or citizen groups) do not possess enough resources to tackle community issues or influence governmental decisions by themselves. Accomplishing something in politics usually requires more than just an individual with a good idea and a desire to see it come to fruition; it also requires coordinated action and significant time and effort on the part of various political actors. Thus, effective citizen participation requires that resources be pooled.

The resources that are most commonly pooled are time and knowledge. Most of the activities listed in Table 7.1 require time to carry them out: it takes time to do research, attend meeting, write letters, and so forth. These activities are most effective with a lot of people (fifty people attending a public meeting is more effective than five), and more people requires more time to organize. Knowledge is another important shared resource. Many participants have knowledge of a particular aspect of an issue but need to rely on others to provide additional information. Also, some participants have the means to disseminate knowledge (usually by being part of an organization), whereas others have knowledge but do not have the means to disseminate it. Sharing knowledge can help citizens gain a fuller understanding of what is going on and also serve to widely disseminate that knowledge.

Pooling resources makes them more valuable. In the aggregate, citizens may have the resources needed to accomplish a political task, but bringing those resources together may be necessary. A coordinated effort that integrates resources from disparate parts of the community will be more effective than if the resources were used in isolation. Social networks aid in this coordination by helping citizens identify what resources they need, who has those resources, and how they can effectively combine their efforts. In other words, social networks facilitate the process by which citizens pool their resources. In this way, social networks are a political resource that enhances the effectiveness of other resources.

A good example of pooling resources was the antigang effort led by Jose Miranda, discussed in Chapter 4. In his efforts to implement his antigang program, he brought together a diverse array of people—from gang leaders to probation officers to city council members to business leaders—to help him implement his plan. Each brought a particular set of resources to the table. Individually, none of these actors could really make an impact on gang activity, but they all had some role to play in Miranda's plan. Without the capacity to bring together resources from a disparate set of groups and organizations, he would not have been able to implement his plans. Some groups and individuals were brought together without the aid of social networks (e.g., the gangs themselves). For others, Miranda's social networks (he was an active member of the chamber of commerce, the Democratic Party, and Latino rights organizations) helped him identify others with political resources and convince them to combine their efforts.

Another example was the effort to establish the artists' village, also discussed in Chapter 4. John Peters, the driving force behind the movement, was able to create momentum by bringing in community groups who had some resources that they could contribute. These groups included arts organizations that could foster activities in the proposed village and neighborhood associations that could offer their political support. The latter group was critical: arts organizations did not have the political clout to make elected officials listen, because most of the organizations were not active in electoral politics and did not command large voting blocs. Neighborhood associations, however, did have this political pull, and their support of the movement gave officials a reason to listen. Once Peters got the neighborhood associations on board (primarily through pitching the idea at their meetings and giving away tickets to art shows), he was able to draw on their social networks to bring in city officials. His ability to utilize the political resources of neighborhood associations to complement the substantive resources of arts organizations made for a powerful coalition, and was a primary reason why the artists' village was eventually supported by the City.

3. Gathering Information

Citizens need information to participate effectively. Collecting information on local issues, however, may be difficult, as officials may not widely broadcast their activities and newspapers do not extensively cover most community issues. Although citizens have their own experiences to draw on, frequently they need to do research to acquire additional information on what decisions are being made, who is making them, and what activities are happening. Gathering this information is a critical part of political participation. Participants cannot simply come up with a plan and then try to get the City or school district to implement it. They need to know what is already being done on the issue, what likely reactions will be within government, who might oppose it, and if there are alternatives being considered. Knowing this information will lead to more effective participation, as participants will have a clearer idea of what they need to do to accomplish their political goals.

Social networks help citizens gather information by creating lines of communication to other people in the community. Networks created through community groups are particularly valuable as a conduit for information. Not only do they link citizens who have mutually beneficial information, but the activities of the groups themselves also serve as venues for information exchange. Commlink (the umbrella organization for Santa Ana neighborhood associations) is a good example of how networks formed through organizations can be valuable to citizens. Commlink holds monthly meetings where each neighborhood has an opportunity to describe what they are doing. They also hold special meetings on issues of concern to neighborhoods, and organize committees and task forces. Most neighborhoods send representatives to Commlink so that they can find out what is going on in the rest of the city, and without the networks created by Commlink, neighborhoods would have a more difficult time learning what other neighborhoods are doing. Commlink is a resource for participants to gather information, and can help them get the information they need to participate.

One example of the importance of gathering information was the effort to implement a new commercial vehicles code, described in Chapter 4. Mike Belliard, a central proponent of the new ordinance, recruited some allies from other neighborhood associations, and after some meetings and discussions, the city council instructed the city attorney to draft an ordinance. The drafting of the ordinance was a collaborative one, with the city attorney and other city officials discussing the details of the ordinance with Belliard and his allies. The citizens who worked on this issue indicated that they had many meetings and conversations with officials in the planning stages. Meanwhile, Commlink held informational meetings where the issue was discussed and invited city staff and elected officials to attend. Commlink also has a committee on Neighborhood Improvement and Code Enforcement (NICE) that stepped up its efforts on this issue. All of this effort put the issue of commercial vehicles, previously a nonissue, on the political map.

The battle over the commercial vehicles code highlights the importance of social networks for gathering information. Belliard used connections with other neighborhood associations, formed through Commlink, to find allies, as well as to find out how this issue affects other communities. He then used his networks with city officials (both elected and nonelected) to find out the current status of the City's commercial vehicles code and why it was not being enforced. Knowing that the old law was unenforceable was important, because it shifted the fight away from getting the City to beef up enforcement (the original tactic) to proposing a new ordinance. Finally, Belliard used his networks with city officials to find out how the ordinance was being written and to know what amendments and changes the city council was planning to make. Most of this information simply was not available to citizens who did not have the contacts within the neighborhood associations and the city government.

4. Disseminating Information to Citizens

Social networks can also be used to let others in the community know about a group's activities. Because the media does not cover community activities extensively, citizens need to find alternative means of letting others in the community learn about their activities. Dissemination of information serves many purposes, from finding allies to increasing public support for a position to agenda setting. Not all issues require that others in the community be aware of what is happening, but in many cases participants will find it advantageous to widely broadcast their activities.

Social networks assist in disseminating information by providing formal and informal channels of communication among groups and individuals in a community, which is more than just letting information travel by word of mouth; it involves providing information to others by speaking at their meetings, calling citizens through phone trees, and similar activities. Letting information travel by word of mouth is passive, whereas disseminating information through social networks is an activity that individuals and groups consciously engage in. While social networks facilitate the spread of information through gossip and casual conversation, they also can be used intentionally to spread information for strategic purposes.

This dynamic can be seen in the attempt to block citywide redevelopment. Dave Orellana, a former redevelopment commissioner and opponent of the plan, used his networks to disseminate information about how it was going to negatively impact Santa Ana neighborhoods. Below is his description of how he got the word out:

> We went to neighborhood groups, various neighborhood associations. We went to, there were some Hispanic organizations. We went and spoke to their folks and their members. Really made it a campaign directly to people. One, we didn't have the capacity or the money to send out letters and stuff. But it was very much that relying on referent authority. Somebody calling me or one of us and saying, "Would you come to my house? I have some people coming over." And these were the folks in the neighborhoods, and every neighborhood has them, where these are the people that the neighbors call up and say, "I'm looking at my ballot [a letter the city sent about the redevelopment plan]. What does this mean?" These were the people who had the spheres of influence within their own neighborhoods. So those were typically the ones to say, "Hey, I've got a question on this. Can you? . . ." "Sure. I'd be happy to come down and talk to you folks."

Using networks to facilitate information flow allows for greater citizen effectiveness. Spreading information through networks compensates for not having the resources to send out letters or communicate through other means. Using social networks in lieu of mass mailings, flyers, or advertisements to disseminate information can save participants time and money. If participants had the financial means to disseminate information through other channels, social networks would not be that valuable as a resource. But because money is often lacking, networks may be the most effective means to disseminate information, and thus an important resource.

5. Communicating with Officials

Up to this point, we have talked primarily about social networks among citizens. Networks between citizens and officials are also an important political resource. Many of the participants in this study had relationships with officials. Frequently, these were formed through belonging to the same organization (e.g., many city council members belonged to neighborhood associations before they were elected and have relationships with neighborhood leaders). Also, some participants volunteer during elections or volunteer to sit on advisory boards. Other ties are formed through past participation and civic activity, as citizens and officeholders may develop relationships while working together on specific policy issues.

These connections provide participants with enhanced access to officials. Of course, many local officials are accessible to citizens absent of personal relationships, and social networks are not required to communicate to officials. But they certainly help. A neighborhood activist put it best when explaining why interpersonal relationships with city officials are important: "It gets me entrée. It means I am generally able to speak directly to the person I want to speak to instead of an intermediary, or an assistant, or a representative, or press official, which I find very helpful." Social networks increase the probability that officials will return phone calls and arrange for private meetings with citizens. They also increase the likelihood that officials will communicate what they know to citizens. As Table 7.1 demonstrates, communicating with officials is a common participatory activity, and social networks can facilitate this communication.

A few examples illustrate this dynamic. Late one night, during a public meeting, the school board asked staff to look into increasing the number of children enrolled in Greenville Intermediate school. The next day, a staff member called the PTA president at Greenville and described what had transpired. Because the request was made late at night (after 11 p.m.), few parents at Greenville knew about it. The PTA president then quickly spread the word and organized vocal opposition to the proposal. The school board, at their next meeting, decided not to take up the issue. Here, we have an example where school staff initiated contact with a citizen participant to inform them of the activities of the school board, based on a previous relationship they had with that individual (the PTA president in the past had supported staff on other issues). Thus, through the relationship that the PTA president had with school officials, he was able to acquire information about an issue of concern, leading to more effective participation.

The space-saver school battle provides another example. In this case, the school district and proponents of the school worked closely together to generate support. The access that supporters had to the school district was critical in letting them know what activities they needed to do and kept them abreast of the latest developments. On the other side, opponents used their relationships with two school board members opposed to the school to get information that they could use in their arguments against the proposal, and information on the latest actions taken by district staff and supporters. These links to officials—both elected and nonelected—and the access that it afforded them made both sides more effective participants.

Summary

Social networks are a political resource because they help citizens accomplish political tasks, such as gathering information, mobilizing citizens, and communicating with officials. This does not mean, however, that citizens will necessarily be more effective at influencing local policy: Just because citizens are able to mobilize more citizens or pool their resources does not mean that this activity will be effective. Thus, we need to make a distinction between citizens' capacity to participate, which is enhanced by social networks, and citizens' effectiveness at influencing policy. Figure 9.1 graphically represents this distinction.

When citizens participate, they engage in a variety of political activities—those listed in Table 7.4 and represented by the leftmost box on Figure 9.1. The reason they engage in these activities is to

Figure 9.1. The logic of nonelectoral participation

accomplish certain political goals. For example, they may circulate a petition to demonstrate support for a proposal to officials or they may organize a protest to demonstrate opposition. By accomplishing these political goals, participants hope to have some influence on policy outcomes, but two factors could block this hope: miscalculation on the part of citizens and officials who choose to ignore the opinions of their constituents. Social networks may be able to facilitate citizen participatory activities, and thus make it more likely that citizens will accomplish their political goals, but it does not necessarily lead to greater effectiveness or impact on policy outcomes. With the assistance of social networks, citizens are able to mobilize more citizens, gather more resources, or disseminate information more efficiently and effectively. This might lead to more influence over local policy, as is hoped by citizens, or it may have no effect. Either way, when considering the implications of social networks we need to keep in mind that while social networks are an important resource, having and using them does not necessarily mean citizens will have greater influence over public policy decisions.

Citizen Participation: Local and National

I would like to begin my discussion of the difference between local citizen participation and its national counterpart with a premise: Citizens are able to engage in most of the same participatory activities nationally as they do locally, but more resources are needed to leverage those activities to accomplish political goals. Citizens can engage in the activities listed on table 7.4 on any level of government. For example, they can contact both national and local officials, and they can circulate petitions on a federal issue just as well as on a local issue. Although some activities may require additional resources on a national level (e.g., attending a public meeting in Washington, D.C. may require travel costs), many do not: for example, citizens can call their local member of Congress as easily as calling their mayor. Size does not necessarily make activities more costly or more difficult. It does, however, influence the ability of participants to accomplish their political goals. In larger governments, participants need more resources to accomplish goals such as demonstrating popular support for a proposal or applying electoral pressure on officials. Participants need to mobilize more citizens, gather more petition signatures, or prompt more people to call an elected official's office in order to have the desired effect. In larger governments, accomplishing the same goals requires greater amounts of time, money, and effort.

In larger governments, however, citizens have more resources to draw upon. When trying to influence national policy, organizations can recruit participants and solicit funds from throughout the country; when operating on the local level, the options for acquiring resources will likely be geographically constrained. In other words, the resources available to citizen participants increase along with government size. Citizens may need more resources when dealing with national issues, but they may have more resources. Thus, the greater resources needed to participate nationally does not mean that citizens will be less effective when trying to influence national issues nor does it support the contention that citizens are less able to engage in national policy making.

The greater resources needed on the national level do not necessarily act as a barrier to accomplishing their political goals, but they alter the process by which those goals are attained. In Santa Ana, participants drew on their social networks to accomplish political goals, using them to mobilize others, to pool resources with other participants, and to disseminate and collect information. Through these methods, participants organized specific participatory activities into general strategies. Participants in Santa Ana did not just go to meetings and contact officials; they also formulated and enacted strategies for leveraging these activities to attain their political goals.

On the national level, however, the process by which citizens' participatory activities are translated into political goals is done through interest groups. Because more resources are needed on the national level, they need to be assembled and utilized through formal organizations rather than through the more informal means of social networks. For example, take the process of mobilizing a large group to contact an elected official in an effort to demonstrate opposition to a policy proposal. Locally, this effort can be accomplished through participants' social networks. As we saw in Santa Ana, participants recruited others by relying on their personal networks, which might be enough to demonstrate opposition in the community. On a national level, to recruit enough people to make an impact requires more than just the handful of people that can be contacted through social networks: interest groups would need to engage in a direct mail campaign or other such device in order to accomplish this goal. Interest groups still rely on social networks, but they do not use them to accomplish the types of political goals that were described above; the necessities dictated by the extent of resources needed to accomplish these goals prevents them from relying on social networks and instead focus on more impersonal and formal means.

The result is the central difference between local and national citizen participation. On the local level, citizens engage in both participatory activities and political strategies; on the national level, citizens still engage in activities, but the strategic function of using these activities to accomplish political goals is relegated to interest groups. This situation exists because nationally, citizens do not have the resources to perform the latter function, whereas on the local level their social networks and other resources provide the means by which they can accomplish their political goals. Locally, citizens are activists, strategists, and organizers, who engage in a host of political activities to support political strategies that they have formulated and organizational efforts they have undertaken. Nationally, citizens are just activists. They attend meetings, contact officials, and circulate petitions, but do not partake in the development of strategy nor organize participatory activity to obtain political goals.

Nationally, lobbyists or interest group staff performed the strategic and organizing functions. A comparison between the use of social networks by citizens and lobbyists may illuminate the limited participatory role that citizens have on the national level. Lobbyists form social networks with elected officials, agency staff, and other interest parties, which have alternatively been called iron triangles, issue networks, and a host of other names (for an overview, see Berry [1997]). These networks, the literature suggests, greatly enhances lobbyists' capacity by easing the information flow between officials and lobbyists, allowing lobbyists to know when actions are taking place and giving them an opportunity to have their voice heard. It also allows lobbyists to pool their resources with sympathetic legislators, agency officials or others to form effective coalitions. Lobbyists are able to form these networks because they have the time and money to spend on developing them. Campaign contributions help gain access to officials, while full-time lobbyists can spend their entire day talking to other participants and collecting information about policies of interest.

Citizens' activities on the local level are very similar to the activities lobbyists engage in nationally. One study of lobbyist behavior (Schlozman and Tierney 1986, 150–51) found that the two most common activities were testifying at hearings and contacting government officials, analogous to the two activities, attending public meetings and talking to officials, which were most common among participants in Santa Ana. Nationally, however, citizens are unable to move beyond the tactical level of engaging in activities because they lack the resources needed to form the politically valuable social networks that lobbyists rely on. Lobbyists, on the other hand, are able to create these networks because they can invest larger amounts of time and money into the effort. Even though the specific activities that lobbyists perform nationally are the same ones that citizens engage in locally, citizens lack the resources that would enable them to move beyond the tactical level and organize participatory activity into strategies for accomplishing political goals.

In sum, citizen participation on the local and national levels shares some commonalities. The specific activities that citizens engage in are the same: they attend meetings, contact elected officials, circulate petitions, and many others. On a tactical level, participation is not all that different. The difference lies in the process by which all of this activity is organized into a coherent participatory strategy. On the local level, citizens, relying in part on their social networks, formulate political goals and organize their activity to accomplish them. On a national level, interest groups mainly perform these activities, limiting citizens' role as strategists and organizers. This result is due to size: as governments get larger and the amount of resources needed increases, the manner in which participation is coordinated and organized becomes more impersonal. The goals pursued may be the same (mobilizing citizens, disseminating information, etc.), but on a national level citizens have less of a role to play.

These differences lead to a different type of citizen engagement with the policy-making process. Citizens are unable to engage the policy-making process on a national level as lobbyists because they lack the resources to do so. Instead, they will most likely play the role of ideologues, pawns, or perhaps watchdogs. The ability to use social networks as a political resource on the local level opens up the possibility of citizens acting as lobbyists, which they readily take advantage of. This analysis of the use of social networks by participants illustrates how they are able to fill the role of citizen lobbyists. They can perform this role because they can use their social networks as a political resource to accomplish their political goals.

Conclusion

In this chapter, I argue that social networks are a political resource that facilitate citizen participation in local politics. Networks can be used to help citizen attain political goals such as mobilizing other citizens, gathering and disseminating information, pooling resources, and communicating with officials. The presence of social networks and the limited resources needed to participate in local politics allowed citizens in Santa Ana to do more than just engage in isolated political activities. Using their social networks they engaged in a process by which they fashioned a strategy for accomplishing their political goals and organized their participation into a coherent whole. This process is analogous to the functions that lobbyists perform on the national level, providing further evidence to support the citizens-as-lobbyist model as the best representation of how citizens engage the local policy-making process.

PART IV

Conclusion

10 The Practice of Local Democracy

The central goal of this book is to explore how citizens engage the local policy-making process: what is the manner in which citizens attempt to influence local policy? In Santa Ana, citizens attempted to influence policy in the same way as lobbyists: they identify political goals, develop strategies, and engage in a variety of political activities to accomplish their goals. They did not approach the policy-making process as either community problem solvers or ideologues, preferring instead to identify specific issues of direct concern to them. They also were not just pawns of some interest group or elected official; although connected to these groups, they acted independently in terms of defining their agendas and pursuing political goals.

To support the claim that the citizens-as-lobbyists model is the most accurate reflection of how citizens engaged policy making in Santa Ana, I explore the issues in which they participated and how they attempted to influence policy decisions. These are the two basic features of citizen engagement with the policy-making process: the patterns of participation across policies and the form of citizen activity in attempting to influence those policies.

Part II examines what issues citizen lobbyists tried to influence and why. I argue that participation patterns are derivative of the opportunities to participate, the relationship of the policy to values held by participants, and the characteristics of policies themselves. Two policy characteristics in particular—directness and clarity of policy impact—best explain which policies generate citizen participation: citizens are more likely to try to influence those policies that have a direct and clear impact on their lives. Policy impact, rather than a general sense of issue salience, is what drives participation because citizens use it to understand costs and benefits of a policy and whether the policy is important enough to spend the time and effort to try to influence.

The presence of policy entrepreneurs also influenced participation patterns. Entrepreneurs, by framing an issue, developing a policy solution, and formulating a strategy to achieve their objective, create and structure opportunities to participate, which provides an incentive for citizens to participate. Local newspapers, however, had minimal impact on the behavior of participants because the coverage was too late and did not provide the information citizens needed to participate. Further, active citizens had other sources of information (primarily social networks and personal experience) that reduced their dependence on newspapers for information. Finally, policies relevant to the urban visions debate were more likely to generate participation, much of which was geared toward promoting a vision of the "good city." The urban visions debate was a central social conflict in Santa Ana, but other cities may have different conflicts that influence participation patterns. The general point here is that participation patterns are influenced by social conflicts, which can prompt citizens to participate on related policies.

As for how citizens participate, they took a multifaceted approach to lobbying local government. Citizens did not stress traditional pressure tactics, such as petitions, protests, and letter-writing campaigns, preferring to utilize other avenues of participation. As far as formal ways to participate, citizens made good use of public meetings, which was the most common activity among participants. Speaking at city council and school board meetings allowed participants to accomplish a host of political goals, such as providing information to officials, criticizing officials, and agenda setting. The many functions that speaking at public meetings serve, along with its relative ease, accounts for why it is was so common.

Informal communication, among participants as well as between participants and officials, also played a crucial role. Contacts between participants and officials (both elected and non-elected) were frequent, despite some complaints that officials were not accessible. Participants also utilized their many organizational affiliations to communicate with other active citizens. These social networks were a valuable resource because they helped participants accomplish their political goals. Without social networks, citizens would have had fewer opportunities to participate and encountered more difficulty in taking advantage of the opportunities that were open to them. Another important aspect of participatory activity on the local level is that citizens have the opportunity to strategize and not just engage in isolated activities. Participants did not just speak at a meeting or add their name to a petition; they were also members of groups that developed strategies for accomplishing political goals. This fact distinguishes local political participation from much participation on the national level, where citizens partake in efforts coordinated by existing organization in which they have no direct input. Rather than just following orders, participants performed the functions that lobbyists perform on the national level: they formulated a strategy and engaged in specific activities to carry out that strategy. To do so, participants relied heavily on their social networks for information and coordination with others active in local politics was a primary means of engaging in political activity.

The patterns and forms of citizen participation in Santa Ana support the citizens-as-lobbyists model described in Chapter 1. Citizens identified issues that were highly salient based on the impact on their daily lives, and lobbied government to influence those issues. The types of issues they pursued and the activities they engaged in were similar to the activities of lobbyists. They engaged the policy process in the same way as lobbyists, with a set of political goals on specific issues of concern. The motivation may have been different (lobbyists get paid to accomplish their goals, whereas citizens pursue issues of importance to them), but the form and pattern of their participation were the same.

Citizen Lobbyists: An Assessment

The ultimate goal of studying citizen participation is to assess its impact on politics and to determine whether it enhances democratic practices in the American political system. To conclude, I examine the benefits and drawbacks of citizen efforts to lobby local government: What benefits are derived from this form of participation and what are its limitations?

The Benefits of Citizen Lobbying Activity

Given citizen lobbyists' immersion in political strategizing, mobilization activity, and the extensive communication between themselves and officials, their political activity serves as a means through which they can learn about the political process. Unlike some of the other ways citizens could potentially engage the policy process, when they do so as lobbyists they place themselves in a position where they can learn about the workings of government. Because they are doing more than just partaking in isolated acts of participation, citizens are able to see how the policy-making process works. For example, one participant made this comment after explaining her efforts to improve a neighborhood park:

> For a playground, imagine, it's about $300,000, and half of it is because of the new disabled requirements and regulations that they have to have in the flooring for safety. It's mind boggling. In fact, I can't even tell you the things that I have to sit through in the committee, that we had to choose, because of all the legislations that have been put in, and that we have to learn what kind of materials that are needed in the playground. You know, when you are sitting there, you're just thinking I want this and this, but by law, you have to do this and this. And the city only has so much money for so many things, and they run out. . . . They [the City's Parks and Recreation Department] told us, well, you know, we only have so much [money], and it will be two or three years before we can do this, or because we have a shortage because of the Orange County bankruptcy. You know, there is so much that people don't realize from the bankruptcy that's taken away from so many things. And I had no idea. You certainly do learn a lot about where our monies come to do some of these projects.

This learning process results from citizens developing political goals and pursuing them through the activities discussed in Chapter 7. Particularly important for this process is the informal communication between participants and officials, as well as the communication among participants, both of which are a means through which citizens learned about politics and policy making. Engaging in political activity does not necessarily foster a learning experience. For example, a citizen who attended a public hearing might not learn anything about policy making; the simple act of attending a hearing, joining a protest, or signing a petition does not expose citizens to much political information. But citizen lobbyists do more than partake in isolated political acts. They move a step beyond that and work with others to develop political strategies to accomplish their goals. It is this activity, where citizens are communicating with others and exchanging information, that provides a real opportunity for citizens to develop their understanding of how the political system works.

Engaging in participatory activities can also enhance civic skills. Speaking at a public meeting, organizing a neighborhood event, or doing many of the other common activities all provide citizens an opportunity to increase skills that are valuable in pursuing their political goals. Most forms of engagement with the policy-making process will provide opportunities for citizens to develop their political skills. So community problem solvers, watchdogs, or even pawns of interest groups will have opportunities to develop civic skills. However, the manner in which citizens engage policy making will influence which civic skills are developed. For citizen lobbyists, networking, organizing, and public speaking skills are the ones that are most likely to be enhanced.

In addition to helping citizens learn about politics and develop civic skills, engaging the policy-making process can also augment social capital. Putnam (2000) suggests that when people are embedded in social networks and interact with others, their trust of others will increase and norms of reciprocity will develop. Although we do not have the data to conclusively demonstrate that social capital was enhanced due to citizen lobbying efforts, we can at least say that the manner in which citizens participated made this outcome very likely. We saw in the previous chapter that citizens use social networks as a political resource, and much of their political activity involved working with other citizens or with officials to accomplish their goals. Further, in Chapter 7 we saw that participants frequently work within community groups (such as neighborhood associations) in their participatory efforts. If social capital theorists are correct, this activity should result in an increase in the stock of social capital. Because they used social networks extensively and worked within community groups, participants should develop a greater sense of trust of their fellow citizens and feel more attached to their community. Citizen lobbyists participated in the types of activities that social capital theorists predict will enhance social capital. Most forms of engagement with the policy-making process will likely have salutary effects on social capital, but the citizen lobbyist role (along with community problem solvers) is particularly beneficial because of the extensive use of social networks and activity within community groups.

The fourth benefit of citizen lobbying efforts is that it provides an additional outlet through which citizens can have their voice heard. Citizens have many opportunities to express their policy preferences, such as through elections or public opinion polls. Engaging the policy making process directly is an alternative way. There are downsides to this method, particularly in terms of participation bias. Participants are frequently not representative of the public at large, and their policy views may not be shared by the wider public. Citizen lobbying may distort policy outcomes in favor of a minority rather than making policy more congruent with public wishes. Thus, there may not be any benefit to the policy-making process itself. However, there are benefits to citizen lobbyists. Even if participation results in biased policy outcomes, it still provides citizens with an additional means of expressing opinions and policy preferences. They are not always successful in accomplishing their political goals, but engagement with the policy-making process provides an outlet where they can attempt to influence public policy.

The Limits of Citizen Lobbying

Citizen lobbying efforts can benefit participants, but they have less value for the policy-making process itself. The activities of citizen lobbyists did not increase the problem-solving capacity of local governments, the reason for which has less to do with participants' activities and more to do with the types of issues that citizens choose to influence.

A basic fact of citizen participation is that citizens need to specialize. Wildavsky (1979, 256–7) perhaps explained it best with his story of "Mr. and Mrs. Model Citizen" who, rather than specializing in one or two issues, attempt to participate on all issues. One night they focus on public safety, the next night air pollution, the third mental health, and so forth. Yet the demands of keeping up with everything take a toll on their private lives. Mr. Model Citizen loses his job because of missing work to attend public meetings, and their children, for whom they have little time given their exten sive civic activities, choose the path of criminal behavior, landing both of them in jail. "To sacrifice private life on the altar of citizen participation seems excessive," comments Wildavsky (1979, 257), and he concludes that having citizens specialize in one or two issues is both necessary and desirable. He suggests that citizens read broadly about current events and participate in those that are of most interest to them.

When citizens decide to participate, what policies do they attempt to influence? The process by which citizens choose their specialties is different than Wildavsky's suggestion that citizens simply pick an issue that interests them. Citizens' participatory decisions involve an assessment of issue salience, which is heavily influenced by the directness and clarity of a policy's impact. Citizens' decisions as to how to specialize is not just a matter of acting on those issues one finds "important," but rather involves a process by which importance is defined and the feasibility of action is assessed. In general, participants defined "important issues" as ones that had direct and clear impact on their everyday lives.

The manner in which citizens decided how to specialize led to a participation pattern featuring extensive activity on neighborhood issues rather than issues with a citywide impact. As we saw in Chapter 3, land use and transportation issues were commonly the focus of lobbying efforts, with less activity on issues such as the city budget. The issues that generated participation were usually narrowly defined and focused on specific governmental decisions, which is largely a function of the influence of directness and clarity on participatory choices. Policies with a direct and clear impact are typically narrowly defined neighborhood issues. Because citizen lobbyists gravitated toward specializing in issues that had a direct and clear impact, most of the policies that generated participation in Santa Ana were of this type rather than issues with a broader, citywide impact.

The manner in which citizens specialized and the issues they chose to influence limited the benefits of their participation for the policy-making process. Specifically, because citizen lobbyists generally focused on narrow neighborhood issues, they did not contribute to the problem-solving capacity of local government. When officials try to address difficult policy problems, they sometimes need the additional resources that citizens can bring in order to formulate effective policy. One of the benefits of participation often cited by scholars is its ability to bring additional resources to the policy-making process (Weeks 2000; Fischer 1993; Durning 1993). Some of the common resources that citizens can provide include information about the nature of the problem, ideas for addressing the problem, and how the community would respond to the implementation of specific solutions. For many issues, officials need to know the information that citizens have to fully understand the problem and develop innovative solutions. In this way, citizen participation can increase the problem-solving capacity of local governments: When citizens participate, local governments are better able to address policy issues because officials have additional resources at their disposal.

On many of the issues citizens attempted to influence, however, government did not need the resources citizens could bring to the process. The issues they chose to influence typically were neither complex nor complicated, and elected officials could easily deal with them without citizen assistance. Although citizen lobbyists brought some information to the policy-making process, for the most part, officials had the information they needed to address the issues at hand. If we think about the issues that generated the most participation in Santa Ana—neighborhood traffic plans, the space-saver school, and other land use and transportation issues—the only real information that citizens provided to officials concerned the amount of support and/or opposition to the proposed course of action. Because these issues were relatively clear and not that complicated, officials did not need additional information from citizens.

Thus, the way that citizens specialized limited their ability to enhance government's problem-solving capacity. Citizens could engage the policy-making process in a way that would bring additional resources to the table. In particular, they could perform the role of collaborative problem solvers, addressing difficult and complex issues facing the community. With this approach to policy making, citizens would be in a better position to contribute to governmental problem-solving capacity. As citizen lobbyists, they did not focus on issues where this potential was fully realized.

This description of the limited value of citizen lobbying efforts for enhancing governmental problem-solving capacity is not meant as a criticism of either the participants or this form of political activity. Rather, it is meant to clarify the role and function that it performs. Citizen lobbying efforts served important functions within the local governmental system by providing a venue where citizens could learn about politics, develop civic skills, build social capital, and have their voice heard on issues of importance to them. However, its value was limited by the types of issues citizens attempted to influence. Understanding this dynamic can help us develop realistic expectations for this form of political activity. Providing citizens the opportunity to participate in the policy-making process is necessary because of the benefits that accrue to participants. But if we desire to increase local government's problem-solving capacity through participation, we need to develop alternative means to do so. The literature is replete with proposals to accomplish this goal through institutions such as deliberative forums, citizens juries, and electronic town hall meetings. The merits of these proposals are beyond the scope of this book. The point here is that if we desire to enhance government's problem-solving capacity, we need to look beyond the traditional means of citizen engagement with the policy-making process described here.

In sum, this book explores the manner in which citizens engage the policy-making process. I argue that the best way to characterize citizens' role is that of a lobbyist. Citizens participate in policy making in the same manner as lobbyists: defining an agenda, developing political goals, and partaking in a variety of activities to accomplish their objectives. They sometimes play other roles, such as community problem solvers or ideologues; however, the dominant mode of engagement is that of citizen lobbyist. There are benefits and limits to this form of participation, and we should be careful to put it in proper perspective. Engagement with the policy-making process is one way citizens can get politically involved, but there are others that have their own set of benefits and drawbacks. If we desire to enhance local democracy, we need to understand what functions different forms of participation can perform, so that we can develop ways to accomplish the democratic goals we seek to achieve.

Appendix

Policies Discussed by Interview Respondents

Policy	Policy area	Mentions
Anti-gang activities	Public safety	1
Antitobacco programs	Other—city	1
Artesia-Pilar playground improvements	Parks and rec.	1
Arts budget in schools	Arts programs	1
Arts movement	Arts programs	3
Bilingual education	School instruction	2
Broadway P-BID	Economic dev.	1
Busing kids to Greenville	Other—school district	1
Centerline (light rail)	Transportation	6
City jail/utility tax	Public safety	2
Citywide redevelopment	Economic dev.	2
Code enforcement	Code enforcement	2
Commercial vehicles code	Code enforcement	3
Condemnation of apartment complex at 2828 N. Bristol	Land use	1
Construction of Centennial Park School	New schools	1
Creation of Historic Resources Commission	Historic preservation	1
Delhi Park Improvements	Parks and rec.	2
Density standards	Housing/overcrowding	1
Eldridge Park improvements	Parks and rec.	1
Empowerment Zone	Economic dev.	4
Extended school year	School instruction	1
Fiesta Patrias (request for city support)	Other—city	1
Floral Park traffic plan	Transportation	2
French Park historical district	Historical preservation	1
French Park traffic plan	Transportation	3
Fundamental schools	School instruction	1
Graffiti removal	Other—city	1
Greenville after-school tutoring	School instruction	1
Hiring of new school superintendent	Personnel	1
Housing issues	Housing/overcrowding	1
Howe-Waffle House preservation	Historical preservation	2
Infrastructure improvements	Transportation	1
Inoperable vehicles	Code enforcement	1

Policy	Policy area	Mentions
Library book budget	Parks and rec.	1
Logan neighborhood rezoning	Land use	1
MacArthur Place mitigation	Land use	2
Main Street pawn shop	Land use	1
McFadden School stoplight	Public safety	1
Measure C	Measure C	11
Minnie Street revitalization/safety	Economic dev.	1
Morrison Park playground improvements	Parks and rec.	1
Northgate Market, French Park	Land use	1
Office tower at One Broadway Plaza	Land use	2
Opposition to the level of compensation for the city manager	Personnel	1
Overcrowding	Housing/overcrowding	3
Permit parking	Transportation	1
Police patrols on Fourth Street	Public safety	1
Police shooting of Jose Campos	Public safety	1
Proposal for a new city library	Parks and rec.	1
Proposed new school on Farmers Drive	New schools	4
Proposed Sports Arena at Eddie West Field (Westdome)	Land use	1
Pushcart regulations	Business regulation	2
Rancho Santiago College swap meet	Land use	1
Redistricting	Other—city	1
Refuse collection contract	Other—city	1
Santa Anita Park improvements	Parks and rec.	1
School uniforms	Other—school district	1
Shelley's liquor license	Business regulation	2
Space-saver school	New schools	7
Special education	School instruction	2
Summer stock	Arts programs	1
Taft School traffic mitigation	Transportation	2
Various police issues	Public safety	1
Veterans drug rehabilitation center at 921 N. Bewley	Land use	1
Washington Square traffic plan	Transportation	2
Wilshire Square lights	Other—city	1
Wilshire Square traffic plan	Transportation	4
Wilshire Square trees	Other—city	1
Wilshire Square vacant lot reuse (garden)	Other—city	1
Total		121

Notes

Chapter One

1. A fifty-sixth respondent asked to do the interview over e-mail. He filled out a questionnaire, but the answers were so short (usually only a few words) that they were not very valuable. The only answers that were used were from Part I, which did not require extensive descriptions.

2. I did not collect extensive demographic information on respondents, although there were some obvious biases. In a city where the majority of residents are renters, almost all of the respondents were homeowners. Also, Hispanics were underrepresented among respondents.

3. The city council generally reported letters received, while the school district did not report any letters.

Chapter Two

1. According to Verba, Schlozman, and Brady (1995), this was the first time that a survey asked this follow-up question.

2. For example, take a community that has a problem with underperforming schools. Typically, in this situation, citizens will lobby government to take action, such as spending more money or reforming the curriculum. From a public acting perspective, citizens would deliberate over what they could do themselves to address the problem, and then act accordingly by, for instance, volunteering at the schools or organizing after-school programs.

3. Ferman (1996) adds that the institutional structure of a city also influences the receptiveness of regimes to citizen participation.

Chapter Three

1. This sentiment was expressed often during participant interviews.

2. For ease of presentation, some similar decisions were combined into one entry if the decisions were on the same topic and made within a few weeks of each other. This accounts for the slight discrepancy between Tables 3.3 and 3.4 in number of policies with over thirty speakers.

3. Measure C was included even though it is an election issue, because it constitutes an attempt to influence a specific local policy.

4. The exception here is bilingual education, mentioned by a few respondents and categorized under school instruction.

5. The list of tools is based on Salamon's (2002, 21) list of common tools, modified to accommodate the local context of this study.

6. Redevelopment policy can have direct impact if council decisions pertain to the condemnation of specific properties.

7. Supporters made lists of improvements that the bond money was going to be used for to make the impacts even clearer. Opponents generally argued that the school board was too corrupt to handle the money wisely and that money could be found elsewhere for the needed repairs.

8. The perception of participants here is more important than the reality of policy impact. Because we are discussing why citizens participate on some issues and not others, the perceptions of participants is what matters.

9. A supporter of the traffic plan argued that the traffic negatively affected the value of her home, although any impact it had was minor.

Chapter Four

1. Most of the analysis is based on interviews with entrepreneurs themselves. Additional information came from other interview respondents and newspaper accounts.

2. All names of participants are pseudonyms.

3. This is the "Main Street pawn shop" issue listed in Table 3.4.

4. The types of activities that Mathews (1999) calls "public acting" and Boyte and Kari (1996) call "public work."

5. For more on the impact of immigration in Santa Ana, see Harwood and Myers (2002).

6. The proliferation of commercial vehicles on residential streets was not a result of overcrowding per se, but rather of the fact that many of Santa Ana's neighborhoods are populated by working-class citizens who drive these vehicles for a living and park them at home when they are not working. That said, code enforcement generally was an issue because of overcrowding, and the only reason that commercial vehicles became an issue is because neighborhood leaders were trying to find ways to reduce visual blight.

7. The citywide redevelopment plan is discussed in Chapter 8.

Chapter Five

1. These arguments are similar to those outlined by Conway (2000).

2. These are rough figures, as the database searches may not have turned up every article that was relevant to Santa Ana politics.

3. The electronic database for *La Opinion* does not go back further than 1992.

4. For city ordinances, the first reading was used as the decision date because second readings are typically pro forma.

5. The school district does not have a standing committee system similar to the city's.

6. "The Art of Revitalization." *Orange County Register*, August 20, 1998, A1.

7. There was one respondent who mentioned that she served on a pedestrian safety ad hoc committee created by the City, but she did not list pedestrian safety as one of the issues she spent the most time and effort on.

8. For example, the 1993 city council decision on the Floral Park traffic plan had thirty-five speakers and over four hundred letters to the council, but had only three newspaper articles.

9. Both the *Los Angeles Times–Orange County Edition* and the *Orange County Register* cover local politics in over thirty cities.

Chapter Six

1. City-as-suburb proponents also supported the artists' village, although their support, at times, wavered. For example, many complained about a coffeehouse that featured live music and "Graffiti art," arguing that it was disruptive to the surrounding neighborhoods. The City eventually took steps to ameliorate the situation, much to the chagrin of cosmopolitans, who saw the coffeehouse as a place where youth could express themselves artistically.

2. For example, at one point there was a controversy over what some perceived as pornographic art being displayed in the artists' village.

3. See Harwood and Myers (2002) for more on Santa Ana's efforts in this regard.

4. The supermarket was eventually built, although slightly smaller to accommodate the adjacent neighborhood.

5. Whether, in fact, the city was giving preferential treatment to Shelley's is questionable. No Hispanic-owned Fourth Street restaurants applied for similar licenses because they were under the impression that they would be denied. Where this impression came from is uncertain. Shelley's opponents claim that it was a logical conclusion given past actions of the City, but supporters contend that if Hispanic-owned restaurants had applied for licenses, they would have received similar treatment.

Chapter Seven

1. The question asked whether they engaged in the activity "once," "more than once," or "never." Because the "once" response was not common, it was combined with the "more than once" category into a simple "yes" response.

2. Many respondents had a broad conception of "protest" to include not just street protests but also attending public meetings en masse and other activities where a large group assembled to oppose a governmental action.

3. The unit of analysis is the 121 policies identified by respondents. Thus, the way to read Table 7.4 is that for each activity listed, there are X number of policies for which a respondent mentioned that they engaged in that activity. For example, for 61 out of the 121 policies, a respondent mentioned he or she attended or spoke at a public meeting.

4. Whether a respondent talked face to face with an official or wrote a letter was more a matter of personal preference than a tactical choice.

5. Especially common were complaints that officials who disagreed with the respondent were not accessible.

6. Networking with officials, however, was not included in this category (it was categorized under "contacting").

7. The types of organizing needed to get out the vote is a little different than for influencing local policy through nonelectoral means. The Measure C campaign involved greater efforts to disseminate arguments for and against the measure, leading to greater use of the media and neighborhood canvassing. But the fundamentals of the organizing campaign—drawing on existing relationships to gather support—were the same.

Chapter Eight

1. I do not know the TV ratings for city council meetings, but I imagine very few people watch them. At the same time, those who do watch are most likely to be those who are politically active, which explains the significant reaction to this meeting.

2. This observation is based on the comments of opponents who were interviewed for this study.

3. Citywide redevelopment had its supporters, but they did not show up at the public meeting because they assumed that the proposal would pass without much fanfare or controversy.

Chapter Nine

1. For examples, see Morris (1984) and Warren (2001).

References

Adkins-Covert, Tawna, Denise P. Ferguson, Selene Phillips, and Philo C. Washburn. 2000. "News in My Backyard: Media and Democracy in an 'All American' City." *Sociological Quarterly* 41 (2):227–44.

Alex-Assensoh, Yvette, and A. B. Assensoh. 2001. "Inner-City Contexts, Church Attendance, and African American Political Participation." *Journal of Politics* 63 (3):886–901.

Alex-Assensoh, Yvette M. 1998. *Neighborhoods, Family, and Political Behavior in Urban America*. New York: Garland Reference Library of Social Science.

Altshuler, Alan. 1970. *Community Control: The Black Demand for Participation in Large American Cities*. Indianapolis, IN: Pegasus.

America Speaks. 2002. "Taking Democracy to Scale: Reconnecting Citizens with National Policy through Public Deliberation." Paper presented at the Taking Democracy to Scale conference, Warrenton, VA.

Anderson, Barbara A., and Brian D. Silver. 1986. "Measurement and Mismeasurement of the Validity of the Self-Reported Vote." *American Journal of Political Science* 30 (4):771–85.

Bachrach, Peter, and Morton S. Baratz. 1962. "Two Faces of Power." *American Political Science Review* 61 (4):947–52.

Bass, Sandra. 2000. "Negotiating Change: Community Organizations and the Politics of Policing." *Urban Affairs Review* 32 (2):148–77.

Berman, Evan M. 1997. "Dealing with Cynical Citizens." *Public Administration Review* 57 (2):105–12.

Berry, Jeffrey M. 1997. *The Interest Group Society*. 3rd ed. New York: Longman.

Berry, Jeffrey M., Kent E. Portney, and Ken Thomson. 1993. *The Rebirth of Urban Democracy*. Washington, DC: Brookings.

Bobo, Lawrence, and Franklin D. Gilliam Jr. 1990. "Race, Sociopolitical Participation, and Black Empowerment." *American Political Science Review* 84 (2):377–93.

Bockmeyer, Janice L. 2000. "A Culture of Distrust: The Impact of Local Political Culture on Participation in the Detroit EZ." *Urban Studies* 37 (13):2417–40.

Booth, John A., and Patricia Bayer Richard. 1998. "Civic Society, Political Capital, and Democratization in Central America." *Journal of Politics* 60 (3):780–800.

Boyte, Harry C. 1989. *CommonWealth: A Return to Citizen Politics*. New York: Free Press.

———. 2004. *Everyday Politics*. Philadelphia: University of Pennsylvania Press.

Boyte, Harry C., and Nancy N. Kari. 1996. *Building America: The Democratic Promise of Public Work*. Philadelphia: Temple University Press.

Brady, Henry E., Sidney Verba, and Kay Lehman Schlozman. 1995. "Beyond SES: A Resource Model of Political Participation." *American Political Science Review* 89 (2):271–94.

Brehm, John, and Wendy Rahn. 1997. "Individual-Level Evidence for the Causes and Consequences of Social Capital." *American Journal of Political Science* 41 (3):999–1023.

Briffault, Richard. 1990a. "Our Localism: Part I–The Structure of Local Government Law." *Columbia Law Review* 90 (1):1–115.

———. 1990b. "Our Localism: Part II–Localism and Legal Theory." *Columbia Law Review* 90 (2):346–454.

Brown, Steven D. 1982. "The Explanation of Particularized Contacting: A Comparison of Models." *Urban Affairs Quarterly* 18 (2):217–34.

Bryan, Frank. 2004. *Real Democracy*. Chicago: University of Chicago Press.

Bryan, Frank, and John McClaughry. 1989. *The Vermont Papers: Recreating Democracy on a Human Scale*. Chelsea, VT: Chelsea Green.

Burr, Jeffrey A., Francis G. Caro, and Jennifer Moorhead. 2002. "Productive Aging and Citizen Participation." *Journal of Aging Studies* 16:87–105.

Calhoun-Brown, Allison. 1996. "African-American Churches and Political Mobilization: The Psychological Impact of Organizational Resources." *Journal of Politics* 58 (4):935–53.

California Attorney General's Office. 2002. "The Brown Act: Open Meetings for Local Legislative Bodies." Informational Pamphlet.

Charity, Arthur. 1995. *Doing Public Journalism*. New York: Guildford Press.

Checkoway, Barry. 1981. "The Politics of Public Hearings." *Journal of Applied Behavioral Science* 17 (4):566–82.

Chess, Caron, and Kristen Purcell. 1999. "Public Participation and the Environment: Do We Know What Works?" *Environmental Science and Technology* 33 (16):2685–92.

Cnaan, Ram A. 1991. "Neighborhood-Representing Organizations: How Democratic Are They?" *Social Service Review* 65 (4):614–34.

Cohen, Cathy J., and Michael C. Dawson. 1993. "Neighborhood Poverty and African American Politics." *American Political Science Review* 87 (2):286–302.

Cole, Richard L., and David Caputo. 1984. "The Public Hearing as an Effective Citizen Participation Mechanism: A Case Study of the General Revenue Sharing Program." *American Political Science Review* 78:404–16.

Conway, M. Margaret. 2000. *Political Participation in the United States*. 3rd ed. Washington, DC: CQ Press.

Coulter, Philip B. 1992. "There's a Madness in the Method: Redefining Citizen Contacting of Government Officials." *Urban Affairs Quarterly* 28 (2):297–315.

Cox, Kevin R. 1982. "Housing Tenure and Neighborhood Activism." *Urban Affairs Quarterly* 18 (1):107–29.

Crenson, Matthew A. 1971. *The Un-Politics of Air Pollution: A Study of Non-Decisionmaking in the Cities.* Baltimore: Johns Hopkins University Press.
————. 1983. *Neighborhood Politics.* Cambridge, MA: Harvard University Press.
Crosby, Ned, Janet M. Kelly, and Paul Schaefer. 1986. "Citizens Panels: A New Approach to Citizen Participation." *Public Administration Review* 46 (2):170–78.
Dahl, Robert A. 1961. *Who Governs? Democracy and Power in an American City.* New Haven, CT: Yale University Press.
————. 1967. "The City in the Future of Democracy." *American Political Science Review* 61 (4):953–70.
DeLeon, Peter. 1995. "Democratic Values and the Policy Sciences." *American Journal of Political Science* 39 (4):886–905.
————. 1997. *Democracy and the Policy Sciences.* Albany: State University of New York Press.
DeLeon, Richard Edward. 1992. *Left Coast City: Progressive Politics in San Francisco, 1975–1991.* Lawrence: University of Kansas Press.
Delgado, Gary. 1985. *Organizing the Movement: The Roots and Growth of ACORN.* Philadelphia: Temple University Press.
De Tocqueville, Alexis. 1956. *Democracy in America.* New York: Penguin. (Orig. pub. 1835.)
Doble Research Associates. 2000a. *Our Nation's Kids: Is Something Wrong?* Report prepared for the Kettering Foundation, Dayton, OH.
————. 2000b. *Public Schools: Are They Making the Grade?* Report prepared for the Kettering Foundation, Dayton, OH.
————. 2001. *Money and Politics: Who Owns Democracy?* Report prepared for the Kettering Foundation, Dayton, OH.
Dreier, Peter, John Mollenkopf, and Todd Swanstrom. 2001. *Place Matters: Metropolitics for the Twenty-First Century.* Lawrence: University of Kansas Press.
Durning, Dan (1993). "Participatory Policy Analysis in a Social Service Agency: A Case Study." *Journal of Policy Analysis and Management* 12:297–322.
Dryzek, John S. 1990. *Discursive Democracy.* Cambridge, UK: Cambridge University Press.
Eksterowicz, Anthony J., and Robert N. Roberts. 2000. *Public Journalism and Political Knowledge.* New York: Rowman & Littlefield.
Elkin, Stephen L. 1985. "Twentieth Century Urban Regimes." *Journal of Urban Affairs* 7:11–28.
————. 1987. *City and Regime in the American Republic.* Chicago: University of Chicago Press.
Erbring, Lutz, Edie N. Goldenberg, and Arthur H. Miller. 1980. "Front-Page News and Real-World Cues: A New Look at Agenda-Setting by the Media." *American Journal of Political Science* 24 (1):16–49.
Fantini, Mario, Marilyn Gittell, and Richard Magat. 1970. *Community Control and the Urban School.* New York: Praeger.

Ferman, Barbara. 1996. *Challenging the Growth Machine: Neighborhood Politics in Chicago and Pittsburgh*. Lawrence: University of Kansas Press.

Fischer, Frank. 1993. "Citizen Participation and the Democratization of Policy Expertise: From Theoretical Inquiry to Practical Cases." *Policy Sciences* 26:165–87.

Fishkin, James S. 1991. *Democracy and Deliberation: New Directions for Democratic Reform*. New Haven, CT: Yale University Press.

———. 1995. *The Voice of the People: Public Opinion and Democracy*. New Haven, CT: Yale University Press.

Freudenburg, William R., and Susan K. Pastor. 1992. "NIMBYs and LULUs: Stalking the Syndromes." *Journal of Social Issues* 48 (4):39–61.

Fuchs, Ester R., Lorraine C. Minnite, and Robert Y. Shapiro. 2000. "Political Capital and Political Participation." Paper presented at the American Political Science Association Annual Meeting, Washington, D.C.

Garreau, Joel. 1991. *Edge City: Life on the New Frontier*. New York: Doubleday.

Gastil, John, and Todd Kelshaw. 2000. "Public Meetings: A Sampler of Deliberative Forums that Bring Officeholders and Citizens Together." Draft prepared for the Kettering Foundation.

Gaventa, John. 1980. *Power and Powerlessness: Quiescence and Rebellion in an Appalachian Valley*. Urbana: University of Illinois Press.

Gaziano, Cecilie. 1985. "Neighborhood Newspapers and Neighborhood Leaders: Influences on Agenda Setting and Definitions of Issues." *Communication Research* 12 (4):568–94.

Giles, Michael W., Douglas F. Gatlin, and Everett F. Cataldo. 1976. "Parental Support for School Referenda." *Journal of Politics* 38 (2):442–51.

Gittell, Marilyn. 1972. *Local Control in Education: Three Demonstration School Districts in New York City*. New York: Praeger.

———. 1980. *Limits to Citizen Participation: The Decline of Community Organizations*. Beverly Hills, CA: Sage.

Gittell, Marilyn, Kathe Newman, Janice Bockmeyer, and Robert Lindsay. 1998. "Expanding Civic Opportunity: Urban Empowerment Zones." *Urban Affairs Review* 33 (4):530–58.

Gormley, William T. 1986. "The Representation Revolution: Reforming State Regulation through Public Representation." *Administration and Society* 18 (2):179–96.

Granovetter, Mark S. 1973. "The Strength of Weak Ties." *American Journal of Sociology* 78 (6):1360–80.

Greenberg, Anna. 2000. "The Church and the Revitalization of Politics and Community." *Political Science Quarterly* 115 (3):377–94.

Greenstone, J. David, and Paul E. Peterson. 1973. *Race and Authority in Urban Politics: Community Participation and the War on Poverty*. Chicago: University of Chicago Press.

Grodzins, Morton. 1966. *The American System: A New View of Government in the United States*. Chicago: Rand McNally.

Gundry, Kathleen G., and Thomas A. Heberlein. 1984. "Do Public Meetings Represent the Public?" *Journal of the American Planning Association* 50 (2):175–82.

Haas, Lisbeth. 1991. "Grass-Roots Protest and the Politics of Planning: Santa Ana, 1976–88." In *Postsuburban California: The Transformation of Orange County since World War II*, ed. Rob Kling, Spencer Olin, and Mark Poster, 254–80. Berkeley: University of California Press.

Haeberle, Steven H. 1989. *Planting the Grassroots: Structuring Citizen Participation*. New York: Praeger.

Haight, David, and Clare Ginger. 2000. "Trust and Understanding in Participatory Policy Analysis: The Case of the Vermont Forest Resources Advisory Council." *Policy Studies Journal* 28 (4):739–59.

Harris, Frederick C. 1994. "Something Within: Religion as a Mobilizer of African-American Political Activism." *Journal of Politics* 56 (1):42–68.

Harwood Group. 1991. *Citizens and Politics: A View from Main Street America*. Report prepared for the Kettering Foundation, Dayton, OH.

Harwood, Stacy, and Dowell Myers. 2002. "The Dynamics of Immigration and Local Governance in Santa Ana." *Policy Studies Journal* 30 (1):70–91.

Hero, Rodney E. 1986. "Explaining Citizen-Initiated Contacting of Government Officials: Socioeconomic Status, Perceived Need or Something Else?" *Social Science Quarterly* 67:626–35.

Hero, Rodney E., and Anne G. Campbell. 1996. "Understanding Latino Political Participation: Exploring the Evidence from the Latino Political Survey." *Hispanic Journal of Behavioral Sciences* 18 (2):129–41.

Hirlinger, Michael W. 1992. "Citizen-Initiated Contacting of Local Government Officials: A Multivariate Explanation." *Journal of Politics* 54 (2):553–64.

Hirschman, Albert O. 1970. *Exit, Voice and Loyalty: Responses to Decline in Firms, Organizations and States*. Cambridge, MA: Harvard University Press.

Hunter, Floyd. 1953. *Community Power Structure: A Study of Decision Makers*. Chapel Hill: University of North Carolina Press.

Jennings, M. Kent, and Gregory B. Markus. 1988. "Political Involvement in the Latter Years: A Longitudinal Survey." *American Journal of Political Science* 32:302–16.

Jones, Bryan D., Saadia R. Greenberg, Clifford Kaufman, and Joseph Drew. 1977. "Bureaucratic Response to Citizen-Initiated Contracts: Environmental Enforcement in Detroit." *American Political Science Review* 71 (1):148–65.

Kaniss, Phyllis. 1991. *Making Local News*. Chicago: University of Chicago Press.

Kathlene, Lyn, and John A. Martin. 1991. "Enhancing Citizen Participation: Panel Designs, Perspectives, and Policy Formation." *Journal of Policy Analysis and Management* 10 (1):46–63.

Kemmis, Daniel. 1990. *Community and the Politics of Place*. Norman: University of Oklahoma Press.

Kemp, Ray. 1985. "Planning, Public Meetings and the Politics of Discourse." In *Critical Theory and Public Life*, ed. John Forester, 177–201. Cambridge, MA: MIT Press.

King, Cheryl Simrell, Kathryn M. Feltey, and Bridget O'Neill Susel. 1998. "The Question of Participation: Towards Authentic Public Participation in Public Administration." *Public Administration Review* 58 (4):317–26.

Kingdon, John W. 1995. *Agendas, Alternatives, and Public Policies*. (2nd ed.). New York: HarperCollins College Publishers.

Kweit, Mary Grisez, and Robert W. Kweit. 1981. *Implementing Citizen Participation in a Bureaucratic Society*. New York: Praeger.

Lake, Ronald La Due, and Robert Huckfeldt. 1998. "Social Capital, Social Networks, and Political Participation." *Political Psychology* 19 (3):567–84.

LaNoue, George R., and Bruce L. R. Smith. 1973. *The Politics of School Decentralization*. Lexington, MA: Lexington Books.

Lawless, Jennifer L., and Richard L. Fox. 2001. "Political Participation of the Urban Poor." *Social Problems* 48 (3):362–85.

Leal, David L. 2002. "Political Participation by Latino Non-Citizens in the United States." *British Journal of Political Science* 32:353–70.

Leighley, Jan. 1996. "Group Membership and the Mobilization of Political Participation." *Journal of Politics* 58 (2):447–63.

Leighley, Jan E. 1995. "Attitude, Opportunities and Incentives: A Field Essay on Political Participation." *Political Research Quarterly* 48 (1):181–209.

Leighley, Jan E., and Arnold Vedlitz. 1999. "Race, Ethnicity, and Political Participation: Competing Models and Contrasting Explanations." *Journal of Politics* 61 (4):1092–114.

Logan, John R., and Harvey L. Molotch. 1987. *Urban Fortunes: The Political Economy of Place*. Berkeley: University of California Press.

Logan, John R., and Gordana Rabrenovic. 1990. "Neighborhood Associations: Their Issues, Their Allies, and Their Opponents." *Urban Affairs Quarterly* 26 (1):68–94.

Lowi, Theodore. 1964. "American Business, Public Policy, Case-Studies, and Political Theory." *World Politics* 16 (4):677–715.

———. 1972. "Four Systems of Policy, Politics and Choice." *Public Administration Review* 11:298–310.

Lukes, Steven. 1974. *Power: A Radical View*. London: Macmillan.

Mansbridge, Jane J. 1980. *Beyond Adversary Democracy*. New York: Basic Books.

Marschall, Melissa J. 2001. "Does the Shoe Fit? Testing Models of Participation for African-American and Latino Involvement in Local Politics." *Urban Affairs Review* 37 (2):227–48.

Marston, Sallie A. 1993. "Citizen Action Programs and Participatory Politics in Tucson." In *Public Policy for Democracy*, eds. Helen Ingram and Steven Rathgeb Smith, 119–35. Washington, DC: Brookings Institution Press.

Martinez, Gebe. 1991. "Santa Ana Council Takes Back Seat in Traffic Issue." *Los Angeles Times–Orange County Edition*, December 15, B3.

Martinson, Oscar B., and E. A. Wilkening. 1987. "Religion, Participation and Involvement in Local Politics throughout the Life Cycle." *Sociological Focus* 20 (4):309–18.

Mathews, David. 1999. *Politics for People: Finding a Responsible Public Voice*. 2nd ed. Urbana: University of Illinois Press.

Mazmanian, Daniel A., and Paul A. Sabatier. 1980. "A Multivariate Model of Public Policy-Making." *American Journal of Political Science* 24 (3):439–68.

McComas, Katherine A. 2001a. "Public Meetings about Local Waste Management Problems: Comparing Participants to Nonparticipants." *Environmental Management* 27 (1):135–47.

———. 2001b. "Theory and Practice of Public Meetings." *Communication Theory* 11 (1):36–55.

McKenzie, Brian D. 2001. "Self-Selection, Church Attendance, and Local Civic Participation." *Journal for the Scientific Study of Religion* 40 (3):479–88.

McLeod, Jack M., Dietram A. Scheufele, and Patricia Moy. 1999. "Community, Communication, and Participation: The Role of Mass Media and Interpersonal Discussion in Local Political Participation." *Political Communication* 16:315–36.

Mesch, Gustavo S., and Kent P. Schwirian. 1996. "The Effectiveness of Neighborhood Collective Action." *Social Problems* 43 (4):467–83.

Mills, C. Wright. 1956. *The Power Elite*. London: Oxford University Press.

Mintrom, Michael. 1997. "Policy Entrepreneurs and the Diffusion of Innovation." *American Journal of Political Science* 41 (3):738–70.

———. 2000. *Policy Entrepreneurs and School Choice*. Washington, DC: Georgetown University Press.

Molotch, Harvey. 1976. "The City as Growth Machine: Towards a Political Economy of Place." *American Journal of Sociology* 82 (2):309–31.

Morris, Aldon D. 1984. *The Origins of the Civil Rights Movement*. New York: Free Press.

Moynihan, Donald P. 2003. "Normative and Instrumental Perspectives on Public Participation: Citizen Summits in Washington D.C." *American Review of Public Administration* 33 (2):164–88.

Niles, Franklyn C., and James Clawson. 2002. "Small Group Involvement and Civic Engagement in America." Paper presented at the 2002 Annual Meeting of the American Political Science Association, Boston, MA.

Olson, Mancur. 1965. *The Logic of Collective Action: Public Goods and the Theory of Groups*. Cambridge, MA: Harvard University Press.

Peterson, Paul E. 1981. *City Limits*. Chicago: University of Chicago Press.

Peterson, Steven A. 1992. "Church Participation and Political Participation." *American Politics Quarterly* 20 (1):123–39.

Piven, Frances Fox, and Richard A. Cloward. 1977. *Poor Peoples Movements: Why They Succeed and How They Fail*. New York: Pantheon.

Pollock, Philip H. 1982. "Organizations as Agents of Mobilization: How Does Group Activity Affect Political Participation?" *American Journal of Political Science* 26 (3):485–503.

Polsby, Nelson W. 1980. *Community Power and Political Theory: A Further Look at Problems of Evidence and Inference*. New Haven, CT: Yale University Press.

Portney, Kent E., and Jeffrey M. Berry. 1997. "Mobilizing Minority Communities: Social Capital and Participation in Urban Neighborhoods." *American Behavioral Scientist* 40 (5):632–44.

Putnam, Robert D. 2000. *Bowling Alone: The Collapse and Revival of American Community*. New York: Simon & Schuster.

Rimmerman, Craig A. 1997. *The New Citizenship: Unconventional Politics, Activism, and Service*. Boulder, CO: Westview Press.

Roberts, Nancy. 1997. "Public Deliberation: An Alternative Approach to Crafting Policy and Setting Direction." *Public Administration Review* 57 (2):124–32.

Rogers, David, and Norman H. Chung. 1983. *110 Livingston Street Revisited: Decentralization in Action*. New York: New York University Press.

Rohe, William M., and Michael A. Stegman. 1994. "The Impact of Home Ownership on the Social and Political Involvement of Low-Income People." *Urban Affairs Quarterly* 30 (1):152–72.

Rosen, Jay. 1996. *Getting the Connections Right: Public Journalism and the Troubles of the Press*. New York: Twentieth Century Fund.

———. 1999. *What Are Journalists For?* New Haven, CT: Yale University Press.

Rosener, Judy B. 1982. "Making Bureaucrats Responsive: A Study of the Impact of Citizen Participation and Staff Recommendations on Regulatory Decision Making." *Public Administration Review* 42:339–45.

Rosenstone, Steven J., and John Mark Hansen. 1993. *Mobilization, Participation, and Democracy in America*. New York: Macmillan.

Rowe, Gene, and Lynn J. Frewer. 2000. "Public Participation Methods: A Framework for Evaluation." *Science, Technology & Human Values* 25 (1):3–29.

Russell, Daniel M. 1990. *Political Organizing in Grassroots Politics*. Lanham, MD: University Press of America.

Salamon, Lester M. 2002. "The New Governance and the Tools of Public Action: An Introduction." In *The Tools of Government: A Guide to the New Governance*, ed. Lester M. Salamon, 1–47. Oxford: Oxford University Press.

Scavo, Carmine. 1995. "Patterns of Citizen Participation in Edge and Central Cities." In *Contested Terrain: Power, Politics and Participation in Suburbia*, ed. Marc L. Silver and Martin Melkonian, 119–30. Westport, CT: Greenwood Press.

Schlozman, Kay Lehman, and John T. Tierney. 1986. *Organized Interests and American Democracy*. New York: Harper and Row.

Schneider, Anne Larason, and Helen Ingram. 1997. *Policy Design for Democracy*. Lawrence: University Press of Kansas.

Schneider, Mark, and Paul Teske, with Michael Mintrom. 1995. *Public Entrepreneurs: Agents for Change in American Government*. Princeton: Princeton University Press.

Selznick, Philip. 1966. *TVA and the Grassroots*. New York: Harper Torchbooks.

Sharp, Elaine B. 1984. "Citizen Demand-Making in the Urban Context." *American Journal of Political Science* 28 (4):654–70.

———. 1986. *Citizen Demand Making in the Urban Context*. Birmingham: University of Alabama.

Shock, David. 2001. "Voter Behavior in School District Property and Income Tax Elections in Ohio: A Test of Rational Choice Theory." Paper presented at the 2001 Annual Meeting of the Northeastern Political Science Association, Philadelphia, PA.

Sirianni, Carmen, and Lewis Friedland. 2001. *Civic Innovation in America: Community Empowerment, Public Policy, and the Movement for Civic Renewal*. Berkeley: University of California Press.

Skerry, Peter. 1993. *Mexican Americans: The Ambivalent Minority*. New York: Free Press.

Soloski, John. 1989. "Sources and Channels of Local News." *Journalism Quarterly* 66:864–70.

Sonstelie, Jon C., and Paul R. Portney. 1980. "Take the Money and Run: A Theory of Voting in Local Referenda." *Journal of Urban Economics* 8:187–95.

Spano, Shawn. 2001. *Public Dialogue and Participatory Democracy: The Cupertino Community Project*. Cresskill, NJ: Hampton Press.

Steelman, Toddi A., and William Ascher. 1997. "Public Involvement Methods in Natural Resource Policy Making: Advantages, Disadvantages and Tradeoffs." *Policy Sciences* 30:71–90.

Stone, Clarence N. 1989. *Regime Politics: Governing Atlanta 1946–1988*. Lawrence: University Press of Kansas.

Swanstrom, Todd. 1985. *The Crisis of Growth Politics: Cleveland, Kucinich, and the Challenge of Urban Populism*. Philadelphia: Temple University Press.

Swindell, David. 2000. "Issue Representation in Neighborhood Organizations: Questing for Democracy at the Grassroots." *Journal of Urban Affairs* 22 (2):123–37.

Taylor, Claire E., Jung-Sook Lee, and William R. Davie. 2000. "Local Press Coverage of Environmental Conflict." *Journalism and Mass Communication Quarterly* 77 (1):175–92.

Thomas, John Clayton. 1982. "Citizen-Initiated Contacts with Government Agencies: A Test of Three Theories." *American Journal of Political Science* 26 (3):504–22.

———. 1986. *Between Citizen and City: Neighborhood Organizations and Urban Politics in Cincinnati*. Lawrence: University Press of Kansas.

———. 1990. "Public Involvement in Public Management: Adapting and Testing a Borrowed Theory." *Public Administration Review* 50 (4):435–45.

Thomas, John Clayton, and Julia Melkers. 1999. "Explaining Citizen-Initiated Contacts with Municipal Bureaucrats: Lessons from the Atlanta Experience." *Urban Affairs Review* 34 (5):667–90.

Thomson, Ken. 2001. *From Neighborhood to Nation: The Democratic Foundations of Civil Society*. Hanover: University Press of New England.

Tiebout, Charles. 1956. "A Pure Theory of Local Expenditures." *Journal of Political Economy* 64 (5):416–24.

Vedlitz, Arnold, James A. Dyer, and Roger Durand. 1980. "Citizen Contacts with Local Governments: A Comparative View." *American Journal of Political Science* 24 (1):50–67.

Verba, Sidney, and Norman H. Nie. 1972. *Participation in America: Political Democracy and Social Equality*. New York: Harper and Row.

Verba, Sidney, Kay Lehman Schlozman, and Henry E. Brady. 1995. *Voice and Equality: Civic Voluntarism in American Politics*. Cambridge, MA: Harvard University Press.

Walters, Lawrence C., James Aydelotte, and Jessica Miller. 2000. "Putting More Public in Policy Analysis." *Public Administration Review* 60 (4):349–59.

Wanta, Wayne, and Y-Chen Wu. 1992. "Interpersonal Communication and the Agenda-Setting Process." *Journalism Quarterly* 69 (4):847–55.

Warren, Mark E. 2001. *Democracy and Association*. Princeton: Princeton University Press.

Warren, Mark R. 2001. *Dry Bones Rattling: Community Building to Revitalize American Democracy*. Princeton: Princeton University Press.

Weeks, Edward C. 2000. "The Practice of Deliberative Democracy: Results from Four Large-Scale Trials." *Public Administration Review* 60 (4):360–72.

Whitt, J. Allen. 1982. *Urban Elites and Mass Transportation: The Dialectics of Power*. Princeton: Princeton University Press.

Wildavsky, Aaron. 1979. *Speaking Truth to Power: The Art and Craft of Policy Analysis*. New Brunswick, NJ: Transaction.

Wilson, James Q. 1974. *Political Organizations*. Princeton: Princeton University Press.

Wong, Kenneth K., and Pushpan Jain. 1999. "Newspapers as Policy Actors in Urban School Systems: The Chicago Story." *Urban Affairs Review* 35 (2):210–46.

Wood, Richard L. 2002. *Faith in Action: Religion, Race, and Democratic Organizing in America*. Chicago: University of Chicago Press.

Wrinkle, Robert D. et al. 1996. "Ethnicity and Nonelectoral Political Participation." *Hispanic Journal of Behavioral Sciences* 18 (2):142–53.

Index

Brian E. Adams is Assistant Professor in the Political Science Department at San Diego State University.